Mourning and Mysticism in First World War Literature and Beyond

Mourning and Mysticism in First World War Literature and Beyond

Grappling with Ghosts

George M. Johnson
Professor and Chair, English and Modern Languages Department
Thompson Rivers University, Canada

© George Malcolm Johnson 2015

All rights reserved. No reproduction, copy or transmission of this publication may be made without written permission.

No portion of this publication may be reproduced, copied or transmitted save with written permission or in accordance with the provisions of the Copyright, Designs and Patents Act 1988, or under the terms of any licence permitting limited copying issued by the Copyright Licensing Agency, Saffron House, 6–10 Kirby Street, London EC1N 8TS.

Any person who does any unauthorized act in relation to this publication may be liable to criminal prosecution and civil claims for damages.

The author has asserted his right to be identified as the author of this work in accordance with the Copyright, Designs and Patents Act 1988.

First published 2015 by
PALGRAVE MACMILLAN

Palgrave Macmillan in the UK is an imprint of Macmillan Publishers Limited, registered in England, company number 785998, of Houndmills, Basingstoke, Hampshire RG21 6XS.

Palgrave Macmillan in the US is a division of St Martin's Press LLC, 175 Fifth Avenue, New York, NY 10010.

Palgrave Macmillan is the global academic imprint of the above companies and has companies and representatives throughout the world.

Palgrave® and Macmillan® are registered trademarks in the United States, the United Kingdom, Europe and other countries.

ISBN 978–1–349–67347–6   ISBN 978–1–137–33203–5(eBook)
DOI 10.1057/9781137332035

This book is printed on paper suitable for recycling and made from fully managed and sustained forest sources. Logging, pulping and manufacturing processes are expected to conform to the environmental regulations of the country of origin.

A catalogue record for this book is available from the British Library.

Library of Congress Cataloging-in-Publication Data
Johnson, George M. (George Malcolm), 1961–
Mourning and mysticism in First World War literature and beyond: grappling with ghosts / George M. Johnson, Professor and Chair, Thompson Rivers University, Canada.
pages cm
Includes bibliographical references and index.

1. World War, 1914–1918 – Great Britain – Literature and the war.
2. English literature – 20th century – History and criticism.
3. Mourning customs in literature.   4. Mysticism in literature.
5. Spiritualism in literature.   I. Title.
PR478.W65J64 2015
820.9'358–dc23   2015001306

Typeset by MPS Limited, Chennai, India.

*Dedicated to my father George James Johnson
And in memory of
Andrew Brink (1932–2011)*

Contents

List of Illustrations	viii
Preface and Acknowledgments	x
Introduction: Attachment, Mourning, and Mysticism	1
1 F. W. H. Myers: Loss and the Obsessive Study of Survival	28
2 Spirit Soldiers: Oliver Lodge's *Raymond* and *Christopher*	60
3 From Parodist to Proselytizer: Arthur Conan Doyle's "Vital Message"	86
4 "Well-Remembered Voices": Mourning and Spirit Communication in Barrie's and Kipling's First World War Narratives	124
5 Mourning, the War, and the "New Mysticism" in May Sinclair and Virginia Woolf	153
6 Purgatorial Passions: "The Ghost" (aka Wilfred Owen) in Owen's Poetry	187
7 "*Misty-schism*": The Psychological Roots of Aldous Huxley's Mystical Modernism	201
8 After-life/After-word: The Culture of Mourning and Mysticism	227
Notes	234
Works Cited	239
Index	252

List of Illustrations

0.1	Sir Thomas Brock R.A. "Aid for the fallen"	x
0.2	John E. Sutcliffe. "A kiss from the trenches"	20
1.1	Frederic Myers	30
1.2	Frederic Myers with his son, Leopold Hamilton Myers	42
2.1	Oliver Lodge with his mother	62
2.2	Oliver Lodge with his family; Raymond seated on floor at left	70
3.1	Arthur Conan Doyle age 6, with his father Charles Altamont Doyle. Reprinted by permission of the Arthur Conan Doyle Collection – Lancelyn Green Bequest, Portsmouth City Council	89
3.2	Arthur Conan Doyle with his sister Annette. Reprinted by permission of the Arthur Conan Doyle Collection – Lancelyn Green Bequest, Portsmouth City Council	91
3.3	Arthur Conan Doyle with a spirit manifestation of his son Kingsley. Reprinted by permission of the Arthur Conan Doyle Collection – Lancelyn Green Bequest, Portsmouth City Council	114
4.1	J. M. Barrie at age 6	126
4.2	Barrie with his mother, Margaret Ogilvy	128
4.3	Rudyard Kipling on his mother Alice's knee in 1866	135
4.4	Kipling, nearly 6, at the time of his stay at "The House of Desolation," Lorne Lodge	136
4.5	Rudyard and Carrie Kipling visiting Dud Corner Cemetery, Loos, in 1930 where John Kipling's name is inscribed on the Memorial Wall. Reprinted by permission of the Mary Evans Picture Library	140
5.1	May Sinclair in 1898. Reprinted by permission of The Rare Book and Manuscript Library, The University of Pennsylvania Libraries	154

List of Illustrations   ix

5.2 May Sinclair with her cat. Reprinted by permission of
     The Rare Book and Manuscript Library, The University
     of Pennsylvania Libraries   161
5.3 Julia Stephen with Virginia as a child, 1884   162
5.4 Virginia peering out behind preoccupied parents
     Julia and Leslie Stephen   163
5.5 Virginia in mourning clothes after the death of her
     mother Julia. Private Collection   164
6.1 Wilfred Owen (center) with his mother Susan, two of his
     siblings, and a nanny. Reprinted by permission of the
     Wilfred Owen Collection, English Faculty Library, Oxford   190
6.2 Wilfred Owen in his officer's uniform. Reprinted by
     permission of the Wilfred Owen Collection,
     English Faculty Library, Oxford   195
7.1 Aldous Huxley at age 8. Reprinted by permission of
     Georges Borchardt, Inc., for the Aldous and Laura Huxley
     Literary Trust, Mark Trevenen Huxley, and Teresa Huxley   204
7.2 Aldous Huxley with his father Leonard   205
7.3 Aldous Huxley with fellow pacifist Gerald Heard in 1937   212

Preface and Acknowledgments

Illustration 0.1 Sir Thomas Brock, R.A. "Aid for the fallen"

A soldier kneels and supports his brother-in-arms as he lies, his body twisted where he has fallen. The soldier has placed his hand over his friend's heart, since he is wounded and dying. The above illustration, Sir Thomas Brock's First World War drawing, "Aid for the fallen" (1914) captures essential features of *Mourning and Mysticism*. Brock's picture depicts a paradoxical moment, of intense bonding between two comrades, but also the breaking of that bond, the moment of its being severed, with sorrow and grief glimpsed in the grim expression on the bereaved soldier's face. And yet, in the ambiguous setting, with a shell burst, or a sky clearing in the left-hand background and deepening shadows towards the right, we might imagine these men in a no-man's land or even a purgatory, waiting for the next stage. If we do, then we are perceiving a mystical quality to this image, an effect enhanced by its loose style, giving the impression of a hurriedly drawn, unfinished sketch. *Mourning and Mysticism* probes such mystical responses to death.

Brock's drawing is appropriate in another sense as well in that it represents the unseen for those at the home front, like Brock, who was sixty-seven when the Great War erupted and who did not visit the front. It was forbidden to take photographs of dead allied soldiers, and soldiers were prohibited from carrying cameras at all after the Christmas truce of 1914 (van Emden 149). The scene thus belongs to the realm of the imagination – a reconstruction of the moment of death as any mother, wife, or other relative would have wanted for their dying loved one: being cared for and comforted by another. Some men did receive this blessing – on the battlefield loyalty and compassion could be limitless. Wilfred Owen, one of the subjects of this book, records cradling his batman "Little Jones" after he had been shot through the head, the blood remaining "crimson" on Owen's shoulder (Owen *Letters* 580). "My senses are charred," was his terse remark (Hibberd 348). Richard van Emden details a case of a German soldier, Emil Loose, who held a British soldier, Raymond Wilson, in his arms as he died. A strange meeting indeed. Loose then wrote to console Raymond's father and eventually met up with him (294–96). Most men, however, did not receive such solace, their bodies being blown to pieces or buried by exploding shells, caught in no-man's land, or destroyed in any number of horrific ways; they died "as cattle," as Owen so ruthlessly put it. These men's bodies – nearly half of those killed – were never recovered, and this distressing situation encouraged mystical responses to loss.

Brock's sketch serves to illustrate another feature of *Mourning and Mysticism*. Brock was a sculptor in the grand, heroic style, most famous for creating the Victoria Memorial in front of Buckingham Palace, as well as Prince Albert for the Albert Memorial and many more. He sculpted memorials of Imperial might and grandeur, but in "Aid for the fallen" he chose to express an intimate emotional moment in shades of soft charcoal, the opposite of austere, colossal statues in stone and bronze. This shift perfectly reflects the main focus of *Mourning and Mysticism* on intimate, emotional, imaginative, transformative responses to loss rather than officially encouraged responses to state sanctioned monuments that sprang up after the war, from the Tomb of the Unknown Soldier to the War Memorial in every Commonwealth village, no matter how small. For a significant minority of people, including most of this book's subjects, such imaginative responses as Brock's proved more effective, ethical, and in some cases therapeutic than stone memorials, designed to evoke abstract values of courage, sacrifice, and honor. Finally, Brock was never considered a war artist in any sense, and neither were most of the subjects in this book considered war writers, with the exception of Wilfred Owen, although several visited the front, and one, Sir Arthur Conan Doyle, wrote a six-volume history of the war. Brock's was an individual response, a first response, in that it appeared in *King Albert's Book*, published after the occupation of Belgium in the fall of 1914, alongside many other artists, musicians, and writers' initial responses, including several under study here: Rudyard Kipling, Oliver Lodge, and May Sinclair.

When an entire culture responds to trauma and loss in mourning, as in First World War Britain, what forces shape that mourning? How are responses to war loss conditioned by earlier responses to loss or by beliefs about the afterlife? What roles do writers play in articulating grief, in mediating collective trauma? When writers express feelings of loss in memoir, fictional or poetic form, how does that affect the mourning process? *Mourning and Mysticism* probes these questions among others. All of the writers in this book grappled with ghosts, most from an early age. Several of them were driven to discover evidence, make arguments for the survival of personality beyond death, and proselytize extensively about their findings and beliefs. They were not alone, since ghosts were thick on the ground in the years leading up to the war, ethereal expressions of a neo-Romantic revival, which renewed interest in philosophical Idealism, with its contention that the Absolute might be glimpsed. However, these were not "the violent old ghosts," as Virginia Woolf put it, of sensational gothic fiction, but those with a psychological dimension, which may or may not "have their origin within us," depending on one's mystical stance (Woolf *Essays* III 324). One only needs to think of the James's ghost stories (Henry and M. R.), or Thomas Hardy's elegies on his first wife, "Poems of 1912–13." The writers in this study wrote out their ghosts in various literary forms and for several purposes, but most often to renegotiate severed relationships, memorialize lost loved ones, and even expunge obsessive or unacceptable memories. In this sense their writing was therapeutic, at least temporarily and partially, but it was not just this, since they brought their talent and skills as artists to bear on their traumas, in order to transcend and transform them. *Mourning and Mysticism* empathetically portrays their sometimes monumental struggles to manage mourning creatively.

This book evolved over many years, but I felt its implications much more deeply after the death of my mother, Eleanor Johnson, in 2009, and then the death of my father-in-law, Alvin Reimer, a few weeks later, when I lived through the emotions of mourning in a way I had not before. To my artist mother I owe the drive to bring this project to completion. I have drawn on my mentor Andrew Brink's pioneering work of applying object relations and attachment theory to literature, and miss our wide-ranging conversations, including those about my plans for this book, after his death in 2011. My father has always been a mainstay in my scholarly work and I owe him a huge debt of gratitude. I have traveled through grief and joy and everything in between with my wife Nina, and thank her for her participation in this project, with ever perceptive comments, and for her patience as I immersed myself in the War and mourning during the months leading up to completing the book. Our children, Sophia and Benjamin, also deserve my sincere thanks for their patience in dealing with a somewhat scattered and, need I say it, preoccupied Dad during the writing months. I learned so much from their response to the loss of their grandparents, and continue to learn every day from their experience of life unfolding.

I also want to recognize the help of my friends and colleagues Genevieve Later, Daniel McBain, Cam Grant, and Leslie de Bont in reading and commenting on parts of this book. I am grateful to Jeffrey Berman for his appreciation of my aims and his perceptive comments as external reviewer for Palgrave Macmillan. Thanks as well to Paula Kennedy, Publisher of Literature and Head of Humanities publishing at Palgrave Macmillan, with whom I worked on my first book for Palgrave, *Dynamic Psychology in Modernist British Fiction*, and who had the faith to give me another crack at publishing with Palgrave. Ben Doyle, Commissioning Editor, and Tomas René, Editorial Assistant have been wonderful to work with in bringing this project to completion smoothly and efficiently. Thanks also to Jo North for conscientious copy editing. For several grants as well as sabbaticals during 2010–11 and the latter half of 2014 that provided some much-needed time to research and write this book, I am grateful to Thompson Rivers University.

Photographs are reproduced by kind permission of the following: Arthur Conan Doyle Collection – Lancelyn Green Bequest, Portsmouth City Council; Harvard Theatre Collection, Harvard University; Wilfred Owen Collection, English Faculty Library, Oxford; Mary Evans Picture Library; the Mortimer Rare Book Room, Smith College; David McKnight, Director, The Rare Book and Manuscript Library, The University of Pennsylvania Libraries; Georges Borchardt, Inc., for the Aldous and Laura Huxley Literary Trust, Mark Trevenen Huxley, and Teresa Huxley. For permission to quote from copyrighted works of Arthur Conan Doyle, I would like to thank the Conan Doyle Estate, Ltd. and Jon Lellenberg for arranging this.

Earlier versions of several sections of this book have appeared as follows: "'Purgatorial Passions': 'The Ghost' (aka Wilfred Owen) in Owen's

Poetry." *The Midwest Quarterly* 51(2) (Winter 2010): 152–68; "Unresolved Mourning and the Great War in May Sinclair's *The Tree of Heaven* and Virginia Woolf's *Mrs. Dalloway*." *May Sinclair: Moving Towards the Modern* (London: Ashgate, 2006), pp. 83–98. I am grateful to these publications for permission to reproduce material.

Finally, I would like to acknowledge my nearest ancestors who fought in the Great War, and somehow survived it: Frank Cooper Johnson (Divisional Supply Column); my great-grandfather Thomas James (120th Battalion, Argyll and Sutherland Highlanders); his younger brothers Cornelius (133rd Battalion) and William James (86th Machine Gun Battalion); and Francis Claude Oliver (102nd Battalion) who did not.

George M. Johnson

Introduction: Attachment, Mourning, and Mysticism

"Then came a War when, bombed and gassed and mined,
Truth rose once more, perforce, to meet mankind,
And through the dust and glare and wreck of things
Beheld a phantom on unbalanced wings..."
Kipling, "A Legend of Truth,"
Debits and Credits (1926) 383

"Sadness is necessary sometimes – like an operation; you can't be well without it. If you think about her, Anthony, it'll hurt you. But if you don't think about her, you condemn her to a second death. The spirit of the dead lives on in God. But it also lives on in the minds of the living – helping them, making them better and stronger. The dead can only have this kind of immortality if the living are prepared to give it them."
Mrs Foxe to Anthony Beavis in Aldous Huxley's
Eyeless in Gaza (1936) 108

"Oh yes, all you English are like that. You lock up your affection, and you sometimes lose the key."
Moonstone channeling Raymond Lodge. Lodge,
Raymond (1916) 135

In 1915, a distinguished-looking man in his sixties sits with his wife in the deepening shadows of the drawing room of Mariemont, his home near Birmingham. He is bearded and balding, his remaining white hair swept back along the sides of his head as if he is bracing against an invisible force. Eyes heavily-lidded, the man leans forward, shoulders stooped, tapping his fingers together. His wife places a hand over his, bringing his tapping to an end and drawing his glance. Her lips are pursed and upturned, giving the slightest hint of hope. They await a communication from their son, Raymond.

Some seven years later, at Crowborough in Sussex in a large gabled house called Windlesham, another man in his sixties, this one with a drooping moustache, sits beside his wife on a sofa. It is December and a log fire flickers in their music room, pushing back the gloom. When an ash-flake flutters free of the grate, the couple, eyes unfocused, do not notice. They are preoccupied with thoughts of the man's son, Kingsley, whose message they anxiously await. Another woman sits with them, muttering to herself. Suddenly a voice, a strange voice, an uncanny voice intones, "Jean, it is I." The wife galvanizes her attention, her hands shaking, as she calls out, "It is Kingsley." The man tentatively asks, "Is that you, boy?" The voice whispers intensely, "Father!" and then, "Forgive Me!" The father clasps his forehead with both hands and says, "There was never anything to forgive. You were the best son a man ever had."

The first father is Sir Oliver Lodge, eminent Edwardian scientist. He received dozens of communications from his son Raymond – an unexceptional experience, except that they were received, not through the Royal Mail, but from the beyond through mediums after Raymond was killed in 1915 in the First World War. The second father, Sir Arthur Conan Doyle, physician and eminent Edwardian author, also received dozens of messages from his soldier son Kingsley – again nothing unusual in that – except that the messages were similarly sent through mediums, as well as Doyle's wife Jean's automatic writing and speaking in the voice of Doyle's guide, "Pheneas," after Kingsley's death in 1918 from Spanish flu. I have here adapted a "conversation" with Kingsley that Doyle recorded in a letter to Oliver Lodge (Lellenberg *Letters* 654). Dozens more could be added to these examples of spiritualism – the practice of contacting the dead through a medium, and to these could be added other forms and techniques of mysticism from automatism to table tilting, widely practiced from the Victorian to First World War era and beyond. Does Doyle and Lodge's involvement in spiritualism represent an unfortunate lapse of judgment, mere eccentricity, even delusional behavior? Was the Edwardian era and its aftermath a culture in the grips of religious crisis, a society made credulous by a desperate need to believe in something?

The cultural historians of these periods tend to think so. Samuel Hynes in *The Edwardian Turn of Mind* writes that Lodge's book of communications, both earthly and unearthly, from his son, *Raymond* (1916), is "sad reading," evidence of

the credulity of belief and of nothing else; and the exposition of Lodge's own theories of life and death are depressing, coming from a man who had once made valuable contributions to scientific knowledge. The book was attacked by scientists as a scandal to the profession, but it had a wide circulation among persons bereaved, as Lodge had been, by the war. (145–46)

Janet Oppenheim in *The Other World: Spiritualism and Psychical Research in England, 1850–1914* operates from the assumption that spiritualism and even its more respectable cousin psychical research lured otherwise discerning people who could not "accept God's absence from the universe" (4) before these fields were "rightly" exposed as pseudo-sciences.[1] Most recently, Marina Warner in *Phantasmagoria* writes "that superrationalist Conan Doyle['s]" "adherence to Spiritualism confounds belief" and that Lodge's faith in survival operates "at a pitch of wishful thinking that is painful to read now. Taking strength from this form of spiritual consolation diverts energy from attacking the cause of the young men's deaths, even in the midst of the most acute suffering" (244). All of these historians – and many more could be cited – assume that their society and they themselves personally have progressed toward enlightenment, rendering the earlier era limited in its understanding. In back-projecting their assumptions and values, they risk misunderstanding and distorting the phenomena under study.

I want to take a different, more sympathetic approach and to argue that the attraction to mysticism in all its varied forms made perfect sense within a culture of mourning, of large-scale loss and bereavement, such as in the aftermath of the Boer War, retreat of Empire and particularly during the First World War and the influenza epidemic that followed close on its heels. It must be kept in mind that the medical profession of the time tended to be suspicious of psychological, introspective approaches to mental health. Bereavement counseling had not developed as a field, psychotherapy was in its infancy and available only to the privileged few, and shell shock (now termed Post-Traumatic Stress Disorder), despite being widespread, was only beginning to be understood as a psychological condition (cf. Johnson *Dynamic* 52, 92). Some forms of mysticism offered a therapeutic means of dealing with the trauma of loss, and so my focus will be on the emotional and psychological reasons why the culture embraced mysticism; thus I will draw on the insights of psychological theories that developed out of the context of this bereavement. An important goal will be to illuminate similarities in responses to loss by the individuals under study, and to show how the resulting collective biography can throw light on hitherto shadowy aspects of this society, as a whole. While some back-projection of values and insights is inevitable, I will attempt to tell the story of this culture of mourning as it unfolded, on its contemporary terms.

Modern warfare and its consequences began at the turn of the twentieth century for the British. The Anglo-Boer war of 1899–1902 arguably represented a watershed war in that the British faced modern guerrilla tactics of warfare and serious questions were raised about the British treatment of prisoners of war that had resulted in high death rates; the war lost popular support and this signaled the retreat of Empire. However, the number of British that perished in that conflict – approximately 22,000 – paled in comparison to the First World War, in which between 722,785 and 744,702 British men died (depending on the historian consulted). A staggering three million Britons out of forty-two million lost a close relative, son or brother (Jalland 35). The secondary bereaved comprised virtually the entire population. British families could barely bring themselves to cast their eyes over the 'Roll of Honour' published daily in the newspapers. In his "Preface" to *Raymond*, Oliver Lodge lamented the appalling "amount of premature and unnatural bereavement at the present time" (vii), and Wilfred Owen famously evoked "each slow dusk a drawing-down of blinds," indicating yet more lost lives ("Anthem for Doomed Youth"). Add to this another 200,000 victims of influenza in 1918–19 (and over 20 million worldwide; Jalland 8), and the magnitude of human loss becomes difficult to comprehend. Perhaps Lady Asquith put it most poignantly when she wrote in her diary in 1915: "before one is thirty, to know more dead than living people" (as quoted in Jalland 36).

The largest-scale response might be termed mysticism in its broadest sense. Mysticism has always been a nebulous term, "so irresponsibly applied in English," often with contempt, as Caroline Spurgeon lamented (1). Nevertheless, it can be defined as an experience of the spiritual life, more particularly the achievement of union or at-onement with God. During the Edwardian period fascination with mysticism rose, in the wake of psychical researcher Frederic Myers's and others' probing of psychical phenomena, and his conception of the subliminal (cf. Chapter 1). William James in his ground-breaking psychological study of religion *The Varieties of Religious Experience* (1902) argued that all forms of mysticism emanated from "that great subliminal or transmarginal region" (426), which needed to be explored further. Evelyn Underhill, the English guru of mysticism, in one of her many books on the topic developed a broad definition of mysticism:

> The expression of the innate tendency of the human spirit towards complete harmony with the transcendental order; whatever be the theological formula under which that order is understood. This tendency, in great mystics, gradually captures the whole field of consciousness; it dominates their life and, in the experience called "mystic union," attains its end. (*Mysticism* x)

For her, it is "a genuine life process and not an intellectual speculation"; in other words it deeply engages the emotional life and ultimately leads to union (*Mysticism* x). The novelist and philosopher May Sinclair, one of the subjects of this study and a friend of Underhill's, distinguished two types. She characterized the old type as being possessed of a diseased asceticism, a denial of the body: "its more abhorrent psychological extravagances are the hysterical resurgence of natural longings most unspiritually suppressed" (*Defence* xviii). Sexual energy is transferred from a human and bodily object to a divine and spiritual one without being transformed; in other words, the instinctual energy is imperfectly sublimated (*Defence* 257). The "New Mysticism," however, she saw arising through the coming together of Eastern and Western mysticism and the maturing of the Western mind: "it has put the disease of asceticism behind it; it is a robust and joyous Mysticism, reconciled to the world" (*Defence* 307). In this form, "Mystic passion embraces while it transcends the whole range of human passion. Like human passion, it works through body, heart, and soul" (*Defence* 311). It reveals separation as illusion and thus surmounts it (*Defence* 315). The "New Mysticism" engages the "psychic powers," involving what psychical researcher Frederic Myers called supernormal phenomena – those which transcend ordinary experience but obey natural laws. She praised "the admirable work done by the Society for Psychical Research ... in collecting and sifting material for Psychology to deal with" (*Defence* 294). In particular, the Society's findings convinced her of the reality of telepathy and mental suggestion, by which "the ordinary methods of communication by speech and sign are 'transcended'" (*Defence* 298–99). Thus, for Sinclair mystical experience could be a sinking downwards, a turning backwards (the old mysticism) or it could be a rising upwards, an accessing of the "untrodden country" of the future, a portent of mankind's spiritual evolution (the new mysticism), or it could be both (*Defence* 292).

Within this definition spiritualism can be included, although Sinclair did not go so far as to accept that there was substantial enough evidence of communication with the dead (*Defence* 351). Spiritualism is a lower form of mysticism in that it involves sensory experience and a dialectic relationship with the being manifested, as Aldous Huxley recognized: "Mystical experience is beyond the realm of opposites. Visionary experience is still within that realm" (*Doors* 110; Sawyer 209), and this is affirmed by contemporary psychologists Edward F. Kelly and Emily Williams Kelly, who demonstrate the importance of mysticism for a twenty-first century psychology based on Myers's conception of the subliminal (524–25). I have adopted this inclusive definition of mysticism rather than employing the term occultism because, as Alex Owen has suggested, occultism generally referred to "the study of (or search for) a hidden or veiled reality and the arcane secrets of existence" (22). This pursuit tended to be intellectual, esoteric, and elitist. The new mysticism, on the other hand, tended to involve synthesis and emotionally engage a wide range of people, both on the home and battlefronts. Evelyn Underhill in her popular book, *Practical Mysticism*, which appeared just after the First World War broke out, wrote that the need for mysticism was even greater during wartime. She noted that,

> it is significant that many of these experiences are reported to us from periods of war and distress: that the stronger the forces of destruction appeared, the more intense grew the spiritual vision which opposed them. We learn from these records that the mystical consciousness has the power of lifting those who possess it to a plane of reality which no struggle, no cruelty, can disturb: of conferring a certitude which no catastrophe can wreck. (ix)

Writing in 1917, May Sinclair argued that the highest state of mystic certainty could occur when the soldier "faces death for the first time. There is no certainty that life can give that surpasses or even comes anywhere near it. And the world has been full of *these* mystics, *these* visionaries, since August 1914. Sometimes I think they are the only trustworthy ones" (*Defence* 302). She might well trust these mystics since she had experienced something similar at the battlefront, as we shall see.

Though there has been some excellent work done on mysticism in war from a cultural studies perspective, including Jay Winter's *Sites of Memory Sites of Mourning* and Jenny Hazelgrove's *Spiritualism and British Society Between the Wars*, on which I have drawn, my focus will be on eminent and not so eminent late-Victorian, Edwardian, and Modernist writers. From numerous candidates, I've selected a range of writers who engaged in a mystical response to mourning, from those like Frederic Myers who died well before the First World War but whose uncanny influence persisted, to fathers or surrogate fathers who lost sons during the war, such as Oliver Lodge, Arthur Conan Doyle, J. M. Barrie, and Rudyard Kipling, to the sisters and friends of soldiers killed, including May Sinclair and Virginia Woolf, to a front-line soldier, Wilfred Owen, and even to a writer disqualified for military service, Aldous Huxley. All of them grappled with ghosts, heard well-remembered voices of those no longer living and had to come to terms with their experiences. Exploring their struggles and solutions will bring into dramatic relief the dilemmas and anxieties of the era. My aim is not to pathologize these writers but to view them as wounded healers whose anxieties and sorrows tap into, reflect, shape, and give voice to socially disruptive group fantasies, to the culture's trauma. English culture became one of mass bereavement and mourning, was under extreme duress and harbored enormous anxiety about the fate of combatants, the threat from its adversaries, and the future of its nation. Myers, Lodge, and Doyle in particular played key roles in extending the possibilities for mourning beyond traditional Christian conceptions through their prolific popular writings. They conveyed evidence for potential psychical extensions of personality, including telepathy, clairvoyance, and automatic writing, phenomena which supported the possibility that personality survived death. All of the writers in this project acted as mediums in the metaphorical sense that Paul Levy describes:

> If we are able to channel and creatively express the spirit of the age from which we are suffering with consciousness, however, we become the "medium" through which the spirit of the age reveals itself to us so as to potentially transform itself, the world around us, as well as ourselves. (3)

As "mediums," they brought their message of the possibility of survival to a wide audience, increasing its horizon of expectations, and they brought the weight of their respectability, in some cases their status as cultural icons, to bear on this question.

But why? Why persist on this quest in the face of ridicule, derision, and damage to that respectability and reputation? I would argue that the source is in their responses to profound early losses, and even in some instances trauma. These responses established a pattern that persisted into adulthood, sensitizing them to later losses and making them not only receptive to, but driven to probe whether communication with lost loved ones was possible. Two overlapping theoretical frameworks, with plenty of empirical evidence to support them, can help us understand the psychological dynamics involved.

Object relations theory and attachment theory, though not a coherent whole, are ideally suited to dealing with the issue of responses to war losses since, in contrast to orthodox Freudian theory, these theories shift the emphasis from psychosexual stages of development to patterns in attachment and responses to separation and loss. As developed by British theorists W. R. D. Fairbairn, D. W. Winnicott, and others, object relations theory proposes that a child's inability to manage adaptive separation from the original caretaker, typically the mother, which serves as a prototype for all subsequent bonds with other people and with the world at large, will lead to later maladaptations and even psychopathology. Negligent as well as over engaged and over controlling caretaking will result in a child internalizing the unsatisfying aspects of the caretaker. According to Fairbairn (1994b), the internalized "object" will be split into exciting and frustrating aspects (170). These conflicting aspects, which arouse love and hatred, will be repressed, split off from the main core of the internalized object, while that core is idealized and is present to consciousness. Fairbairn (1994a) describes this internal configuration as the schizoid condition of withdrawal of affect (25–26). The most traumatic source of the failure to adapt is the death of either of a child's parents, which frequently leads to later depressive episodes.

D. W. Winnicott's concept of the transitional object contributes to our understanding of the separation process. Normally these objects, represented in a concrete form by infants' special toys and in a symbolic way as an intermediate area of experience reflected, for example, in a child's babbling, provide a bridge between the mother and the outside world, or between the familiar and the unfamiliar. These objects, and the accompanying symbolic activity, play a comforting role when the mother is absent and so facilitate the separation process (Brink *Creativity* 64–65). However, in individuals whose early object relations have been disrupted, transitional objects can counter depressive feelings of body disintegration and loss of self. They may become the focus of particularly intense and ambivalent, divided feelings of hatred and love toward the lost person. In imaginative individuals the transitional experience sparks off exceptionally creative symbolic play to heal those divisive feelings and to control depressive anxiety. In later life, art forms can become transitional objects (Rose 354). These theories are also particularly apropos because they developed in part as an attempt to deal with responses to Second World War trauma. Interestingly, even as far back as the Edwardian period, anthropologists Robert Hertz and Arnold van Gennep started to view death itself as a transitional experience. In 1907 Hertz argued that funeral rites served to transition "the status of the dead from the realm of the living into an afterlife; the identity of the deceased was not lost, but, rather, reconstituted into something meaningful" for the society (Strange 16). Van Gennep in 1909 suggested that the corpse possessed an intermediary status before burial and immortality. Mourners underwent transitional experience from the world of the living to a separate state of mourning and then a return to the society of the living once the rites of disposing of the dead were complete (147–48). In object relational terms we could argue that transitional experience learned as a child comes into play again when imagining the transition of the loved one from alive to the intermediary state of being a corpse to this person's status as immortal or beyond earthly existence.

John Bowlby also began to develop attachment theory in the context of mass bereavement, but in post-First World War Britain (Newcombe 2). Based on evolutionary biology, attachment theory postulates that forming emotional bonds is fundamental to human behavior (and can be observed in neonates) and that it is an adaptive strategy (Bowlby *Secure* 120–21). Infants form attachments initially for protection, and in maturity the attachment extends to reproduction, the two major organizing functions of human behavior (Crittenden *Assessing* 36). Attachment theory, as elaborated by Mary Ainsworth, Mary Main, Patricia Crittenden, and others, furthers our understanding of the connection between childhood separation anxiety and traumas in attachment, and adult attachment patterns and complications in mourning. Based on study of infant–caretaker interactions and on longitudinal study of patterns of attachment into adulthood, these researchers have discovered that initial caretakers, typically mothers, tend to "transmit" their attachment patterns to their infants (Crittenden *Assessing* 38). The pattern a child learns and adopts tends to persist into adulthood through internal working models that a child develops, which "contain *expectations* and *beliefs* about (1) one's own and other people's behaviour; (2) the lovability, worthiness and acceptability of the self; and (3) the emotional availability and interests of others, and their ability to provide protection" (Howe 35). Adults tend to impose their pattern on any new relationships they might develop (Bowlby *Secure* 127). These clinicians delineated three major infant attachment patterns that can predict later behavior: Secure (designated by the letter B), Anxious Avoidant (A), and Anxious Resistant (C). According to Andrew Brink in *Obsession and Culture*, creators typically manifest a more complicated avoidant-resistant (A/C) pattern, a classification developed by Patricia Crittenden (25). These complicated but enriched individuals are dominantly avoidant (in adulthood termed dismissive), but also show resistance. Crittenden claims that this more sophisticated group employs self-protective strategies that alter according to conditions (*Assessing* 230).

In childhood, the insecure avoidant pattern (observed in approximately one-third of infants according to Crittenden [*Assessing* 32]) develops when a parent's love and acceptance is conditional as long as the infant does not make too many demands (Howe 44). The infant learns to minimize overt shows of attachment behavior and displays of negative affect, which only result in a parent's "irritable attempts to control, deny or dismiss the infant's need or anxiety" (Howe 44). These children learn to defend against frustration in attachment by dismissing attachment, suppressing feelings, and relying on cognition in relationships: "feeling is thus impoverished, dismissed into an inner world of thwarted attachments and angry resentment at unfulfilled needs" (Brink *Obsession* 24). Avoidant children typically develop considerable capacity to read others' emotional states for protection (although not their own; Howe 102). In adulthood, avoidant, or dismissive, "refers to both dismissing the perspective, intentions, and feelings of self and also preoccupation with the perspectives, desires, and feelings of others" (Crittenden *Assessing* 41).

However, those who manifest the avoidant-resistant (A/C) pattern also show resistance, manifested in marked ambivalence toward and manipulation of relationships, and preoccupation with past family relationships and experiences. They may have parents who present very different dangers to them and so they use a different strategy for dealing with each one. Another possibility is that one parent will present widely varying behavior, making a range of adaptive behavior necessary (Crittenden *Assessing* 234). Oscillating positive and negative feelings in early relationships may be exaggerated when a child is genetically predisposed to a disorder such as manic-depression, and/or suffers trauma (Crittenden *Assessing* 34).

William James wrote that "the great sense of terror in infancy is solitude" (as quoted in Howe 6), and the permanent loss of an attachment figure is a huge challenge for any child. Crittenden claims that, "loss is the universal and ultimate danger. Loss of an attachment figure during childhood threatens personal survival" (*Assessing* 251). However, for those insecurely attached, loss or other trauma, including abuse, poverty, and severe illness can be especially difficult to cope with and "can lead to behaviours that are angry, obsessive and compulsive" (Howe 121). Repeated losses or trauma compound the difficulties. Patricia Crittenden claims that an "especially threatening" situation occurs when early danger

> is repeated at later ages. Loss of an attachment figure in childhood that was followed by loss of other attachment figures would be an example of an extremely and repeatedly traumatizing set of dangers that would require extensive effort to resolve, that is, to enable the individual to feel safe. The effect might be to exaggerate use of the individual's existing strategy by making it more rigidly self protective. (Crittenden *Assessing* 250)

Avoidant types tend to bottle emotions, but, in order to maintain composure, arousal and stress levels tend to be high and grieving remains unresolved (Howe 121).

However, there is considerable evidence to suggest that creative behavior can ameliorate the effects of repeated trauma from loss. In both object relations and attachment theory, infants first form symbols as a substitute when the care-giver is absent. If the care-giver and infant are emotionally mis-matched and disruptions in attachment are chronic, the infant feels anxiety. Imagination serves to counteract anxiety. In later life, the drive to control anxiety can result in obsessional behavior, even addiction to creativity itself, a compulsion to create (Kavaler-Adler, *Compulsion* 2). The less rigid and controlling a person is, the more potential there is for what Andrew Brink refers to as an open obsessional response (*Obsession* 16, 25). If a person develops the capacity to express feelings through words, then this can help increase flexibility and adaptability. Writing functions like play and can in effect become therapeutic, at least temporarily. Writers can develop the capacity to renegotiate severed or damaged attachments in the imagination and through creative expression. Early trauma sensitizes writers to loss, so that losses later in life will activate distressing and unresolved memories, causing them to erupt into present consciousness. Nevertheless, writers have the facility to manipulate imagery and symbol in order to manage anxiety by shifting it into fictional situations and in some cases onto fictionalized characters within the ordered form of a novel, play, or poem. A number of researchers have studied the significance of early loss in future achievement, eminence, and creativity. Measuring eminence by inclusion in encyclopedias, Eisenstadt et al. found that, "by age ten 25.0 percent of the subjects had one parent dead, and by age fifteen 34.5 percent had one parent dead" (*Parental* 11) and this is more than twice the rate of parental death from the general population based on census data (*Parental* 19). Of 563 products of eminent subjects, 439 products were published or performed after the father died. Out of 516 creative products of eminent subjects, 312 products appeared after the mother died (Eisenstadt, *Understanding* 3). The implication is that creativity arose out of early loss or a later grief reaction.

All of the writers in the current study are Victorian by birth, the oldest, F. W. H. Myers, being born in 1843 and the youngest, Aldous Huxley, being born in 1894. His death, in 1963, is also the latest of those studied. With the relatively low life expectancy for this period, of 44 for males and 47 for females in 1900, though rising to over 60 by 1930 (Jalland 7, 5), one might expect that children would lose parents while relatively young, especially since the average age at first marriage was approximately 26 for women between 1900 and 1920, and for men 27.2 in 1900 rising to 28 in 1920 (Tomka 52–3).[2] Even so, there are an exceptional number of contemporary writers (British or living in the British Isles) who lost parents in childhood, including Elizabeth Bowen (1899–1973), Gerald Bullett (1893–1958), Thomas Burke (1886–1945), Frances Hodgson Burnett (1849–1924), Agatha Christie (1890–1976), Joseph Conrad (1857–1924), Caradoc Evans (1878–1945), E. M. Forster (1879–1970), Kenneth Grahame (1859–1932), Edmund Gurney (1847–1888), Rider Haggard (1856–1925), Radclyffe Hall (1880–1943), Frank Harris (1856–1931), A. P. Herbert (1890–1971), William Hope Hodgson (1877–1918), A. E. Housman (1859–1936), Laurence Housman (1865–1959), Christopher Isherwood (1904–1986), James Laver (1899–1975), C. S. Lewis (1898–1963), John Masefield (1878–1967), Somerset Maugham (1874–1965), George Moore (1852–1933), Edwin Muir (1887–1959), E. Nesbit (1858–1924), Mollie Panter-Downes (1906–1997), Eden Phillpotts (1862–1960), J. B. Priestley (1894–1984), Herbert Read (1893–1968), Dorothy Richardson (1873–1957), Henry Handel Richardson (1870–1946), Bertrand Russell (1872–1970), Siegfried Sassoon (1886–1967), Henry de Vere Stacpoole (1863–1951), Frank Swinnerton (1884–1982), P. L. Travers (1899–1996), Mary Webb (1881–1927), and Francis Brett Young (1884–1954). Numerous others experienced differing forms of trauma including abuse or severe illness, such as Stella Benson (1892–1933), Robert Graves (1895–1985), and H. G. Wells (1866–1946). Of the writers in this study, Frederic Myers, May Sinclair, Virginia Woolf, and Aldous Huxley lost a parent before adulthood. The others suffered a variety of traumas, including the loss of a sibling, in the case of Barrie – with a crippling effect on his mother; physical abuse at the hands of maternal substitutes or at school – extreme even for the period – as in the case of Rudyard Kipling, Oliver Lodge, and Arthur Conan Doyle; or trauma resulting from the need to suppress what was considered socially unacceptable and in fact illegal behavior, as with Wilfred Owen's homosexuality. With all of the subjects, trauma was enhanced and complicated by other factors including parental alcoholism in the case of Sinclair and Doyle, descent into poverty resulting in frequent moves and decreased familial stability, again in Sinclair's and Doyle's situations, workaholic parents in the case of Lodge's parents and Woolf's father, and sexual abuse, in Woolf's case.

One of the most significant features linking all of the writers under consideration is that they had already developed an avoidant-resistant pattern of attachment by the time trauma struck, making it a real challenge to surmount trauma, and especially repeated trauma. Nevertheless, this pattern of attachment offered them several advantages as they learned to transform trauma through imaginative writing. As Howe notes, "dismissing individuals are particularly vigilant in monitoring other people's facial expressions and body language for any potential sign of attachment relevant cues, particularly negative ones" (108). These skills of observation and awareness of conflict are essential tools for the writer. Since the nervous systems of dismissive types are over-sensitized or hyper-aroused they tend to be highly reactive, so that past "fears of danger, isolation and hurt" erupt into consciousness, but this also gives them access to these powerful emotions and the urge to manage them by fictionalizing them (Howe 185). Their considerable capacity for thinking about feeling is essential when transforming emotion recollected in tranquillity, as Wordsworth put it, into coherent fictional form. They also tend to maintain distance from intimacy as a defense against threat, giving them the solitude necessary for writing (Howe 106, 123).

Researchers determine attachment patterns in adults typically through interviews, such as the Adult Attachment Interview. This discourse is analyzed to determine patterns or constructs. A psychobiographer can similarly analyze patterns or constructs from a writer's oeuvre, though without the same precision that an interview with a living person can provide. Avoidant or dismissive adults have been subdivided according to dominant constructs within their discourse. One pertinent pattern, "Role Reversal, occurs when a subject recounts being endangered and needing comfort and protection, but being placed in the position of having to provide these to the parent instead" (Crittenden *Assessing* 73). J. M. Barrie provides a striking instance of this. Another, "Neglect," pertains to subjects whose parents are psychologically distant, "unaware of, and inattentive to, their children's needs. Parents who retreat from the family into excessive work are often neglecting, as are parents who are depressed" (Crittenden *Assessing* 74). Both Oliver Lodge and Virginia Woolf record instances of this pattern. In the "Performance" construct, acceptance and love for the child hinges on demands of excessively high performance, leading to compulsive overachievement, identified by its association with danger (Crittenden *Assessing* 75). Most of the writers under consideration demonstrate some aspect of this construct, but Arthur Conan Doyle in particular records significant evidence of it; many of his adventures, both in the world and in writing, involved an element of danger. In general, avoidant types tend to inhibit display of negative feelings and withhold parts of the story they do not want to discuss. They tend to substitute "startlingly vivid, intrusive, and recurrent images" of the context of an emotional situation, such as images of comforting places, instead of emotion experienced by the speaker in reaction to attachment figures (Crittenden *Assessing* 90), as will be seen clearly in Myers's autobiography. When these figures are discussed, it tends to be in a distanced manner, so the subject will refer to "the parents" rather than "my parents," a habit Doyle developed in referring to his mother as "The Ma'am," and a moniker also occasionally used by Kipling. Also typical is false positive affect, that is, using "inappropriate positive affect at times when negative affect would be more appropriate, particularly when danger is discussed," and these tend to be made in parenthetical statements (Crittenden *Assessing* 89). Striking examples of this appear in Virginia Woolf's writing. Avoidant-resistant interviews typically involve more sophisticated strategies, including idealization, oscillation of thought, and false cognition, and "can swing between denotative and evocative extremes" (Crittenden *Assessing* 231). Crittenden claims that, "in terms of images, they both avoid affectively rousing descriptions and, when it is not possible to fail to recall, they also use sensory images of desired comfort or vivid images of the things that they fear or that elicit anger" (*Assessing* 231). In fiction, these strategies can result in vivid, unpredictable, imaginatively engaging, and appealing prose.

When trauma occurs on a mass scale, as it did during the First World War, those insecurely attached will face greater challenges in coping than those securely attached, but even the protective strategies of those securely attached will be activated and the weaknesses and fault lines in them will show under the strain (Howe 82). Kai Erickson defines "collective trauma" as "a blow to the basic tissues of social life that damages the bonds attaching people together and impairs the prevailing sense of communality" (460). Despite the relevance of object relations and attachment theory, its established body of evidence and potential contribution to understanding death and mourning in the wake of trauma, rather surprisingly the historians who have examined these topics in the period leading up to and including the First World War, including Julie-Marie Strange, Jay Winter, and Pat Jalland, have ignored these theories, even in the case studies presented within their larger analysis of society as a whole.[3] However, even on the level of English culture we might speculate that on the home front the avoidant-resistant mode would be fully activated, perhaps even dominant, as civilians engaged in patriotic behavior (to the extent of being held in the hypnotic sway of patriotism), suppressed emotions, kept a stiff British upper lip and yet were preoccupied with lost loved ones, and increasingly demonstrated ambivalence towards the war as the horror of it became known. Although the phrase stiff upper lip apparently originated in the United States in the early nineteenth century, by the late nineteenth century it was firmly British and associated with the "play up and play the game" ethos driving the expansion of the British Empire. Interestingly, the findings in the present study roughly align with Jalland's that in the post-war period the stiff upper lip dominated, that is, there was a shift to a culture of avoidance and reticence in dealing with death (xiii).[4] But she does not probe the psychology of this. Nevertheless, the shift is not surprising considering the vast numbers of abruptly severed early relationships brought about by the deaths of fathers and husbands at war (Jay Winter [*Sites* 46] estimates that in all the nations involved in the First World War six million children lost fathers and three million women lost husbands).

If mysticism was a widespread response to this trauma, as I am arguing, can object relations and attachment theory shed any light on why or how mysticism met the needs of those suffering? I believe they can, without reducing the mystical impulse to a psychological construct or, worse, a manifestation of pathology. I take heed of Aldous Huxley's argument that mysticism cannot be reduced to any particular discourse that would explain it away (as quoted in L. Huxley *Timeless* 195). Aldous Huxley warned in particular about the "depth psychologist, who assures us that mystical experiences are simply the revivals of some obscure memory of infantile bliss at the mother's breast, or, better still, a fetal bliss within the womb. (What utter Bosh! But let that pass.)"

(as quoted in L. Huxley *Timeless* 195). My approach aligns with Huxley's and also with William James in *The Varieties of Religious Experience*. For James, religious experience is "the subconscious continuation of our conscious life" and also a connection with the "more," beyond his power to analyze or judge (*Varieties* 512). In other words, the psychological dimension of mysticism does not preclude the spiritual dimension. James suggested that mystical states arose from the subliminal (*Varieties* 426). He cited Myers's view that the subliminal was "the enveloping mother-consciousness in each of us" ("Frederic Myers's" 218), a revealing analogy in the light of object relations and attachment theory. Mystical experience arising from the subliminal invariably involved "reconciliation," strove towards unity, and conveyed a sense of security (*Varieties* 388; Browning 258). Myers claimed that mystics, like geniuses, have greater access to the transcendental realm through the subliminal (*Human* II 286), and psychologist Edward Kelly concludes that for Myers there was a fundamental connection between genius and mysticism (Kelly 493). Evelyn Underhill claimed that "the essence of the mystic life consists in the remaking of personality: its entrance into a conscious relation with the Absolute. This process is accompanied in the mystic by the development of an art expressive of his peculiar genius: the art of contemplation" (*Mysticism* 448). This art she compares with poetry writing and other forms of creation. Mysticism, then, plays a reparative, restorative, and also creative role, enhanced in the face of loss or other trauma. While not embracing the concept of mysticism or spiritualism, David Howe, a contemporary attachment theorist, recognizes that it is natural for bonds to continue after death. He claims that, "in the case of the death of a loved one, for many people, although by no means everyone, even though the loss is acknowledged and understood, a kind of continuing bond, perfectly normal and healthy, often exists with the deceased for months, even years" (84). He also comments that in old age, "God and other religious figures increasingly serve attachment functions" (94).

Mysticism, including spiritualism, has a particular attraction for avoidant-resistant individuals, especially when confronted with unexpected recurrent loss. As Knight Dunlap notes, mysticism is derived from the Greek *mysterion*, itself "derived from the term *myo*" which means "to be mysterious or secret"; literally, "to keep one's mouth shut" (13). Mysticism is inward looking and makes consciousness central, the supreme reality, rather than the external world (Kelly 574). Since they cannot convey their experience directly, mystic writers resort to symbolism and mythology (Spurgeon 6), aligning with the narrative strategies of avoidant-resistant types. Yet mysticism in James's view does not lead to detachment or indifference but to renewal of engagement in life. It must serve the strenuous life (Browning 265–66). Michael Eigen argues that "Mystical moments also involve a sense of movement between dimensions of experience, and between self and other" (31), and he notes that Winnicott showed that "transitional experiencing" opened new relations between self and other and new ways of experiencing the world (32); thus mysticism offers the opportunity for therapeutic growth. In spiritualism the "other" communicated with from the beyond has an ambiguous status, both there, in the voice or script, but at a remove since vocalized through a medium or conveyed in script as in automatic writing, and thus disembodied. In this sense, connecting to a loved one through a medium is a transitional experience, where the medium, and the voice or script of the loved one, become a symbolic substitute for the embodied person. Spirit communication, typically fragmentary and symbolic, requires an act of creativity where imagination fills in its gaps and absences, and anxiety generated by preoccupation with attachment can be diminished. Of the forty-two writers listed above (including the four in the present study) who experienced early loss of parents, at least 75 percent turned to some form of mystical writing, whether expressed in the fantasy or supernatural genres, or through autobiographical descriptions of mystical experiences, as in the case of Russell (Brink *Russell* 63–66), or in writing about mysticism, as did Sinclair in *A Defence of Idealism* and Bullett in *The English Mystics*, or in some combination of these forms.

Further, mysticism and spiritualism, far from being delusional or pathological responses to loss and mourning, can in some instances represent a more ethical form of mourning (because intimately honoring the individuality of lost loved ones) than officially sanctioned representations of mourning such as war memorials. Far from functioning as a wasteful diversion "from attacking the cause of the young men's deaths," as Warner claims (244), sustained spiritualist connection could allow the mourner to take responsibility for the lost loved one, to find expression for the compassion or other feelings they may not have been able or willing to express while the person lived. Recent theorists of mourning and the role of elegy support this viewpoint. Clifton Spargo states that "a resistant and incomplete mourning stands for an ethical acknowledgement of [the identity] of the other whom one mourns" (13). Patricia Rae, following Derrida, suggests that the dead are placed in an imagined space within the self (17). This is analogous to the object relational transitional space. The placement can be achieved by the device of prosopopeia, the self-conscious fiction of an apostrophe to an absent, deceased, or nameless entity, which posits the possibility of the latter's reply and confers upon it the power of speech (17). Virginia Woolf's *Jacob's Room* and Wilfred Owen's "Strange Meeting" are the most obvious examples of this, but spirit soldier memoirs, such as Lodge's *Raymond*, in effect accomplish something similar depending on how one views the status of the messages from the beyond. As will become clear, all of the writers in this study developed some form of resistant mourning expressed in their writing, which ran counter to mainstream culture, whether this took the forms of spiritualist scripts, as in the case of Doyle, or innovative fiction, as in Woolf's war novels.

Traditionally, historians such as Jay Winter have viewed war memorials as serving the role of helping the bereaved recover from their loss (96) in a "highly personal" way. The war memorial "used collective expression, in stone and in ceremony, to help individual people – mothers, fathers, wives, sons, daughters, and comrades-in-arms – to accept the brutal facts of death in war" (94). Memorials do not express anger and triumph, suggesting their existential purpose. We do know that memorials attracted huge numbers of people to pay their respects. The temporary cenotaph in London attracted half a million people in a week, so the decision was made to make it permanent (Hanson 419). When the tomb of the Unknown Warrior was constructed in 1920, over one million visited it in a week (Jalland 61). Neil Hanson notes that reporters "accorded the Cenotaph an almost mystical significance," one registering "moments of silence when the dead seemed very near, when one almost heard the passage of countless wings – were not the fallen gathering in their hosts to receive their comrades' salute ...?" (as quoted in Hanson 418). Not surprisingly, the designer of the Cenotaph, Edwin Lutyens, embraced spiritualist and theosophical ideas, through his wife's commitment to theosophy and his friendship with spiritualists, including Oliver Lodge (Winter 103). Will Longstaff painted several war memorials, including the London Cenotaph in "The Immortal Shrine," with ghosts of soldiers marching past them, perhaps suggesting the mood the monuments evoked or implying that memorials do not express all regarding mourning and that the unseen were more significant than the memorials themselves.

Nevertheless, Winter does not demonstrate that the meaning of war memorials was "highly personal" by providing actual testimony from the bereaved to support this (94). Memorials may have provided a temporary salve, but as Jalland argues they were a mixed blessing and did not mitigate the grief of all (62, 68). Several writers, including

Owen and Huxley in this study, were highly critical of memorials and resisted this conventional form of mourning. Owen expressed his cynicism about memorializing soldiers in his "Dulce Et Decorum Est." The inscription, "Dulce et decorum est/Pro patria mori" (it is sweet and right to die for your country), such as one might find on a memorial, closes this angry poem about a gas attack. He put the lie to traditional rhetoric associated with war, and this poem became an anthem in the post-war period. Aldous Huxley satirizes the mixed motives, which have nothing to do with actual feelings of loss, of those involved in creating a war memorial in his novel *Crome Yellow* (99–100). Siegfried Sassoon perhaps most specifically satirizes the function of memorials to erase memory of individual anguish and death in "Memorial Tablet (Great War)" and "On Passing the New Menin Gate," the memorial inscribed with thousands of names of soldiers who died at Ypres. He closes "Menin Gate" with the bitter question: "Was ever an immolation so belied / As these intolerably nameless names? / Well might the Dead who struggled in the slime / Rise and deride this sepulcher of crime" (Sassoon). Kipling's attitude towards memorials is more complicated, since on the one hand he composed or selected official inscriptions for the Imperial War Graves Commission, but he also felt compelled to write his own "Epitaphs of the War," each one evoking an individual response to death, some from a dead soldier's perspective, and some conveying his own anger and bitterness, such as "Common Form": "If any question why we died / Tell them, because our fathers lied." In his poem "London Stone," his bleak name for the London Cenotaph where the poem is set, grief threatens to overwhelm, through the repeated parenthetical and yet exclamatory refrain "(Grieving! – Grieving!)." Gathering at the Cenotaph for the Armistice ceremony is only effective for a few minutes:

> For those minutes, let it wake
> (Grieving! Grieving!)
> All the empty-heart and ache
> That is not cured by grieving

This is because grieving "must last our whole lives through." Only the realization that others similarly suffer "may ease the grieving," but this is tentative and the implication is that the grieving will never end, a clearly resistant attitude towards mourning.

Jenny Hazelgrove claims that spiritualism acted as a living memorial to the dead and performed an identical function to commemorative art such as memorials (35), but she fails to make the distinction that spiritualism was much more personal and did not rely on appeals to general ideals of duty, sacrifice, and love of one's country. As has been suggested, spiritualism allowed development and revision of an intimate relationship over time. Further, its controversial status challenged the status quo and denied state efforts to manage sorrow (Rae 18). Chronic, irreconcilable mourning as expressed in spirit soldier memoirs or imaginative work in general (Illustration 0.2) could in effect act as a route to justice by articulating injustice and in resisting "normal" mourning.

Spiritualism did not suddenly rise up during the war but had been gaining momentum since its modern incarnation in the United States in the mid-nineteenth century. The phenomenon was so widespread in

Illustration 0.2 John E. Sutcliffe. "A kiss from the trenches"

late nineteenth-century England that in 1882 the Society for Psychical Research (SPR), comprising many eminent members of society, was formed to investigate the claims of survival beyond death as well as other psychic phenomena. Of the writers in this study, Frederic Myers was instrumental to the development of the SPR, Lodge and Doyle became prominent members, Sinclair and Huxley belonged, and the rest, except for Owen, engaged with its findings to one degree or another. Psychical research gave spiritualism a new respectability, but it also exposed charlatans in the movement, most famously Mme. Blavatsky. A number of spiritualists, including Arthur Conan Doyle, found the rigors of psychical research annoying and preferred to accept spiritualism as a belief system. Most of the writers considered in this study had at least encountered psychical research or spiritualism or both prior to the war, though, like Doyle, their attitude may well have been ambivalent.

During the war a number of conditions arose which drew large numbers of people towards spiritualism, aside from the obvious condition of sudden mass traumatic bereavement. First, a huge number of soldiers' bodies (nearly half of those killed) were not recovered or were unrecognizable, so the comfort of literally mourning over the body of the loved one in the home was lost (Jalland 374). Rudyard Kipling, the most famous of parents in this tortuous situation wrote that, "We are a very large band now – we parents who do not know where our dead are laid: and I think, it is that indignity which moves us as much as anything" (*Letters* 379–80).

Second, in early 1915 transport of soldiers to England for burial was prohibited (Jalland 188), and this was reconfirmed in December 1917 (van Emden 251). After the war, the Imperial War Graves Commission prohibited exhumations to bring soldiers' bodies back to England and elsewhere (van Emden 252). The official reasons given were that only the wealthy would be able to afford to bring their loved one's remains home, which went contrary to the principle of equality of treatment, and emptying so many graves would involve a colossal amount of work and would disrupt the cemeteries that had been offered to Britain by the nations where the battlefields lay. Unofficially, it was thought that those less fortunate might agitate for government support to repatriate their lost loved ones, and this would be too costly, and that a continuous stream of coffins arriving in Britain would be overwhelmingly demoralizing (Hanson 352). These decisions further contributed to removing the comfort and certainty of placing the body in a sacred place, usually nearby the home. As Julie-Marie Strange states, war "stripp[ed] bereavement bare," and "the absence of a corpse rendered customary rights of mourning obsolete" (272–73). Without a body onto which to project feelings, mourners shifted focus to the soul or spirit, and yet the manifestation of a spirit whether in auditory or visual form still satisfied the human need for tactile representation of the lost loved one.

Third, traditional mourning rituals were no longer considered appropriate, since soldiers had fallen "in a sacred cause," and sorrow was not considered correct "as for those who come to a less glorious end" (Lerner 101). Fourth, the traditional Christian church did not adapt quickly to the radically changed circumstances of mass bereavement and thus failed to provide adequate comfort for the bereaved. Rene Kollar notes that in 1914, for instance, public prayer for the dead was uncommon in the Church of England, although it became widespread by the end of the war (17). As Jenny Hazelgrove argues, spiritualism met the needs of mourners because it was more fluid and nimble than traditional religions and had a capacity to absorb and explain traditional beliefs (14). However, spiritualism also had the ability to absorb scientific or at least arguably scientific findings on psychic phenomena and notably on the concepts of telepathy and ether, developed by Frederic Myers and Oliver Lodge respectively.

Ironically, spiritualism itself took on the form of a religion. In 1914 the Spiritualists' National Union claimed 145 affiliate societies; in 1919 the number had increased to 309, and by 1937 there were 520, for a total of about 250,000 members (Jalland 371), with as many more spiritualist meeting places not associated with the union and as many as 100,000 home séance circles (Hazelgrove 14, 15). Rene Kollar notes that, "most spiritualist societies and organizations began to view themselves as churches" and articulated "a fundamentally religious point of view" (xii). Main proponents, such as Oliver Lodge and Arthur Conan Doyle, viewed spiritualism as an extension of Christian faith. Lodge wrote that there is nothing in the spiritualistic creed "which is alien to the Christian faith" ("Christianity" 171), and Doyle regarded it "as a scientific development of the attitude and teaching of Christ" (*History* II 272). Doyle repeatedly made great efforts to show that spiritualism could unify, renew, and revitalize Christianity (*New* 58; *History* II 262–77). As Rene Kollar has shown, the Church of England took spiritualism seriously. In the 1920 Lambeth Conference and the 1939 Archbishop's Committee on Spiritualism, the church reported favorably on the claims of spiritualism "and even argued that spiritualism might indeed complement Anglicanism and help Christians" come to terms with war loss (x). Nevertheless, these reports were not made public until 1979, and point to spiritualism as a site of anxiety and conflict. The Catholics tended to be more hostile to spiritualism, and in 1926 the Catholic

Crusade Against Spiritualism viewed it as a cult (Kollar 19). From another angle, scientists and rationalists could also be quite hostile, G. Stanley Hall claiming for instance that "Spiritism is 'The common enemy of true science and true religion'" (as quoted in Hess 17).

The controversy surrounding spiritualism certainly kept it at the forefront of public debate, but it was not the only other response to loss besides the state-sanctioned memorials and ceremonies. Other behaviors confirm the inadequacy of memorials as sufficient for mourning. Large numbers traveled to soldier cemeteries in France to search for loved ones' graves, beginning as early as 1919 when the Church Army took 5,000 families (before June), although some had wanted to travel to the battlefield while the fighting still raged (van Emden 284). Tens of thousands visited during the 1920s (van Emden 287), and by 1931, 140,000 made the pilgrimage per year (Wilkinson). Others obsessively reconstructed the last days and hours of lost loved ones, including Kipling (Jalland 44). They created remembrance books and household shrines (Jalland 63).

With their great facility in writing, the subjects in this study primarily exercised creative expression as their form of resistant and ethical mourning. At their best, they took a sacramental approach to the supernatural, in Glen Cavaliero's terms, where the uncanny is viewed as the province of the imagination (21). Through their published writing, all of them helped shape responses to loss in their culture, but three of them in particular, Myers, Lodge, and Doyle, contributed significantly to making mysticism (incorporating psychical research and spiritualism) a high-profile response to war loss. Chapter 1 chronicles Frederic Myers's quest to establish continuity between natural experience and what he called supernormal experience, in order to prove that human personality survived bodily death. Driven by the tragic suicide of the love of his life, Annie Marshall, Myers's enormous labors in psychical research set the agenda for a significant twentieth-century approach to loss and mourning. Chapter 2 probes Lodge's extension of Myers's research in his theory of the ether. Lodge suffered neglect from preoccupied parents and extensive bullying at school, but when he was contacted at his first séance by his Aunt Anne, the one person who had nurtured him and expanded his educational horizons, he became committed to psychical research and spiritualism. His huge scientific reputation enhanced psychical research's credibility, and he popularized arguments for survival in his numerous pre-war publications, as well as in his most famous book, his pioneering spirit soldier memoir of his son, *Raymond* (1916). Chapter 3 traces the trajectory of Arthur Conan Doyle's interest in psychical research and spiritualism, from early skepticism and parody to unabashed proselytizing after he suffered multiple losses of loved ones during the war. Doyle's responses to loss were shaped by an unstable early home life, including his father's alcoholism, poverty, and his mother's enmeshed relationship with Doyle. Similarly to Lodge, Doyle suffered severe punishment at school, against which he rebelled, a stance he continued to take when championing various causes, including spiritualism. Doyle became the leader of the spiritualist movement during and after the war, doing more than any other single person to popularize it. Chapters 4 and 5 deal with pairs of writers – J. M. Barrie and Rudyard Kipling, and May Sinclair and Virginia Woolf respectively – because their responses to loss and their engagement with mysticism bear some striking similarities. Both Barrie and Kipling had complicated relationships with their soldier sons (or surrogate sons, in the case of Barrie) and both faced huge challenges in coping with the sons' loss. Their ambivalent attitude towards mysticism prompted them to explore a variety of responses through enigmatic plays, stories, and poems. Although May Sinclair was pro-war and participated briefly in an ambulance unit, while Woolf was a pacifist, both explored fleeting transcendent connections between people beyond death. Their initial explorations of war loss enabled them to probe more fully childhood losses in subsequent autobiographical fiction. Chapter 6 explores archetypal war poet Wilfred Owen's particular form of mysticism, his obsessive use of ghosts and phantasms in his poetry to mask anxiety about homoerotic impulses. Chapter 7 probes lost generation satirist Aldous Huxley's response to a triple trauma in early life. During and after the war he savaged mysticism in his writing, but anxiety about the possibility of another war brought on depression and exploration of mysticism in modernist fiction as a successful reparative strategy.

Although these writers expressed their mystical impulse in very different styles and forms, and they belong to different generations, in some instances their devotion to mysticism fostered creative networks extending even to uncanny connection between them. This is particularly true of the later-Victorian men, Myers, Lodge, Doyle, Barrie, and Kipling. Myers mentored both Lodge and Doyle and they considered him a genius. His profound influence on Lodge extended beyond the grave, since Myers purportedly took Oliver's son Raymond under his wing in "Summerland," as Lodge referred to the afterlife. Doyle's and Lodge's conversation about spiritualism at their Knight of the Garter ceremony in 1902 made that event worthwhile, according to Doyle. The two corresponded about mediums and séances for years, though Lodge was more conservative in his claims about spiritualism and spirit photography and said of Doyle that he lacked the wisdom of the serpent (as quoted in Higham 302). Doyle wished that Lodge had left out his philosophical musings in *Raymond* to make it more accessible to the common man, but he greatly admired Lodge's courage in conveying his personal experience of spirit communication. Lodge on his part read Sherlock Holmes to his children (*Past* 249), and to his wife Doyle's spiritualist novel *The Land of Mist* in which Lodge is praised as "the first brain of Europe" (*Land* 244; Hill *Letters* 230). Doyle held a great deal of respect and affection for his fellow Scotsman J. M. Barrie and he even collaborated with him on a play, *Jane Annie, or the Good Conduct Prize*, though it was a "dreadful failure" (Barrie *Greenwood* 183). Barrie impishly sent to Doyle his short story, "The Adventure of the Two Collaborators," in which they enlist Sherlock Holmes to discover why it failed (Stashower 143). Perhaps more profoundly, Doyle saw in Barrie's dynamic mother something of his own, claiming that she was "wonderful with a head and a heart – a rare combination which made me class her with my own mother" (*Memories* 249). He was full of praise for Barrie's portrait of his mother, *Margaret Ogilvy*, which Doyle described as "so fine a work" (Lellenberg *Letters* 384). Doyle highly admired Kipling (Stashower 185) and they corresponded for years; Kipling on his part was a fan of Doyle's. Their interest in the paranormal drew them together; Kipling paid tribute to Doyle in his psychic detective story, "The House Surgeon," by naming the house Holmescroft (Ricketts 209). Barrie and Kipling came to know one another while writing for W. E. Henley between 1888 and 1897, when they were considered members of "the Henley Regatta" writers group (Ricketts 161). May Sinclair was perhaps more on the fringes of male-dominated literary circles, but in her autobiographical novel *Mary Olivier*, her protagonist possesses a row of Rudyard Kipling's books (301). We do get glimpses of her sharing the high table with the Doyles at a Society of Authors dinner in 1912 (Boll 95), or meeting with Virginia Woolf in 1909, when significantly they discussed mystical moments of ecstasy (Woolf *Letters* I 390).

These writers read and quoted from one another, mostly approvingly, but with occasional criticism. On one occasion Barrie wrote of Kipling that, "his chief defect is ignorance of life," but he made the astute observation that Kipling's genius lay in the short story (Ricketts 130, 173). May Sinclair drew Lodge's ire when in 1917 she reviewed Charles Mercier's *Spiritualism and Sir Oliver Lodge*, but she made amends by apologizing (Boll 112). Woolf drew on Sinclair's essay "The Novels of Dorothy Richardson," in which Sinclair was the first to apply "stream of consciousness" to the novel, in "Modern Fiction," one of Woolf's polemics attacking the Edwardians as materialists (Zegger 98; Silver 18–19,

155–56). In another of these she lambasted Doyle's Sherlock Holmes stories, stating that "to me Dr. Watson is a sack stuffed with straw, a dummy, a figure of fun" (*Essays* III 426).

As a post-war intellectual, Huxley entered the literary circles in which Virginia Woolf traveled, notably at Lady Ottoline Morrell's Garsington, and he admired Virginia Woolf's language, though not what he viewed as her detached characterization (Murray 246). Although in one novel he has a character scorning the Edwardian Peter Pan generation (*Time* 304), he himself discovered the superiority of Victorian Frederic Myers's description of the subliminal and extensions of human personality over Freud's and even Jung's psychology. He confirmed Lodge's vision of the posthumous state as expressed in *Raymond* (Huxley *Doors* 112). Virginia Woolf was more ambivalent about "these psychical people" as she referred to the psychical researchers, but she learned about them through her friendships with the Strachey brothers and Leo Myers, Frederic's novelist son, a contemporary of Woolf's. In a letter she referred to Leo as "the son of the man who saw ghosts" (*Letters* III 54), a significant epithet given that she grappled with plenty of ghosts herself. Wilfred Owen is perhaps the odd man out since he had just started to meet the London literati (though he was thrilled to catch a glimpse of Rudyard Kipling; Owen *Letters* 337) and had only published five poems by the time of his early death.

Nevertheless, most of the writers under study drew on a psychologically informed common mystical discourse framed by psychical researchers, including Frederic Myers and William James, and students of spiritualism such as Lodge and Doyle, although they may not have read directly in this field and may have felt doubts or ambivalence about the findings; thus the incidents and tropes used to express loss and mourning take on recognizable forms, such as "the crisis apparition" and the "spirit communication." These writers experienced mystical states and were drawn to this discourse in their attempts to articulate it because of their experience of early disruptions in attachment, including various types of trauma such as death of loved ones. Their insecure attachments sensitized them to later loss, but they developed the capacity to manage threatening feelings of anger, anxiety, and isolation through writing about it, whether in autobiographical, informational, or fictional forms. Losses during the First World War reactivated unresolved mourning and fostered preoccupation with severed relationships, but mysticism in various forms enabled them to renegotiate and in some cases extend these relationships. In some situations this enabled them to engage in a more ethical form of mourning by honoring the individuality of lost loved ones. This could prove more therapeutic than officially sanctioned representations of mourning such as war memorials. They might even achieve at-onement, or atonement, with the lost other. With several, their resistant form of mourning appears to have succeeded and enabled writers to then access and creatively renegotiate earlier childhood trauma, as we shall see. For others this was not an unmitigated success, since it could be argued, for instance, that Arthur Conan Doyle's resistant mourning became obsessive in its refusal of closure, or that Kipling's search for his dead son's body became obsessive and unproductive. These writers expressed for many the chaotic feelings associated with traumatic bereavement and they suggested possibilities for healing. They extended the horizon of expectations of their readership regarding survival and associated beliefs and helped to alter the important cultural practice of mourning by bringing the imagination to bear on the grieving process.

In *Mourning and Mysticism* I have chosen a collective psychobiographical approach because I feel that these writers' sustained and courageous grappling with ghosts of their pasts requires psychological probing based on findings from the most pertinent theories about loss and creative repair. In this decision I fly in the face of most of the writers in this book who cautioned against employing a biographical, let alone a psychobiographical approach to their lives. "May God blast anyone who writes a biography of me" cursed J. M. Barrie, in perhaps the least subtle of these excoriations (Chaney i). Their anxiety is not surprising given their avoidant pattern to emotional turmoil and their protective strategies of concealment. They all harbored secrets of great magnitude and paradoxically invested heavily in maintaining privacy despite in most cases being public, even iconic figures. One wonders how they would have coped in the internet age – presumably they would have avoided as much of its invasiveness as possible. Nevertheless, I will try to avoid what Frederic Myers cautions against, that there is "hardly a good easy man among us but might be analysed into half neuropath and half Philistine, if it would serve a theory" (*Human* I 92).[5] These writers are without exception complex, but focusing on loss and responses to it brings into relief patterns relatively consistent over time. Short, chapter-length biographies best capture these where full-length biographies might obscure them in the mass of detail usually presented chronologically. In this spirit of enquiry and sympathy for these writers faced with seemingly insurmountable challenges, let us now turn to their lives.

1
F. W. H. Myers: Loss and the Obsessive Study of Survival

> "I know no man who seems to have lived more consistently in a sort of rapture of thought, without weary or discontented interludes, but in an impassioned ecstasy of sweetness. In this he was a mystic, and his joyful serenity of mind is just what one finds in the lives of mystics."
>
> A. C. Benson "Frederic Myers" 183

> "The reader need not suppose that I expect his admiration. But if he on his part be psychologically minded, he will prefer that idiosyncrasy should not be concealed. If he is to be interested at all, it must be in the spectacle of a man of sensuous and emotional temperament, urged and driven by his own personal passion into undertaking a scientific enterprise, which aims at the common weal of men ... what has been accomplished did in fact demand, – among many nobler qualities contributed by better men, – that importunate and overmastering impulse which none can more fiercely feel than I."
>
> Frederic Myers, introduction to "Fragments of Inner Life" 2

The young boy sits on a wooden chair in a sparsely furnished rectory, his mother presiding over him. The boy looks up, bible in hand, and asks his mummy whether bad people go straight to hell. His mother purses her lips and looks away before telling him that evil people might be destroyed at death. His lip quivers as he asks whether they would have the same fate as the mole he had seen crushed by a cartwheel, and she reluctantly says perhaps. Tears well up and he staggers to his feet, as if reeling from shock. His mother's forehead creases, but before she can respond he has darted out the French window to the garden. She calls out Freddie, but he takes no notice, instead running to his favorite spot, under a great clump and tangle of blush roses. There he sobs, and through his tears looks down on the black pool of Bassenthwaite Lake and then up towards Skiddaw mountain, its shoulders and peak cloaked by cloud. He becomes entranced by the clouds' movements until the peak emerges, as high as heaven, and his tears subside.

Some days later, his mother gently pushes him forward into the sickroom, where the pale and shrunken figure of his father lies, barely recognizable from just a few months before. Then, his father had paced in the study, declaiming Virgil and emphasizing the stresses with his hand. Freddie flushes, remembering how his father had scolded him for not having done his exercises as well as he might have, and he wonders whether this neglect has helped bring on his father's sudden illness. Freddie sits beside his mother, holding her hand, as she with her other hand holds her husband's until it grows cold, and the breath ceases. His mother tries to control her crying, and Freddie places a kiss on her cheek. In the days that follow, he appears at just the right moments, when his mother is borne down by her tragedy, head in her hands, and he caresses her or reads from a little book of Christian Meditations. One time, when overpowered with grief, she murmurs "there can never be joy again." Freddie says earnestly, "You know, God *can* do everything, and He might give us, just once, such a vision of him as should make us happy all our lives after."

Young Freddie grew up to be Frederic W. H. Myers (Illustration 1.1), and the scenes I have reconstructed here capture something of the most critical moments of his early childhood. Myers recounts that he felt "the first horror of a death without resurrection" when he saw a dead mole before age six, and how his "brain reeled under the shock" of being told by his mother that a soul might be annihilated. In a journal, his mother recounted his sensitivity to the death of an unnamed baby cousin and to another called Harry. She also noted how much of a comfort he was to her in her "deep sorrow" after the loss of her husband (Gauld 43). Those losses, particularly of Myers's father, which also entailed the loss of his beloved early environment, combined with his mother's emotional overinvestment in her eldest son, provide the sources for his obsessional quest to prove the survival of personality beyond death. Myers possessed "a sensuous and emotional

Illustration 1.1   Frederic Myers

temperament," as he himself realized, and he learned early on to channel some of this emotion into poetry, increasingly so after he experienced the greatest loss of his adult life, the suicide of his cousin Annie Marshall, for whom he had developed an intense platonic love. From this point on, his response to loss was increasingly avoidant-resistant, as his unresolved mourning and preoccupation with death was directed into his gargantuan labors at psychical research and the dynamic psychology that he constructed. To observers, such as A. C. Benson quoted in the epigraph, he could appear to be "a mystic," living "consistently in a sort of rapture of thought" (183), but his wife, Eveleen was less than thrilled with this detachment.

From the 1880s Myers developed his theory of the subliminal self, with its emphasis on the limitless potential of the psyche, and he also probed many other psychical phenomena, including telepathy, automatic writing, and crisis apparitions, through publications of the Society for Psychical Research, which he helped found in 1882, but also in respected literary publications. Myers, aided by his socially ambitious wife, became the nexus for the fascination with psychical phenomena in the later Victorian period. He was well connected not only with the literati, but also with the philosophers, scientists, and mental scientists intrigued by this pursuit. Although Myers died of a respiratory ailment at a relatively early age, his magnum opus, *Human Personality and its Survival of Bodily Death*, published posthumously in 1903, collected hundreds of cases demonstrating extensions of personality into the realm of spirit, thus supporting his survival of personality thesis. Partly because of its controversial nature, this work was hugely influential to the point where one historian, John Cerullo, has referred to the period from 1903 to the 1920s as "the Age of Myers" in psychical research (103). Myers's work acted as a bridge to the next generation of writers, the Edwardians and emerging modernists, and interest in it surged during and after the war as society attempted to cope with the mass trauma of war loss. Following Myers's lead to one degree or another, writers such as Barrie, Doyle, Kipling, Sinclair, Woolf, Blackwood, and Huxley in this study, and many more besides, considered various extensions of consciousness within a construct of realism, as no longer belonging to the realm of gothic fantasy, and articulated the real possibility of telepathic or spirit communication between the living and between the living and the dead. Interestingly, Myers's voice persisted beyond death as well, since it was purportedly channeled by an astonishing array of mediums; Myers thus had a further impact on mystical responses to loss of writers such as Sir Oliver Lodge, as detailed in Chapter 3.

In his autobiographical "Fragments of Inner Life," Myers invites scrutiny, suggesting that readers "will prefer that [his] idiosyncrasy should not be concealed" (2). However, just before this he states:

> I hold that all things thought and felt, as well as all things done, are somehow photographed imperishably upon the universe, and that my whole past will probably lie open to those with whom I have to do. Repugnant though this thought is to me, I am bound to face it. I realize that a too great discrepancy between my account of myself and the actual facts would, when detected, provoke disgust and contempt.

This statement implies an anxiety about exposure, a repugnance to it, but also a fear of discrepancy, or hypocrisy. What underlies this anxiety? Did Myers have secrets? What is the nature of his self-proclaimed idiosyncrasy? A careful examination of biographical details and the patterns that emerge, through the lens of object relations and attachment theory, can reveal new insights. In the first full-length biography of Myers, Trevor Hamilton counters an earlier biographer Fraser Nichols's speculation that the seeds of Myers's future troubles at Cambridge "were unwittingly planted by the love of a too-doting mother for her brilliant child" (12). Hamilton asserts:

> in the light of other comments on the character of Mrs Myers, this is probably a superficial Freudian speculation. Myers grew up in a very supportive environment, had considerable natural gifts, a strong physique, and optimistic temperament, and huge energy. (12)

Myers's environment may have been supportive up to a point, but it also was exceptional, even for the Victorian period. Myers's father, also Frederic, born in 1811, excelled academically. He became a scholar at Clare College, Cambridge, where he received scholarships and "the Hulsean essay prize in 1830," later becoming a fellow there (Hamilton 10). Myers took religious orders, and in 1838 became the perpetual curate of St John's, Keswick. He married at 28, but his wife Fanny died the next year. He then married Freddie's mother Susan two years later, and so loss and grief would have been embedded in the relationship from its beginning. Whereas he was tolerant, liberal in his religious views, and committed to educating his parishioners, his wife was much more of an evangelical. Both were ambitious, particularly in regards to Freddie. At a very early age Frederic senior taught Freddie the classics, inspiring him with a love of Virgil (10).

Susan concerned herself with Freddie's religious education, emphasizing a literalist understanding of the Bible as well as self-improvement in preparation for the afterlife (Hamilton 12). This education she began when Freddie was just two years and nine months old, and she had him reading the Bible at just over four (Gauld 38). In the journal she kept from the time Freddie was one year and six days old until two months after her husband died when Freddie was eight, she recorded his responses to her teaching, such as his shock and grief "when good men do anything wrong," or his "burst of tears" when she told him that the dead mole had no soul and so would not go to heaven (Gauld 39). She soon realized that he possessed a sensitive nature: "and along with this delight is a proportionate pain when he is disappointed in anything he has set his heart upon – or when his will is crossed, or his fancy, in anything" (Gauld 41). Gauld comments that "the preoccupation with death and the afterworld which Freddie had, as a result of his mother's teachings, by then acquired would now strike the most religious people as altogether morbid, and at times it undoubtedly caused him great unhappiness" (Gauld 42). Her control and cosseting also provoked rebellion in him, and she noted: "he is not grateful or humble as I sh. [sic] like to see him" (Gauld 40). Gauld comments that "he remained careless of parental instructions, and was arrogant and overbearing with other children" (41). Trevor Hamilton cites a family friend who claimed that Mrs Myers "was a cold, hard, woman," and that "Frederick [sic] Myers and his brothers were brought up very carefully if anything too carefully. They were almost prigishly [sic] brought up" (11). Myers himself referred to her character as of "'the old school'; – a character of strong but controlled affections, of clear intelligence, unflinching uprightness, profound religious conviction" ("Fragments" 7). Another factor that may have provoked testing behavior is that Frederic had two brothers who came close on his heels, Ernest, when Freddie was one year and eight months old, and Arthur, when Freddie was just over two. The demands on Susan's time would have increased enormously when her husband suddenly fell ill in the spring of 1851, and then permanently after he died in July 1851. Married just nine years, Susan must have felt abandoned, and she wrote in her diary of her "overwhelming grief," "deep sorrow," and great sadness (Myers 8). Part of her response was her dogged ambition to have his biography published, at which she failed, and to have published his unpublished writing, *Catholic Thoughts* (1873) and *Lectures on Great Men* (1856) at which she succeeded. His death also necessitated a move away from the beloved Lake District, first to a small house in Blackheath, and then, in 1856, to Cheltenham, where her sons could attend Cheltenham College as day boys, since, as Myers put it, "she wished to keep her sons with her" (7–8). Most importantly, again in Myers's own words, she "made our welfare the absorbing interest of her life" (7). Myers's sense of loss is implied in his retrospective, romantic description of the Keswick Parsonage garden where he claimed "my conscious life began": "The memories of those years swim and sparkle in a haze of light and dew. The thought of Paradise is interwoven for me with that garden's glory" ("Fragments" 7).

The consequences of Myers's enmeshed relationship with his mother begin to be seen in his precocity and, in Hamilton's words, "considerable, possibly even overweening, sense of his own worth and status" (16).

While Myers's "awe-struck joy" and "reverent emotion" at first learning and hearing Virgil's poetry is associated with his father, the contents of his own earliest poems would seem to draw on preoccupations and feelings associated with both parents. In 1857, at age fourteen while at Cheltenham, he penned two poems about Belisarius, the Byzantine general unjustly imprisoned and betrayed by his adulterous wife. At first glance these seem unusual subject matter for a youth, but Myers's father had written a volume on Great Men, and Frederic senior may have been presented as one by Susan. Both poems suggest that fame will outlast shame and ensure survival. One ends: "Not in vain to mourn and struggle, not in vain in shame to die / For my fame shall live beyond me, and the recompense is nigh" (60). Both poems also blame women for wrongs done: "It was a woman drove me into penury and night" (53). His other early poems focus on death and subsequent glory, such as his memorial for Robbie Burns (penned at age fifteen), "the Death of Socrates" (age sixteen), and "The Prince of Wales at the Tomb of Washington." The last-mentioned features Washington's communication from beyond the grave that he does not want pardon for revolting from his father's rod, and he compares this to a family dynamic: "Neither can one consent for ever bind / Parent and offspring, but they shall at length / A closer union in disunion find, / In separation strength" (87). It is tempting to speculate that Myers might here be trying to justify or rationalize the loss of his father. Interestingly, in the poem the Prince does not respond to the voice of Washington, but "In solemn silence turned him from the spot" (90).

"The Prince of Wales" was the first poem to gain Myers notoriety when he went up to Cambridge at the early age of seventeen. Myers won the Chancellor's medal for it in 1861 and he recited it at the Cambridge Senate house in an "uncompromising singsong" which was "received with an ominous sound of decided disapproval, compounded of laughs, groans, catcalls, and hisses," according to a contemporary, E. M. Oakley (83–84). However, at the end of the recital he received "a regular ovation" (84). Oakley claimed that Myers "was popularly regarded in the University as a *rara avis in terris*, certainly eccentric, probably negligible" (83). However, his self-absorption and arrogance would lead to much greater notoriety when he was accused of plagiarizing a number of lines from an Oxford Prize Poem collection (Beer 120) in his poem which won the Camden medal for classical verse (the second time he had won this prize). Myers was excelling at Cambridge as an intellect, an athlete, and in religion, so that he came to be known as "the superb," as he noted in his daily diary (as quoted in Hamilton 21). Evidently this went to his head, as he recollected: "Having won a Latin prize poem, I was fond of alluding to myself as a kind of Virgil among my young companions. Writing again a similar poem, I saw in my bookshelves a collection of Oxford prize poems which I picked up somewhere in order to gloat over their inferiority to my own" (as quoted in Beer 122–23). He deliberately "forced" into his poem the best lines (which he referred to as "collecting gold from Ennius' dung heap"), and then was surprised when he was forced to resign the prize and a vote was taken on whether he would be prevented from taking his degree (Beer 122). In an explanatory letter to his uncle, Myers admitted to being "foolish, reckless, & headstrong" and of "acting on crude and sometimes presumptuous opinions without considering or regarding what others will think" (as quoted in Beer 125). He also acknowledged the momentous consequences: "my name has been held up to scorn and reproach in a great number of newspapers[,] for example Athenaeum, (as I am told), Guardian ... many of my acquaintance have had their opinion of me greatly shaken & my mother has been and is seriously distressed" (as quoted in Beer 126). Nor was this an isolated incident, as Myers himself recollected: "many another act of swaggering folly mars for me the recollection of years which might have brought pure advancing congenial toil" (as quoted in Beer 123). Myers was definitely manifesting a resistant dimension in his personality. Hamilton documents that Myers cultivated an anti-intellectual front and that he went through a temporary homosexual phase. He stresses that "Myers had a desire to posture and shock as a young man (and occasionally throughout his life)" (24). By the time Myers graduated from Cambridge at twenty-two with two first-class degrees and a reputation as an intellect and poet, "he was without intellectual and emotional security" (Hamilton 33).

His arrogance and isolation mark a typical avoidant response to unmanageable and misunderstood feeling, and this pattern strikingly emerges in two voyages he made, to Greece and America. During the years from sixteen to twenty-three he seems to have projected much of his emotional turmoil into his passion for Hellenism. For him "the classics were but intensifications of my own being. They drew from me and fostered evil as well as good; they might aid imaginative impulse and detachment from sordid interests, but they had no check for lust or pride" (10). In 1864 he traveled to Greece hoping to increase his intimacy with Greek culture, but he left "with such a sadness" because he realized that his longing for the past was an "unnatural passion" ("Fragments" 11). Agnosticism set in as he traveled through America in 1865; he recounted that "during that time alone in my life [I] felt a numb indifference to both past and future" (12). A striking incident at Niagara Falls captures both his reckless nature and his depression. He decided to swim across the river below the falls late at night and alone, asking himself before he plunged into these dangerous waters, "What if I die?"; his answer "was blank of emotion" (12).

On his return to England he was converted to Christianity "in its emotional fulness" [sic] by Josephine Butler, "an ardent and beautiful woman, much older than myself" and the first of several unattainable women, some with a connection to his mother Susan, for whom Myers felt a sensual attraction ("Fragments" 12–13). The Myers family had known the Butlers in Cheltenham from 1857, when Frederic developed an adolescent crush on this young married woman, but also apparently tried to provoke and shock her (Hamilton 35). As a young man he was drawn closer to her by loss. Susan Myers was the godmother of Josephine's daughter Eva, and she arranged for the Butlers to borrow her brother's house in the Lake District for a holiday. On returning to Cheltenham, as Hamilton recounts, "little Eva died in a fall from the top of the hall stairs. Susan Myers strongly supported Josephine through grieving and helped her to try to assuage her grief by throwing her energies into good and charitable works" (35). Her loss, grieving, and beauty aroused Myers to a "passionate intensity" of belief in her and the Christianity she espoused (as quoted in Hamilton 36). They wrote rapturous letters to one another and made hospital visits to the poor and dying (on one occasion a dying prostitute) (Hamilton 37), but Myers mainly channeled his emotion for Josephine into long sensuous religious poems, including "Translation of Faith," "St John," "Ammergau" (in which he desires to merge with Mother Nature), and "St Paul." The last-mentioned was dedicated to Josephine in September of 1867 and ironically became his most famous poem, going through four editions by 1890 and over a dozen reprints into the 1920s. Myers presents Paul as a loner, "without cheer of sister or of daughter, / Yes, without stay of father or of son," without friend but Christ (105). About women, Paul asks, "What was their sweet desire and subtle yearning, / Lovers and women whom their song enrols? / Faint to the flame which in my breast is burning, / Less than the love wherewith I ache for souls" (106). Hamilton remarks that Myers "at this stage in his life, seems to have been very unstable and to have suffered great swings of emotions and intellectual position" (35). He was obviously sensitized to loss and suffered repeated bouts of depression, yet continued to provoke, shock, and cultivate "an artificial and overblown spiritual intensity" (39), expressed in florid, inflated poetic rhetoric. Nevertheless, in one poem from January 1871, "On Art as Aim in Life," he expresses insight into the therapeutic role of art. In "dark places truth lies hid," but Art can alleviate suffering: "such be thy sorrows, yet methinks for them / Thine Art herself has help and requiem," bringing about repose. In "a lovely dream" of creation:

> What place for anger? What to thee is this
> That foe and friend judge justly or amiss?
> No man can help or harm thee; far away
> Their voices sound and like thin air are they;
> Thou with the primal Beauty art alone,
> And tears forgotten and a world thine own.
>
> How oft fate's sharpest blows shall leave thee strong
> With some re-risen ecstasy of song! (*Collected* 196)

In writing poetry, one removes "far away" to an inner world where not only are tears forgotten, but fate's sharpest blows are renegotiated or re-orchestrated in "some re-risen ecstasy of song!"

Despite the reprieve of poetry, Myers was to suffer further blows in his relational life. He was strongly attracted to physically beautiful women, and noted in his diaries that he proposed marriage to a Miss E in 1871 but was rejected and had an unsuccessful dalliance with a Miss Drew in 1872, among others (Hamilton 39). Throughout these years, he maintained very close relations with his mother. In one letter to her he wrote that, "we have drawn so very close together, and feel the essential unity of our inmost affections and hopes" ("Fragments" 1904 30). He also assured her "that some close affection will be raised up for me to make even this earth a home –" ("Fragments" 1904 31; Beer dates this 1879, 169). As it turned out, his mother played an instrumental role in the development of his relationship with the second unattainable woman who, despite this, would become the love of his life, Annie Marshall. Annie had recently married into his mother's Marshall family when he met her at a luncheon in June 1867. Her husband Walter Marshall was wealthy but had begun to manifest symptoms of manic depression (Hamilton 40). Myers fell in love with Annie when he met her again in February of 1871 at Vevey, which he recollected in a poem of that title. She was lovely "and full of tears unshed; / And my soul sprang to meet her, and I knew / Dimly the hope we twain were called unto" ("Fragments" 24). After June of 1872, when he met her in London, his encounters with her increased, and he even went on holiday to Madeira and the Canary Islands with her and her husband (Hamilton 41). He repeatedly admired her blue eyes and childlike ways, but he claimed that they maintained a platonic love, as he expressed in the poem "Honour," which he claimed "breathes the sadness of a passion accepting moral barriers" ("Fragments" 17) and, from the poem itself, where honor "is enough for her and for him" (19). Part of her attraction must have been her vulnerability and her struggle with losing her husband to increasingly erratic behavior and madness as she became the mother of five of his children. Frederic commented that "the combination of her innocent look, her loveliness, & the tremor of a hidden tragedy which hung over her eyes" fascinated others, and presumably himself ("Fragments" 26). By 1876 Walter's behavior had become extravagant, and at one evening gathering when he began using violent language to Annie, Myers contacted Annie's father and Walter's brother (Beer 157). They had him committed temporarily, and he admitted that he had contracted syphilis when he was 21. After this his symptoms were treated as indicators of the onset of General Paralysis of the Insane and responsibility for him was taken out of Annie's hands (Beer 163). Both Annie and Myers had suffered illness and bouts of depression during this period, probably relating to the impossibility of their relationship as well as guilt, and it appears that they decided not to see one another while Walter remained confined (Beer 161). On 2 July 1876 Myers parted from Annie to travel to Norway with his brother, while Annie returned to a Marshall family house near Hallsteads in the Lake District accompanied by Frederic's mother Susan. Annie had drawn on Susan's support throughout these years, but when they arrived Susan recorded in a letter to Frederic that Annie

> grew silent towards me, after having been *quite* frank & loving – & I could not with all my entreaties get her to speak what was in her mind, after she had once said that she saw she had been quite wrong in everything – in this last step for W. (the certif.) & altogether @ religion – in rejecting Xianity. (as quoted in Beer 164)

One wonders whether Annie's realization that "she had been quite wrong in everything" included Myers now that he was no longer present, and whether this was the source of her change in attitude towards his mother. When Susan sensed that Annie's mood was improving, she left her to travel to Edinburgh. While there, she heard that Annie had committed suicide by wounding herself in the jugular vein and then drowning herself in the lake (Beer 164–65). Her despair about her marital situation and guilt in her role at having Walter confined against his will would have contributed to provoking this act, but there was also mental instability in her family "since two of her sisters died insane" (Hamilton 46). Susan broke the news to Frederic, including the detail that his letter to her had come "too late & is burnt" (as quoted in Beer 164).

To say that Myers was devastated would be an understatement. Annie's loss and the possibility of reuniting with her in the spirit realm would haunt and preoccupy Myers for the rest of his life and would drive his obsessional quest to explore the supernormal dimension of the human psyche and prove that human personality survived bodily death. Her death exacerbated his anxiety about and sensitivity to loss developed from his response to his earliest losses, and the tragedy shaped his relationships from this point forward, particularly that with his eventual wife. Myers's immediate response to Annie's loss was a feeling of the "saddest separation," but once he returned from Norway his mourning was complicated by the fact that he could not express it to all. In a chapter of his autobiography "Fragments of Inner Life" devoted to "Mourning" he wrote that, "the story of my sorrow was such, – the affairs of others were so mingled with it, – that there were few to whom I could speak it out. But I felt that I must tell Lady Mount-Temple all" (27). His confessor was a motherly figure and a spiritualist, who fostered his feeling that "between souls that cling aright there can be no enforced separation" (27). Aside from this talking cure, he appears to have adopted the avoidant response to loss in which his feelings were turned inward in solitude. Myers had always been a devotee of Wordsworth and he quoted his poetic mentor in describing this: "the years which followed upon this tragedy may best be described in a phrase of Wordsworth's, as 'a sinking inward into myself from thought to thought, a steady remonstrance, and a high resolve'" (27). Like Wordsworth, he also returned to the scene of his loss, and he recorded that, "some of the serenest hours of those mourning years were spent in that Valley in the grounds of Hallstead's, on Ullswater, which has been the setting of much of my inward life" (28). Not only was this where Annie, whom he calls Phyllis in his autobiography, had committed suicide but it was also a similar setting to where she had spent her childhood. If "serenest" seems an odd word here, it must be realized that his strongest emotions about Annie and her loss were channeled into a series of poems he wrote and included in his autobiography. In the first, "Love and Death," he captured the intensity of his feeling for Annie:

> All human passions merged in one; –
> The whole soul in one act set free; –
> Mother for daughter, sire for son,
>   Feel faintlier what I feel for thee. (19)

He expressed the immediate impact of her death in another one: "Then came the news that, on me hurled, / At once my youth within me slew, / Made dim with woe the reeling world, / And hid the heaven that shone therethrough" (22). He figured himself as a ghost to express the longer-term effect of her loss:

> And still I roam, with shades a shade,
>   Their mourning pathways to and fro;
> I wait till this confusion fade,
>   These dreary phantoms melt and go;
> Till out of gloom a star shall glow,
>   A stillness gather in the stir,
> And longing eyes her eyes shall know,
>   And wounded heart be whole with her. (22)

The hope of a reunion in the spirit world, "an immortal security" (28), dominated his thinking and helped him move forward.

Marriage, and a profound affinity

He continued to be attracted by beautiful young women, and after two years he evidently was casting about for a wife. Caroline Jebb, the wife of a friend, wrote about a trip that Myers took to America: "I am sure he is gone over with many ideas of amusing himself. *He* does not see that his girth is wide his hair thin, his 35 years fully printed on face and figure, and that the only kind of person fitted to *attract* him, would scorn him" (as quoted in Beer 170). Despite the fact that his youth was slain, on his return Myers managed to attract a beautiful young woman, Eveleen Tennant, whom he first met on his birthday, 6 February 1876, at George Eliot's home and whose portrait by Millais he had seen at the Royal Academy when with Annie (Beer 170). He rapidly courted Eveleen and proposed within six weeks. When he announced the engagement to his mother he stressed that his feeling for Eveleen was different "from the ponderings over possible attachments, and attempts to feel them, which we know so well" (as quoted in Hamilton 48). As Hamilton notes, it was almost as if Myers "had been trying to make himself fall in love" (40). When he married, on 13 March 1880, Myers was 36, a poet and intellectual, while Eveleen was only 21. Aside from wondering whether Myers's hasty actions represented an expression of genuine feeling, one has to ask what might have attracted Eveleen to Myers. She may have been impressed by his worldliness, but a more distinct possibility is that at least in part she was drawn to him by their mutual experience of loss. Her father had died in

1873 and the family was female dominated, with four girls and only one boy. She may also have found a father figure in Myers. We do know that her family was suspicious of Myers's motives, especially since she was wealthy. Her brother Charles investigated Myers's character and financial resources, but Eveleen's mother liked Myers and appreciated his intellectual and creative qualities (Hamilton 50–51). Eveleen not only provided Myers with financial security, but also many important society connections. Her granddaughter Deenagh Goold-Adams recalled that Eveleen had ambitions, that "she wanted fame, fortune and beauty for herself and all her dear ones and would fight for that with any weapon that came to hand" (Hamilton 57). Apparently, also, the couple's feelings for one another were very strong, at times tempestuous since both were "volatile personalities," to the extent that this became public and was satirized by another Cambridge poet J. K. Stephen (Hamilton 52). Flaws such as this appeared early in their marriage. Eveleen did not appreciate Frederic's absences either from his job as Inspector of Schools or involving psychical research, and she was possessive of him with his friends, particularly Edmund Gurney (Hamilton 53). For his part Myers insisted on spending as much time as he liked with his mother and on taking holidays with his brother Arthur, whose illness required Myers's support (Hamilton 53). Myers's avoidant stance became apparent as well with their children, Leopold (born 1881), Silvia (born 1883), and Harold (born 1886). Myers tended to be distant and authoritarian with them, and was particularly harsh towards Leo[1] (Illustration 1.2), whereas Eveleen would appear to have fulfilled her emotional needs through them, becoming possessive with them (Hamilton 54). According to Hamilton, she felt intellectually inferior to Myers and that she did not measure up to other accomplished women in his life, such as the intellectual psychical researcher Eleanor Sidgwick, Henry Sidgwick's wife, and even to Myers's determined and shrewd mother. Perhaps as a response to her emotional isolation, she developed an interest in and considerable talent for photography (Hamilton 54). She also garnered attention through "strategic illnesses," preventing Myers from yet another psychical research trip (Hamilton 59).

However, perhaps her husband's most galling flaw was that he remained obsessed with Annie Marshall, a situation that determined Eveleen's actions even beyond the death of Myers (Beer 171; Hamilton 283–92). To his credit Myers had told Eveleen about Annie before their marriage, but in a letter to Henry Sidgwick in January of 1880 he rationalized that Eveleen

> was a gift to me from Annie, – a pure child chosen by her whom I worship to be my companion thro' this world, till we meet 'where

Illustration 1.2 Frederic Myers with his son, Leopold Hamilton Myers

no loves are mutually exclusive, but each intensifies all'. This is what I have said to Evie, and her look and answer are treasured deep in my heart. I twice took Annie to look at Eveleen's picture [by Millais] as a girl of 16 in 1875, – and she admired as I did the glowing innocence of those child-eyes. They would've loved each other; – and I believe they will. (as quoted in Hamilton 56)

With all the trials in their marriage and particularly Myers's obsession with psychical research, a direct consequence of his preoccupation with Annie, Eveleen's attitude towards her changed drastically. In 1893, just after Myers had turned fifty, and on the seventeenth anniversary of the day, 2 July, when he had last laid eyes on Annie, he penned his autobiography, "Fragments of Inner Life." Its content and structure confirm Myers's preoccupation with Annie. Most of its forty-odd pages are devoted to her – in the thirteen poems included totaling 192 lines, in references to other poems about her, and in passionate description of her attributes and the pain he felt at her loss. His obsession was such that he calculated "Only on 426 days of my life – now numbering more than 18,000 days, – did I look upon her face, but that was enough" (39). For him Annie was his one profound affinity which he believed had preceded his earth life and was eternal: "I felt that if anything still recognizable in me had preceded earth life, it was this one profound affinity; if anything were destined to survive, it must be into the maintenance of this one affinity that my central effort must be thrown" (38).

Eveleen, on the other hand, merited only two paragraphs, one in a chapter titled "Marriage and Friends" which begins "Life and activity on earth should be elevated, but not impeded, by devotion to souls elsewhere" (29). He then gives the briefest factual account of his marriage and family, without any sense of excitement or joy, before concluding "I will not now dwell on this tranquil period of domestic happiness" (29). Subsequently, he spends more space listing his friends before being compelled to return to Annie in relating a curious incident when Myers observed admiration and pity in an unknown "high-bred beautiful" woman's face when she encountered Annie (Phyllis) in the street. Myers sensed an endless spiritual kinship with this woman, possibly suggesting a need for confirmation of his theory of eternal spiritual affinity ("Fragments" 30). He ends the chapter with several poems, the first of which he claims "is a picture of myself, idealized as a gorilla; – a grotesque form in which I can best summarize the profound discordances, the upward struggle, of that inward life of which fragments have been given here" (31). In "From Brute to Man," a gorilla, "his gleaming heart within" cries out as a strange light rises in him and "was a soul" (31). The other paragraph in which Eveleen is discussed similarly veers off course. Myers begins with, "My wife is beloved and loving; my three children are an unfailing joy" (41). He observes the latter playing on the lawn, but concludes, "this cannot be *my* destiny which is fulfilling itself in earthly felicity; it is the destiny of these innocent spirits linked with mine; but for me it is something accidental and posthumous, and presently it must fade away" (41). In the next paragraph he reveals that, "the love of life burns strong as ever within me; – the love of life elsewhere!" (41). This autobiography was not an impulsive gesture dashed off in a fit of nostalgia, since Myers had twenty-five numbered copies printed, six for friends, four for his wife and children, and the rest to remain in his study. However, he stipulated that his friends were not to open their sealed copies until after his death, and "anything to whose publication [Eveleen] may object" should not be published during her lifetime ("Prefatory Note").

We can only imagine her reaction on reading this autobiography after Myers's death in 1901. We do know that she "fought tigerishly," in Hamilton's words (286), and unsuccessfully, to gather up all copies of "Fragments" from Myers's friends, including William James and Oliver Lodge, and that she had published a highly expurgated version in 1904 along with a selection of his poems, but not those referring most explicitly to Annie Marshall. In her "Preface" she only admitted that, "a few passages have been omitted from [the autobiographical chapters] on account of their references to people still living" (Eveleen Myers "Preface"). Her attitude towards her husband's legacy was definitely ambivalent. On the one hand she tried to control what was made public about him and his work, and was jealous of his intense relationships with various mediums who frequently brought him messages purportedly from Annie. (Eveleen destroyed some of his records of the most important sittings; Hamilton 286.) She also disdained and felt hounded by the many mediums who claimed to have had messages from him after his death, and even attempted to prevent publication of their results (Hamilton 284, 290). On the other hand, similarly to Frederic's mother in regards to his father's legacy, she was determined that Frederic's memory live on, continued to edit editions of his prose and poetry, and hoped for an edition of his letters to be published. More surprisingly, she took over Myers's diary after he died and used it to record her own attempts to become a trance medium to channel Myers's voice. These sessions were successful enough to frighten her children (Hamilton 284). She also traveled to the USA eight months after Frederic died to hear communications from him through one of the most famous mediums, Mrs Piper, which were apparently also successful (Hamilton 288).

Psychical research: ardent passion and assurance of things unseen

Eveleen Myers's intense reaction to Myers's preoccupation with Annie after her death for the rest of his life only underlines the importance of this loss to his writing and particularly to his work in psychical research. Myers recollected that "during that period of ardent passion [for Annie], I received my first assurance of things unseen." He added that, "I felt with Plato that Love is an inlet into the spiritual world" ("Fragments" 40). Although Henry Sidgwick sparked his scientific interest in psychical research in 1871, Myers recounted that "It was not until the autumn of 1873 that I came across my first personal experience of forces unknown to science" ("Fragments" 33). At a séance a large hairy hand materialized, but when Myers grasped it with both hands it "became smaller and smaller like a new-born baby's" before disappearing (Eveleen Myers, as quoted in Hamilton 88). The image is significant, since what would become Myers's obsessive pursuit of psychical research was all about connecting with others in the spirit world, particularly Annie, only to feel that connection slip away at various points in this pursuit. On 30 July 1877 Annie Marshall first communicated with Myers from the beyond (Hamilton 102), and he would receive messages from her periodically, notably after he had gone through periods of intense doubts about his researches, as in September of 1893 when in a séance with a famous medium, Mrs Piper, Annie's communication "left little doubt – no doubt – that we were in the presence of an authentic utterance from a soul beyond the tomb" (Myers, as quoted in Hamilton 212).

Myers himself was aware of the dangers of this deeply personal motivation. In an address to the Society for Psychical Research in May 1900 he said,

> the danger, then, for our research will lie not in lack but in excess of motive; our minds may be biased in their judgment of evidence by deep instinctive desire. For my own part I certainly cannot claim such impartiality as indifference might bring. From my earliest childhood – from my very first recollections – the desire for eternal life has immeasurably eclipsed for me every other wish or hope. Yet desire is not necessarily bias; and my personal history has convinced myself – though I cannot claim that it shall convince others also – that my wishes do not strongly warp my judgment, – nay, that sometimes the very keenness of personal anxiety may make one afraid to believe, as readily as other men, that which one most longs for. (*Human* II 294)

This awareness would stand him in good stead as he sifted through thousands of pieces of evidence, separating the charlatans from those possessed of genuine extrasensory powers, in his ambition to provide support for the theory that personality survived bodily death in some form. This is not to say that his ardent belief did not occasionally occlude his scientific objectivity, and there are instances when Myers and other psychical researchers were clearly duped. Nevertheless, Myers courageously and exhaustively examined and tested phenomena not normally perceivable by the five senses, including telepathy, crisis apparitions, and hallucinations, considering them as extensions of the powers of human consciousness. In so doing he constructed an inclusive psychology, yet one which admitted the limits of current understanding, and in fact the first British dynamic psychology, articulating processes of mental development and activity, as I have detailed elsewhere (*Dynamic Psychology*). Myers thus invested what he called "supernormal" phenomena with more legitimacy than they had previously held, and psychical research very nearly became an orthodox part of the burgeoning field of psychology, gaining the support and participation of many famous scientists, psychologists, and philosophers of the day, including William James, Henri Bergson, and Sigmund Freud, as well as the fascination of writers. At the very least psychical research kept debates about the psychical, spiritual, and mystical dimensions of human beings at the forefront of British culture from the 1880s to the First World War and beyond. Although Myers's work was eclipsed for a variety of reasons (cf. *Dynamic Psychology*), there recently has been a revival of interest in his findings, and a number of his concepts have been shown to have validity, particularly those pertaining to mysticism, as we shall see. In the remaining portion of this chapter I intend to summarize those concepts that proved most significant in shaping cultural responses to loss, mourning, and mysticism, as well as to comment on Myers's psychological investment in them. I will conclude by showing how his voice persisted beyond death, thus furthering mystical responses to loss.

In the 1870s Myers became involved in the investigation of mediums at séances, under the guidance of Henry Sidgwick, with other Cambridge-connected men and women, including Myers's intimate friend, Edmund Gurney, who had provided a sort of marriage testimonial for Myers to the Tennant family (Hamilton 49). This was while Myers was developing a career as a School Inspector. The so-called Cambridge group did not achieve their goal of demonstrating the dominance of spirit over matter, and a physicist, William Barrett, became the leading psychical investigator (Hamilton 102). He was the instigator of developing a society for objective examination of supernormal phenomena, which became the Society for Psychical Research in 1882, with Henry Sidgwick as its first President. Although the Society initially included spiritualists and set up committees to investigate a diverse array of phenomena, from haunted houses to physical manifestations, Myers focused on what was first called thought-reading or thought-transference, which Myers renamed telepathy, a concept that rapidly entered culture generally (Hamilton 121).

Telepathy: "true security"

Myers defined telepathy as "the communication of impressions of any kind from one mind to another, independently of the recognized channels of sense" (*Human* I xxii). The word telepathy is derived from "feeling at a distance," and his choice of this word is significant when we consider the psychological needs that the concept met for Myers. Myers, Gurney, and others in the thought-transference committee began investigating cases and presented the ones they collectively agreed were the most substantial in their major work, *Phantasms of the Living* (1886). The majority of the 703 cases were crisis apparitions, impressions or apparitions of living people "coinciding with some crisis which those persons were undergoing at a distance," particularly the crisis of death (*Human* I 247). *Phantasms* concluded that there was some evidence for both experimental and spontaneous telepathy. The results were encouraging, suggesting that mind could operate independently of the brain and matter. The difficulty was in determining how the process worked. Myers held, and continued to hold for the rest of his life, that a "psychical invasion" takes place, transmitted through a spiritual ether (or metetherial environment, as he phrased it) (*Human* I 247). For Myers, the evidence for telepathy allayed his separation anxiety, reaching back into his earliest childhood, and provided him with a certain form of attachment security. Telepathy functioned as a kind of transitional experience in Winnicott's terms, a sensory replacement for an absent loved one which overcame solitude. In 1900 he concluded that "the worst fear is over; the true security is won. The worst fear was the fear of spiritual extinction or spiritual solitude; the true security is in the telepathic law" (*Human* II 281). Myers had desperately wanted to have experienced a crisis apparition when Annie died, as he expressed in his poem "Feror Ingenti Circumdata Nocte." At the time of her death, "No sound or sight, no voice or vision came":

> Yet surely once thou camest! and the whole
>   Dark deep of heaven sighed thy tale to tell;
> Lost like Eurydice's thy spirit stole

Wildered between the forest and the fell; –
Only mine eyes were holding, and my soul
Too roughly tuned to feel thy last farewell ("Fragments" 21)

Despite the failure of communication with Annie, Myers argued that love is a kind of telepathy: "Love is a kind of exalted, but unspecialized telepathy; – the simplest and most universal expression of that mutual gravitation or kinship of spirits which is the foundation of the telepathic law" (*Human* II 282).

His sense of security was challenged again when his most intimate friend, Edmund Gurney, passed away suddenly in June of 1888 from an overdose of chloroform, probably accidentally, though he overworked himself and was a manic-depressive (Hamilton 166). Eveleen Myers described the "terrible grief" Myers felt at the loss of this dear friend: "Freds [sic] mind and his [Gurney's] mind were at a complete unity together. No words of mine can describe dear Freds [sic] grief" (Hamilton 167). Not only did Myers lose one of his few intimate friends, but psychical research lost an assiduous researcher. There were, however, two consolations. Like Annie, Gurney began to send messages to Myers, which "clenched" his belief in survival, through one of the most accomplished mediums examined by the SPR, Mrs Leonora Piper ("Fragments" 41). Also, Oliver Lodge, who had known Gurney, became interested in telepathy and, after Gurney's death, a collaborator with and a new friend for Myers, "an unusual experience for a man who kept himself in cordial remoteness from the herd," as Trevor Hamilton puts it (206).

Subliminal consciousness and the subliminal self

Myers's examination of telepathy, crisis apparitions, and other supernormal phenomena led him to the stance that what lay beyond consciousness was far more complex and dynamic than the prevailing psychological thinking allowed. W. B. Carpenter, for instance, had developed the idea of unconscious cerebration, which held that abnormal mental phenomena originated in pathology (Hamilton 126). Other doctors and mental scientists emphasized that these phenomena represented signs of degeneration. Myers took a broader view, arguing that very often these phenomena suggested extensions of powers. For example, automatic writing, where people wrote without knowing what they wrote, and in some cases material they could not have known, suggested that mental activity could operate productively outside of primary consciousness and could even "give us true telepathic messages, or perhaps messages of high moral import, surpassing the automatist's conscious powers" (*Human* I 74). From the late 1880s, Myers developed his main innovation, and the one underpinning his theory of personality, his conception of the subliminal self (Kelly 114–15). In several articles published from 1892 to 1895 he proposed that:

> the stream of consciousness in which we habitually live is not the only consciousness which exists in connection with our organism. Our habitual or empirical consciousness may consist of a mere selection from a multitude of thoughts and sensations, of which some at least are equally conscious with those that we empirically know. I accord no primacy to my ordinary waking self, except that among my potential selves this one has shown itself the fittest to meet the needs of common life. ("Subliminal" I 301)

Below the threshold of the ordinary, empirical consciousness, which he named the supraliminal, was psychical action that he called subliminal. The spectrum of consciousness in the subliminal extended from automatic physiological processes no longer required as part of memory in order to survive, to psychic impressions "which the supraliminal consciousness is incapable of receiving in any direct fashion," such as telepathic and clairvoyant messages ("Subliminal" I 306). Dreams, which gave indications of "intensified power," were a good example of how more than one level of subliminal consciousness could be involved simultaneously.[2] This subliminal self consisted of "an aggregate of potential personalities, with imperfectly known capacities of perception and action, but none of them identical with the assumed individuality beneath them" ("Subliminal" I 308). Myers preferred this term to secondary self, then in common use, which gave the impression that there could only be one other self.[3] The number of potential personalities and streams of consciousness was apparently limitless. Myers rejected the idea of unconscious mental events, since he believed that all psychic events could potentially figure in a stream of consciousness. Also, although the subliminal self could be diseased, it was not necessarily inferior to the supraliminal self. On the contrary, Myers believed that messages from the subliminal self could indicate expansion and evolution of the personality, as found in the visions of genius ("Subliminal" I 317) and mystical insights. As well, Myers viewed the supraliminal as a spectrum "bounded at one end by organic functions which we cannot by any effort assume under conscious control, and at the other end by the highest efforts of reason to which the mind can attain" ("Subliminal" II 328), though he later added at this end "the rarest, most precious knowledge" that comes through "subliminal processes of telepathy, telaesthesia, ecstasy" (*Human* I 72). He hypothesized that this spectrum was not continuous, but rather that there were gaps and interruptions in perceptions at this level. Thus for Myers, human beings are "multiplex" and "polypsychic" in that subliminal consciousness could emerge in an endless variety of ways, but he also argued that humans have an overarching unity, the Subliminal Self (capitalized), soul, or spirit, which includes both the subliminal and supraliminal consciousness and awareness of both of these, and originates in a spiritual world, (a world of ether), and a metetherial, transcendental environment (*Human* I 34, 215; Kelly 364). Overall, Myers's conception of the subliminal was not reductive, but exploratory, emphasizing potential and extensions of capacity. Whereas physicians focused on morbid symptoms, he wrote that:

> The business of the psychologist [is] to look out for extensions of capacity – to recognize evolution. And these morbid visions take on a new importance if they are regarded as indications of a power of visualization, of combination, of invention, existing in subliminal strata of our being, and accidentally revealed by the volcanic upheaval of fever. ("Subliminal" I 315)

Genius: "a stage of integration slightly in advance of our own"

For Myers, genius was an important topic since it revealed extended capacity, and he made a significant contribution to this field beginning as early as 1892. For him, genius was not a product of psychic conflict or neurosis, but the genius "is for us the best type of the normal man, in so far as he effects a successful cooperation of an unusually large number of elements of his personality – reaching a stage of integration slightly in advance of our own" (*Human* I 72), though the genius is prey to the "degeneration and insanities" emanating from subliminal uprushes (*Human* I 56) because of the dynamic interaction between supraliminal and subliminal mentation (Kelly 477). Geniuses are more highly evolved, demonstrating greater complexity of perception and greater concentration of will and thought, in the direction humanity as a whole is heading (Myers I 77–78). The enhanced faculties of genius are not new but are revealed, brought "above the threshold of supraliminal consciousness" (*Human* I 118). The genius is "more readily permeable to subliminal uprushes, takes the chance of wider possibilities, and moves through life on a more uncertain way" (*Human* I 116). A team of contemporary psychologists, after a comprehensive review of Myers's research on genius, has recently concluded that "Myers correctly anticipated most of what we think has been best in the first century of psychological work on creativity" (Kelly et al. 492).

Genius and mysticism

Myers argued that beyond intellectual genius there existed "'moral genius,' 'the genius of sanctity,' or that 'possession' by some altruistic idea which lies at the roots of so many heroic lives" (*Human* I 56). The "Ancient Sage" or mystic, regardless of religion, has had greater access than most human beings to the transcendental realm through the subliminal (*Human* II 286). Kelly et al. conclude that "Myers led the way in exposing an inescapable connection between genius and mysticism at the foundations of human personality" (493). They emphasize the point that for Myers "mysticism does not imply supernatural intervention" (491). However, in his chapter on "Trance, Possession and Ecstasy," Myers argued that recorded instances of ecstasy suggested

> actual excursions of the incarnate spirit from its organism. The theoretical importance of the spiritual excursions is, of course, very great. It is, indeed, so great that most men will hesitate to accept a thesis which carries us straight into the inmost sanctuary of mysticism; which preaches 'a precursory entrance into the most holy place, as by divine transportation.' (*Human* II 259)

Myers proposed that in ecstasy "a spirit from inside can go out, can change its centre of perception and action, in a way less complete and irrevocable than the change of death" (*Human* II 259). In support of this Myers observed that "the evidence for ecstasy is stronger than the evidence for any other religious belief" and that ecstasy has been recorded in all religions (*Human* II 260). He gives examples of "strong souls" who have experienced it, from Elijah to Plato to Buddha, and Mahomet, to Joan of Arc to Kant, Wordsworth, and Tennyson (*Human* II 261). Furthermore, these mystics evidently had an extraordinary capacity to receive transmissions from the spiritual realm, and humanity as a whole has this potential:

> in a universe where instantaneous gravitation operates unexplained – where a world of ether coexists with the world of matter – men's minds must needs have a certain openness to other mysterious transmissions; must be ready to conceive other invisible environments or co-existences, and in a sense to sit loose to the conception of Space, regarded as an obstacle to communication or cognition and possibly of Time as well. (*Human* II 262)

Myers drew on a Romantic analogy as "our simplest guide":

> As is the memory and the foresight of a child to that of a man, even such, I suggest, is the memory and the foresight of the man's supraliminal self as compared to the retrocognition and the precognition exercised by an intelligence unrestrained by sensory limits; – whether that intelligence belong to the man's own subliminal self, or to an un-embodied human spirit, or possibly to spirits higher than human. I maintain that in this thesis there is nothing incredible; – nay, that it is the necessary corollary of belief in the existence anywhere of any extension of the powers which we habitually exercise. (*Human* II 263)

Thus, Myers argued that the Subliminal Self "unrestrained by sensory limits" possessed much greater powers and potential than the supraliminal self. From the Subliminal Self spiritual excursions could be made outside the physical body and the Subliminal could also receive messages from the spiritual realm. Mystics had a more highly evolved capacity for this. In the "Epilogue" to *Human Personality*, Myers reaffirmed that, "Observation, experiment, inference, have led many inquirers, of whom I am one, to a belief in direct or telepathic intercommunication, not only between the minds of men still on earth, but between minds and spirits still on earth and spirits departed" (II 287). He expressed confidence that the laws of the spirit world would "more and more be tested by modern experience and inquiry" (II 288) and laws established, analogous to those of Energy and Motion. There would be "an ultimate incandescence where science and religion fuse in one; a cosmic evolution of Energy into Life, and of Life into Love, which is Joy" (II 290). Throughout this last section Myers himself sounds mystical with his incantatory prose and his emphasis on the evolution of Love, "which is Joy at once and Wisdom" (II 291). Myers predicts that "Inevitably, as our link with other spirits strengthens, as the life of the organism pours more fully through the individual cell, we shall feel love more ardent, wider wisdom, higher joy; perceiving that this organic unity of Soul, which forms the inward aspect of the telepathic law, is in itself the Order of the Cosmos, the Summation of Things" (II 291). In "pervading ecstasy" the soul merges with the Great or World-Soul, about which he quotes Plotinus (II 291).

Myers's later years

In his later years Myers could give the appearance of a mystic,[4] as he did to A. C. Benson, who knew Myers as a father, when his son came to be a boarder at Benson's Eton house in the 1890s. He describes Myers as

> seem[ing] to hold himself aloof, and to be preoccupied in larger designs. I knew nothing then of his inner hopes and quests; but though his whole life was nurtured on emotions and ecstasies, there was never anything in the least emotional or effusive about his talk. He was essentially reserved; and there is one thing that always struck me very forcibly about him, and that was the extreme serenity and tranquillity of his face and bearing. (179–80)

He adds, "I know no man who seems to have lived more consistently in a sort of rapture of thought, without weary or discontented interludes, but in an impassioned ecstasy of sweetness. In this he was a mystic, and his joyful serenity of mind is just what one finds in the lives of mystics" (183). In this aloofness, preoccupation, reserved nature and "rapture of thought" we can see strong elements of avoidant-resistance. Myers was clearly absorbed in his inner life. According to Benson, Myers's "was a self-centred life, though not an egotistical one" since his focus was on what he might become in a spiritual sense (184).

In order to discover this, Myers continued to work obsessively at psychical research. In the 1890s he worked with the extraordinary mediums Mrs Piper, Eusapia Palladino, and Mrs Thompson, as Trevor Hamilton has detailed, as well as exposing numerous frauds (206–9, 213–21, 221–27). This work continued to cause tensions in his marriage, mainly because Eveleen Myers was jealous of Myers's contact with Annie Marshall through these mediums (Hamilton 224). After succumbing to influenza and then pneumonia in March 1898 and influenza again in 1899, Myers was found to have Bright's disease, a chronic kidney condition, which "led to enlargement of the heart and degeneration of the arteries" (Gauld 332).

A rest cure at the Riviera was prescribed, although while there he continued to work with Mrs Thompson (Hamilton 224). After returning home, he again suffered symptoms of Bright's disease, including in October 1900 severely restricted breathing, called Cheyne-Stokes (Gauld 333), and traveled once more to the Riviera. From there at the suggestion of William James he went to Rome in January 1901 to try a serum purported to improve the arteries. After a temporary improvement, he succumbed to pneumonia and died on 17 January 1901. James was deeply impressed by Myers's "serenity, in fact his eagerness to go, and his extraordinary intellectual vitality up to the time that the death agony began" (as quoted in Gauld 333-34). Myers was only 57 years old, but his "obsessive involvement in psychical research," as Hamilton puts it, led to overwork and exhaustion (306). After he had been told by the medium Mrs Thompson that "he would awaken in Annie's arms on 6 February (his birthday) 1902," he interpreted this to mean that he would die then and planned out the rest of his work on *Human Personality* accordingly (Gauld 333).

The "problem of Myers" and his "posthumous activity"

Myers had left the task of completing his magnum opus to Richard Hodgson and Alice Johnson, but there was dissent between them and work proceeded slowly, to Eveleen's great frustration. Nevertheless, praise of Myers's work came quickly and from well-respected sources. His friend Sir Oliver Lodge claimed that Myers's "grasp of science was profound" ("Conviction" 46), that what he had seen of *Human Personality* suggested that it was "likely to be an epoch-making work" (51) and that Myers "had an imagination wider than that of most men" (56). The father of modern psychology William James thought it probable "that Frederic Myers will always be remembered in psychology as the pioneer who staked out a vast tract of mental wilderness and planted the flag of genuine science upon it" ("Frederic Myers" 225). Myers first mapped out the subliminal region, so future research into its precise constitution deserves to be called "the problem of Myers" (218). Myers "also invented definite methods for its solution. Post-hypnotic suggestion, crystal gazing, automatic writing and trance speech, the willing game, etc. are now, thanks to him, instruments of research" (218). James himself drew on Myers's conception in his ground-breaking study of religion and mysticism *Varieties of Religious Experience* (1902). All types of mysticism "spring from the same mental level, from that great subliminal or transmarginal region of which science is beginning to admit the existence" (426). He also cited Myers's broadminded ideas on prayer, that it brings "a real increase in intensity of absorption of spiritual power or grace" necessary to maintain our spirit, regardless of the object of our prayers (*Varieties* 467). Recently, psychologists Edward Kelly et al. argue that "a large proportion of James's late work revolves specifically around his attempts to draw out in detail consequences for the psychology of religion, and for the epistemology and metaphysics, of Myers's theory of the Subliminal Self" (558). James's key development is a transmission or filter model of consciousness where mind is not generated by the brain but instead is focused, limited, and constrained by it (Kelly xxx).

James was only one of a number of prominent psychologists, social scientists, physicians, and philosophers to test the implications of Myers's psychical theories, including Henri Bergson, Theodore Flournoy, William McDougall, Sir Cyril Burt, and J. C. Flugel.[5] Other psychologists and psychoanalysts, including James Ward, James Sully, Sigmund Freud, and Carl Jung, engaged with some aspects of Myers's theory without completely embracing psychical research. During his lifetime Myers, along with other members of the prestigious Society for Psychical Research, had worked tirelessly to move their research into a central position in the burgeoning discipline of psychology partly through their extensive participation in the first four International Congresses of Physiological (later Experimental) Psychology. According to the French Nobel prize-winning (1913) physiologist, Charles Richet,

To Myers the success of the International Congresses of Experimental Psychology at Paris [1889], London [1892], Munich [1896] and again at Paris last year [1900] was largely due. He compelled the adherents of the classical psychology and philosophy to pay attention to the new problems which he presented to them. (*Journal of SPR*, April 1901 56)

Historian John Cerullo claims that, by the 1896 Munich Congress, psychical research "was on the verge of offering the psychological profession as comprehensive an interpretation of personal identity as had yet been had" (99). Although not all psychologists and other thinkers were convinced of Myers's theories, his development of England's first dynamic psychology kept debates over psychical, spiritual, and mystical dimensions of humanity at the forefront of social science as well as culture, as I have argued elsewhere (*Dynamic Psychology*).

Following Myers's death, the Society for Psychical Research also followed up on his ideas. In 1912 it formed a medical section specifically to test and publish on therapeutic applications of Myers's subliminal. These psychologists and physicians included Lloyd Tuckey, Milne Bramwell, V. J. Wooley, Constance Long (a translator of Jung), T. W. Mitchell, and William McDougall. Prominent Oxford psychologist and SPR member William Brown published extensively on the implications of Myers's theories for psychotherapy. In 1932 he reviewed the evidence collected by the Society over the past fifty years and declared that it was "Sufficient to make survival [of the soul after death] scientifically extremely probable" (as quoted in Shepard 182).

Myers's writings about extensions of human capacity, such as telepathy, as evidence for the survival of personality beyond death had an impact far beyond the world of academia. As a promising poet and man of letters, Myers's connections with the literary and artistic world were extensive, and his marriage to Eveleen Myers with her family connections and later connections in the burgeoning world of photography only increased his network and influence. Biographer and friend of Myers, A. C. Benson, claims about the Myers's Cambridge home that "the people one met there were not of the familiar academical kind, but men and women who brought you the rest of the larger world with them, and with a halo of interest in fame about them" (177–78). During his lifetime Myers corresponded and exchanged ideas with, and in some cases befriended, numerous renowned contemporaries, including Robert Browning, George Meredith, Arthur Conan Doyle, George Eliot, Henry James, John Ruskin, Robert Louis Stevenson, Leslie Stephen, Alfred Tennyson, and Mark Twain. Myers convinced Doyle to join the SPR after he read in *Light* about how Doyle was convinced by séances, and this led to Doyle's long, though somewhat ambivalent association with the Society (Hamilton 74). As a young man at Cambridge Myers discussed "God, Immortality, Duty" with George Eliot, whose grave countenance he dramatized as "like a Sibyl's in the gloom" (Hamilton 77). It was at her house on his thirty-sixth birthday that he met again and became interested in his future wife Eveleen. In the case of Henry James and Robert Louis Stevenson, Myers queried them about psychical aspects of their fiction. The list could go on. A diverse array of transitional and early twentieth-century writers engaged with Myers's evidence for survival of human personality, some becoming members of the SPR, including J. D. Beresford, Algernon Blackwood, Frances Hodgson Burnett, Lewis Carroll, Radclyffe Hall, Andrew Lang, May Sinclair, Hubert Wales, Oscar Wilde, and W. B. Yeats, while others assimilated aspects into their writing, including Grant Allen, J. M. Barrie, Arnold Bennett, R. H. Benson, Stella Benson, Marjorie Bowen, G. K. Chesterton,

Agatha Christie, Marie Corelli, Walter de la Mare, William De Morgan, Goldsworthy Lowes Dickinson, George du Maurier, Lord Dunsany, E. M. Forster, Roger Fry, Charlotte Haldane, Robert Hichens, William Hope Hodgson, Aldous Huxley, M. R. James, Rudyard Kipling, D. H. Lawrence, Stephen Leacock, Vernon Lee, John Masefield, Stephen McKenna, Elinor Mordaunt, Arthur Morrison, E. Nesbit, Beverly Nichols, Oliver Onions, Barry Pain, Forrest Reid, Saki, M. P. Shiel, James Stephens, Lytton Strachey, Netta Syrett, Evelyn Underhill, Hugh Walpole, Rebecca West, Charles Williams, and Virginia Woolf. To date I have discovered over fifty fictionalized psychical cases, most based on Society for Psychical Research cases published by Myers or summarized in *Human Personality*, and one, Doyle's "The Parasite," even featuring a fictionalized portrait of Myers (cf. Johnson "Apparition").

However, perhaps the most fascinating instances of his wide-ranging influence are what Sir Oliver Lodge refers to as Myers's "posthumous activity" ("Conviction" 10), his communications from the beyond. These began almost immediately after his passing and became so numerous that Eveleen Myers felt hounded by the "spiritualistic paparazzi," as Hamilton puts it (288). Myers himself on the other side purportedly felt similarly, as received through Mrs Thompson: "They keep on calling me. I am wanted everywhere ... Do appeal to them not to break me up so" (Lodge, *Survival* 1909). On 27 February, Eveleen received a letter from Alec Yorke, one of Queen Victoria's courtiers and Myers's friend, who claimed that in séances it was revealed that "Fred is resting so peacefully" (as quoted in Hamilton 283). One of the earliest and most prolific mediums was Mrs Verrall, who produced over one thousand messages (Hamilton 292). Several of these mediums had literary connections, including Mrs Holland, who was Rudyard Kipling's sister, Alice Fleming (and who began channeling Myers messages in 1903), and Mrs Zoe Richmond, wife of Kenneth Richmond, a psychotherapist and collaborator with novelist J. D. Beresford. One, Mrs Willett, Winifred Coombe Tennant, was a relative by marriage, the wife of Myers's brother-in-law Charles (Hamilton 293).[6] These mediums began receiving overlapping messages independently and in different locations, as far flung as India, where Mrs Holland lived, and these became known as cross-correspondences. Over a half dozen mediums produced over nineteen volumes of automatic scripts (Hamilton 298). Then there were independent mediums, such as H. A. Dallas and Geraldine Cummins, who published their communications from Myers.[7] The latter's book of scripts was so convincing to Eveleen Myers that she bought twenty-seven copies and offered Cummins residence in her house to be near the recipient when her husband's messages came through – an offer Cummins declined (Hamilton 300). These scripts have continued to have an impact on writers. Novelist Rosamond Lehmann discovered Myers's psychical insights through Cummins's scripts and subsequently introduced psychical phenomena into her fiction, for instance in *A Sea-Grape Tree* (1976). When reading Cummins's *Beyond Human Personality*, Lehmann recalled that:

> It was as if an actual current of spiritual energy were flowing from me to the pages; as if I understood and were in harmony with the imaginatively creative nature of the alleged communicator, F. W. H. Myers. In short, it was, for me, an experience of picking up the truth; and I did not attempt to interpret it: I just went on reading and re-reading; and each time I did so, even at my flattest, the same sympathetic vibration kindled, and sustained me. Everyone has their first teacher in this or any other field, and he was mine ... (Lehmann 126)

Hamilton details that Myers's messages have continued to be recorded nearly up to the present, in *The Scole Report* (1999), for example (Hamilton 300). The most famous of Myers's messages, however, and the most pertinent for this study, came to Sir Oliver Lodge, as we shall see. Lodge had "no doubt" that "the activity of Myers" continued beyond the grave ("Conviction" 10, 11).

With such a legacy from beyond the grave, and yet Myers's relative obscurity in history, how can we discern the fundamental dimensions of the earthly Myers? Alan Gauld asserts that Myers was "endowed with a remarkable, indeed a dangerous assortment of irreconcilable qualities" (334) and this complexity may help explain how Myers could be seen as a mystic by A. C. Benson, and by others a sensualist, a passionate truth-seeker and yet self-absorbed and a poseur, who "rang a little false" (Jane Harrison as quoted in Beer 184). He seemed to relish being center stage and yet was aloof, snobbish, and reserved, even secretive. Oliver Lodge asked "To how many was he really known? I wonder. Known in a sense he was to all, except the unlettered and the ignorant. Known in reality he was to very few" (*Survival* 345). Nevertheless, through the lens of attachment theory and object relations it has been shown that early losses and his mother's evangelical indoctrination and emotional overinvestment in him after the death of Myers's father had a profound effect on this sensuous and sensitive boy. His anxiety about annihilation at death along with his rebellious response to his mother's mixed signals, cosseting and yet preoccupied with her grief and her other children, led to his developing an avoidant-resistant pattern of attachment. He channeled strong emotion, including arrogance (distancing him from others) along with frustration and anger, into precocious poetry. As a young man, sentimentality and sensuality masked his lack of understanding of genuine feeling and an emotional void. It is hard to imagine how someone could become more preoccupied with a relationship than Myers after the death of the love of his life Annie Marshall. Anxiety and desire to renegotiate this thwarted attachment drove him to pursue psychical research, to the detriment of his relationship with his wife and children. This preoccupation generated at least one source of his mysticism. Nobel Laureate Charles Richet claimed that "if Myers were not a mystic, he had all the faith of a mystic and the ardour of an apostle, in conjunction with the sagacity and precision of a *savant*" (as quoted in Melton 918). Perhaps this observation best helps explain how Myers's practice and advocacy of psychical research proved so influential on his contemporary culture. Through his relentless probing of the subliminal and various extensions of human capacity, such as telepathy and automatic writing, Myers demonstrated that humanity possessed largely untapped powers and he convinced many that these should be treated seriously and examined scientifically. He advocated that it was possible and worthwhile to communicate with those who had passed over, and his stance transcended any particular religious dogma, though he felt that his discoveries aligned with the essence of Christian teaching. His ironically posthumous magnum opus *Human Personality and its Survival of Bodily Death* as well as the many communications purportedly received from him in the afterlife helped set the agenda for a significant twentieth-century approach to loss and mourning. In the spiritual realm at least, the early twentieth century can indeed be seen as the age of Myers.

2
Spirit Soldiers: Oliver Lodge's *Raymond* and *Christopher*

> Aunt Anne "ostensibly took possession of the medium, and in her own energetic manner reminded me of her promise to come back if she could, and spoke a few sentences in her own well-remembered voice."
>
> Lodge *Past Years* 277

> "Of all my sons, the youngest, when he was small, was most like myself at the same age. In bodily appearance I could recognize the likeness to my early self, as preserved in old photographs; an old schoolfellow of mine who knew me between the ages of eight and eleven, visiting Mariemont in April 1904, remarked on it forcibly and at once, directly he saw Raymond – then a schoolboy; and innumerable small mental traits in the boy recalled to me my childhood's feelings."
>
> Lodge *Raymond* 8

A spindly boy stands awkwardly, one hand gripping the other held tight to his chest. He watches, terror mounting in his eyes as the flushing schoolmaster sits at his desk stabbing at the boy's essay with a pen. Other boys, sitting on wooden forms at long desks, furtively glance up from their work until one of the other masters at the back of the room catches sight of their disobedience and cracks the offender's desk with a cane. The room is spartan and filthy, and the boys shiver, not only with fear, but also because it is a chilly late October day and the inadequate stove will not be lit until 5 November, an annual ritual. The master at the front of the room suddenly stands, his jowls vibrating, and screams "Failure! Hands!" The boy, quivering and with tears rolling down his cheeks, presses his hands to his chest but the headmaster wrenches them away, grasps a cane and brings it down repeatedly on the boy's hands. A red weal appears and the boy's hands curl up, but they are ripped open again by the headmaster who commands, "Stay!" Blow after blow falls until the boy can barely stand, and the headmaster cuffs him before pushing him back to his bench, where the boy huddles, unable to write.

Several evenings later the boy, the smallest of his classmates, tosses in bed in an early restless sleep. The dormitory door bangs open and another boy enters, flops into his bed and calls out an obscenity to the small boy. He adds, "Put the candle out." The slumbering boy murmurs, "sleeping." The other gets up, pulls a leather strap from under his pillow, and goes to the small boy's bed, shouting that he get up. The figure on the bed huddles and the older boy pounds the younger's ear with his fist. When the small boy tries to defend himself, the older thrashes him with the strap on the head and groin. The following Saturday, the small boy seems reluctant to peel off his clothes for his weekly bath, so the housemaid undoes his buttons for him. Her hand flies to her mouth when she sees his bruises and scars, and she sinks to her knees, weeping. He stands before her, listless and silent (*Past* 38).

That spindly young lad represents something of what Oliver Lodge experienced at age eight. He repeatedly described his school days at Newport grammar school in Shropshire from age eight to twelve as "undoubtedly the most miserable part of my life" (*Past* 34). Lodge remembered being frequently thrashed, not only on the hands but on the head, shoulders, and the backs of the legs (*Past* 37, 58). To make matters worse, the headmaster and principal perpetrator was his uncle (*Past* 34). Intense bullying by other louts at the school further compounded his misery. Lodge claimed that, "I had more illnesses at Newport than in the rest of my life, or so it seems" (*Past* 35). His horrible situation pushed him to the brink of suicide (*Past* 59). Lodge developed an avoidant-resistant response, claiming that, "I learned to suppress my feelings, until for the most part they became extinct" (*Past* 57). His preoccupation with this trauma can be seen in the amount of space he devotes to it in his autobiography, *Past Years*, in his fervent advocacy of educational reform throughout his life, and perhaps most strikingly in eruption of emotion about this trauma into various narratives, notably his soldier biography, *Christopher* (1918). Undoubtedly these years of being beaten and bullied constituted the defining trauma of his early life.

However, Lodge had already learned avoidant-resistant behavior in his family life, since his parents had been "lost" to him from his

Illustration 2.1 Oliver Lodge with his mother

earliest days, as both were intensely preoccupied with work, as well as, in his mother's case, with a large family (Illustration 2.1). Although Lodge claimed that he was "deeply enamored" of his mother (*Past* 52), significantly he did not tell either parent about his traumatic school experiences (*Past* 59, 60). It would be another female figure, his Aunt Anne, who rescued him from the path prescribed for him of following in his father's footsteps into the family business. She recognized his potential and facilitated his education in London, where from age fifteen he took up his "real education" (*Past* 65). Lodge had to rebel from his family in order to pursue his passion for physics, but he was driven and went from strength to strength as a scientist, first proving the existence of electromagnetic waves and then contributing to the development of radio-telegraphy, as well as making a wide range of technical innovations, from the moving coil loudspeaker to increasing X-ray efficiency, to inventing an automobile ignition system. Lodge's avoidant-resistant pattern of attachment was transformed into what Lodge referred to as "brooding," an obsessive pondering over elementary phenomena without being distracted by "transient happenings" (*Past* 343). This habit was key to his success as a scientific thinker, and also helps explain why he repeatedly did not follow through with developing the technical details through arduous experimentation.

Although he had been interested in psychical research as early as 1882–83, significantly he became devoted to it after he was contacted at his first sitting with a medium by his Aunt Anne, "a perfect godsend" (*Past* 11) and emotional bond to his vocation, who had died suddenly of cancer. Other near-death and significant losses propelled him on his quest to discover whether personality survived death, notably the loss of his son Raymond in the First World War in 1915. Lodge believed that he was forewarned of this calamity by his mentor in psychic matters, Frederic Myers, who had continued to send messages through mediums after his death in 1901. Raymond in turn communicated through mediums to his father, but ironically Lodge had repeated the pattern of his own father, chronically overworking, and not seeing or getting to know his son as much as he should have, as he admitted (*Raymond* 9). When Lodge published the memoir *Raymond* (1916), the book enabled Lodge to renegotiate his distant relationship with his son, to take responsibility for the loss as both father and non-combatant, and to find a larger purpose for this life, seemingly prematurely cut off. By this time Lodge had become a cultural icon, both for his scientific achievements and accessible syntheses as well as for his social commentary, including his popular books outlining his arguments for belief in survival of personality beyond death. *Raymond* generated controversy but also became popular, a number of editions being printed, and itself acting as a kind of spirit medium, bringing his son's life and afterlife to a wide audience. It facilitated collective grieving and spawned many other spirit soldier memoirs.

From this point on Lodge became increasingly in demand for speeches on spiritualism and he continued to produce books and articles at an astonishing rate, keeping him at the forefront of English culture. He had developed a theory of ether as applied to the physical world as early as 1882 (Rowlands) and then extensively in the 1890s when he carried out what he believed to be his most important physics experiments to discover whether this medium for electromagnetic waves would be dragged along with the momentum of a rapidly spinning disc (Jolly 107–8). The results were inconclusive, but Lodge felt that with more sophisticated equipment than was then available the ether would eventually be detected, even though Einstein's special theory of relativity rendered it unnecessary and arguably unprovable (Jolly 110). Most importantly, he theorized that the ether was the medium not only for physical phenomena, but also for the spirit world, and he became absorbed in developing this speculation in his later years. His commentary on survival and the ether sounds increasingly mystical, as we shall see, and he became a modern-day prophet or sage who kept debates about psychical research and spiritualism at the forefront of English culture and imbued them with scientific respectability. As J. Arthur Hill puts it, Lodge became "the chief reconciler of Science and Religion in later days" (Hill 252). Similarly to Myers, his enormous impact continued to be felt after his death, as numerous mediums have recorded messages from him almost up to the present day.

Oliver Lodge's family background and early life would have made it seem highly unlikely that he would attain his eventual position as an eminent scientist and psychical researcher, although his propensity for overworking might have been predicted. Oliver's paternal grandfather was born in Ireland, but became a vicar and the headmaster of a local school in Barking, in Essex. However, Lodge's father, also Oliver, was left to fend for himself as the twenty-third of twenty-five children born to two of the vicar's three wives, the eldest child being fifty-six when the youngest was born (*Past* 13–14). In his autobiography, Sir Oliver comments that the Lodge men were tall, "energetic men, all of them, and seemed to live for work, rather than for sport of any kind, as far as I could make out" (*Past* 16). Sir Oliver's father followed this pattern to an extreme. He lived a "strenuous life," leaving school at fourteen and working in a railway office where he voluntarily undertook extra work and "practically spared time for nothing else" (*Past* 18, 21). He married twenty-three-year-old Grace Heath in 1849, and on the day after his marriage returned to work but was sent back home to the relief of Lodge's mother Grace, "who felt rather chagrined at his absorption in the official work. She, however, soon threw herself into that work with great energy and ability" (*Past* 21). Like her husband, Grace had come from precarious economic and emotional circumstances. Although her father had also been a vicar and headmaster, he died early, leaving his large family in poverty. His wife retired to a "house of refuge" with one daughter, and several other daughters were placed in an orphan school. Grace was the youngest (*Past* 11–12). It would seem that their insecurities at least partially explain their drivenness. Lodge repeatedly uses the word "strenuous" to describe the household and in particular his father's obsession with work (*Past* 18, 20, 25). Oliver was born on 12 June 1851, the first of seven sons and a daughter who appeared at short intervals, the second son being born within two years of Oliver's birth. Several years later Oliver's father obtained a position as a blue clay agent in the Potteries, and then acquired several other agencies, necessitating a great deal of travel, while Grace took on the responsibility of the bookkeeping at home, "in spite of her large family" (*Past* 24). Lodge comments, "That it was wise of my mother to undertake so much office work may well be doubted. Some of us boys were pressed into the service from time to time ..." (*Past* 24). As the eldest, Oliver bore the burden of premature responsibility, and yet also suffered neglect, for which he places most of the blame on his father. He states:

> I wish my father had not been so utterly busy and absorbed in his work. The strain of life made him sometimes irritable; and we never got to know him properly till near the end, when we treated him with reverence. The constant labour sometimes threatened to spoil the happiness of home. (*Past* 31)

Lodge idealized his mother, and it seems likely that she over-invested her emotion in him, given that her husband was so frequently absent. Lodge recollects that:

> My mother, too, was overworked, but her disposition was different. She was naturally placid and affectionate to an extraordinary degree. And my love for her – I might say our love for each other – was of the utmost vividness and reality. I believe she used to think I could do nothing wrong. (*Past* 31–2)

She even went so far as to claim that the example of Oliver contradicted the doctrine of original sin (*Past* 32). Nevertheless, how much time would she have been able to spend with him?

We do get a glimpse of Oliver's response to this overworked and anxiety-laden family through a number of behaviors and incidents. Lodge mentions that he had a speech impediment that persisted for some years, not being able to pronounce the hard k and g (*Past* 23). Oliver ill-treated dogs and other animals on several occasions. At age three, he recalls, "I had a toy whip given me, and I must needs exercise it on a dog: this time it was a nursemaid who remonstrated, and asked how I would like the whip applied to me ... It is strange, but I didn't realize that it hurt the dog" (*Past* 29). Lodge explains away this cruelty as representing the child's savage stage in evolution, but could it not be an expression of his anger and frustration? Another incident, one of Lodge's earliest recollections, captures his avoidant response to neglect. It could almost be an illustration of Winnicott's strange situation. At the Crimean War peace celebrations in February 1856 when Oliver was just four, his father told him to stand near a Russian gun (which in itself caused him some anxiety) "till he came for me." Oliver senior listened to speeches, adjourned for lunch, "went away with the bigwigs, and in the evening went home" (*Past* 22). When his mother asked where the boy was he replied, "forgotten all about him," and he returned to Stoke to fetch him. Lodge records that, "however, I still stood, on the burning deck, so to speak, long after the crowd had all dispersed; I don't remember being even distressed at the long wait" (*Past* 23). On another occasion his father shipped him off to Ireland "on a cheap excursion" with an acquaintance, without sufficient funds. Oliver recounts that, "the experience was horrible" and had a long-lasting impact (*Past* 29). He claims that "it rained nearly all the time, we were thoroughly wet through, and half starved. For months afterwards I felt a shivering down the backs of my legs" (*Past* 30). Lodge developed a lifelong anxiety about travel, claiming that "my favorite nightmare was connected with the losing of trains or luggage or people, and having all sorts of maladventures connected with journeys" (*Past* 30). To make matters worse, Oliver senior's stinginess in time and money was combined with a particular overweening ambition for his son. Lodge writes that his own desires were neglected:

> though I pined for a lathe, I never had one. My father was too busy to attend to my requirements in any such direction. Moreover, he was anxious for me to succeed him in the business, and he looked forward to the time when he might call it Oliver Lodge & Son; which later on he did ... (*Past* 30)

Biographer W. P. Jolly summarizes Lodge's early childhood as "a pleasant and satisfying time" (12), but this is not what Lodge's own recollections suggest. Rather, the picture that has emerged is of an eldest son, pressed into early responsibility as a tool in the family business, but whose needs (even basic ones of correction of a speech impediment) and desires were neglected. He was shy and early on learned an avoidant response to abandonment. Later, he admitted "his dislike of children's parties – indeed, in my own case, a party of any kind" (*Raymond* 8).

Lodge summarizes his own early life thus: "I must say that home life was rather spoilt by the incursion of business into it" (*Past* 52). Lodge's parents' preoccupation with work likely contributed to their failure to scrutinize the school to which they sent Oliver when he was eight. He records that they were "glad of the opportunity" and no doubt the convenience and thrift of sending him to a school run by a relative, Oliver's uncle, who had recently married one of his mother's sisters (*Past* 34). Oliver must have felt betrayed by his uncle and by his family, especially since the uncle, never named by Lodge, "seemed to take a pride in not sparing him" frequent lashings and beatings (*Past* 37). A sense of Lodge's enduring anger emerges in his masterly understatement that "I don't think he could have known how much it hurt. In later life I once offered to show him, but he declined, and would not hold out his hand" (*Past* 37). The sadistic treatment by both schoolmasters and the "ruffians," in imitation of their masters, led, Lodge says, to the "obliteration of any spontaneity of joy in life" (*Past* 57). Avoidant behavior was reinforced, since Lodge reflected that "avoidance of the cane was the only motive for learning in those few dreary years: everything was worked on the principle of repulsion instead of attraction – an expensive and ineffective variety of force" (*School Teaching* 16). Violence bred violence, Lodge recalling that he and another boy went about destroying birds' nests, their occupants and the adults, and that they kept lists of each day's work (*Past* 48). From his extensive descriptions there can be no doubt that the "stupid system" in which he found himself trapped was extreme, even for the time (*Past* 54). Perhaps even more shocking is that his parents did not seem to discern his agony, or if they did (and Lodge does say that his mother "could not but know that I was unhappy" [*Past* 60]) refused to act on it so that Lodge was forced to spend four years there. These four years he compares to "something like the years of the war" in his "mingled feelings" to them (*Past* 60).

Finally, Lodge received respite at age twelve when his father summoned him to Edinburgh, where Oliver senior had fallen from his horse and broken his arm (*Past* 42). However, once again he may have demonstrated neglect or at least self-absorption, since the boy "was sent about to explore the city by myself" although he enjoyed this (*Past* 42). This sojourn marked the end of his schooling at Newport, but he was subsequently offered a place at a Rectory school at Coombs, where he remained until his "schooling was cut short" at fourteen when his father, whose arm had not mended properly because of overwork, decided that Oliver should enter the family business. Recall that Oliver senior had entered the workforce at fourteen, and he held "that a boy was no good in business unless he entered it at fourteen, began low down, and went through the whole mill" (*Past* 51). Lodge claimed that he did not rebel from his mother, but from this point on he actively rebelled against his father's plans for him, although he had to spend "seven of the most critical years, from the age of fourteen to twenty-two" in the business before he "managed to escape" (*Past* 52, 30). Lodge's regret at the time spent at this drudgery is palpable, but it would have been life-long regret if it had not been for the intervention of his remarkable Aunt Anne.

Lodge introduces her on the first page of his autobiography, before either parent, and he claims that "she must figure in it many times," which she does (*Past* 12). He is full of praise for her, referring to her as "a woman of great natural ability as well as of considerable education" and as "ever-remarkable" (*Past* 12, 42). Clearly he had a close emotional and intellectual bond with her. Her trajectory is truly remarkable, especially for a woman in that period. She was one of the Heath daughters who landed in the orphanage after the death of her father, but the recently widowed Queen Adelaide visited the school, took a fancy to the girl, and "invited her to become a Woman of the Bedchamber" at Court (*Past* 11). She thus moved in some influential circles. After the Queen died in 1849, Anne was left some money, invested it wisely and gained "a small independent fortune" (*Past* 12). She had directed Lodge's informal education at various points, teaching him about steam engines and later setting him problems to work out in the field of astronomy, an educational strategy he heartily commended (*Past* 43). When he was fifteen or sixteen she invited him to spend a winter with her in London, where she encouraged him to attend lectures and take notes. Claims Lodge, "it was her influence that made me study thoroughly all that I attempted" (*Past* 66). Significantly, she also directed his religious education, having "strong evangelical leanings" herself and introduced him to the Reverend James Moorhouse, later Bishop of Manchester, an eloquent speaker, whom Oliver listened to, "rapt," and whose confirmation classes he attended. Lodge claimed that "to him I owe much" (*Past* 12).

From this point on, Lodge attended lectures of every kind, from chemistry to constitutional history to geology to steam, but when he returned home this had to be done discreetly, since "all my work was an interruption to business" (*Past* 67). These years Lodge starts to describe as "strenuous," ironically just as he had described his father's obsession with work: "it was a strenuous but enjoyable time; I lived for work" (*Past* 85). After he obtained a teaching apprentice position in London, against his father's wishes (*Past* 70), he gradually gained a foothold in the world of scholarship. He presents himself as a shy loner, who "never took time off or associated with other students" (*Past* 83). His ambition was huge, but thwarted by demands from home. He had wanted to attend Cambridge, but failed to obtain an exhibition which would have given him the financial resources, so instead attended University College in London. Lodge summarizes this time as "an odd life. For I was a kind of rebel from home, and my expedition to London was not regarded with paternal approbation" (*Past* 83). Not until 1873 at twenty-two years of age did he finally manage to break away from the family business (*Past* 39).

He was so shy and focused on work that he did not have a personal life until shortly before marriage. He appears to have remained sexually naïve, even though he taught an all-girls' class at Bedford College (albeit with a female chaperone, who knit during his lectures!), where he was affectionately known as "Noll-Lodge" (*Past* 92). Perhaps his curiosity was sublimated by an interest in the theatre at the time (*Past* 84). He states adamantly that, "I had no adventures of any kind" (*Past* 117). He did encounter prostitutes as he walked home, "but this was horrifying, and I used to run to escape them" (*Past* 117). This was until he was twenty-five, when "I began to be seriously afraid that I should succumb to temptation. Curiosity was a sort of raging fever, for it is not good for man to live alone" (*Past* 121). He had no access to women of his class, even at home, with the exception of the woman who would become his wife, whom he had known since they were both twelve. She began to take an interest in him, noting that "Oliver has improved" when she saw him at a lecture on the geysers of Iceland, during his Christmas break in 1875 (*Past* 120). Like Oliver's own mother, Mary Marshall had lost her father at an early age, in her case soon after her birth. Interestingly, her mother's premonition of her husband's death was one of the first psychic stories Oliver was told (*Past* 118). However, unlike Lodge, she was an only child, "much indulged by her mother and her loving elderly step-father, who had married his young wife when she was left a widow with a baby daughter" (Jolly 45). She had an artistic bent, so when Lodge told her about the Slade School of Art at University College, she enrolled in March 1876 (Jolly 37). Although Lodge kept a diary of his encounters with Mary, demonstrating his preoccupation with her, he recorded mainly events rather than his emotions, perhaps yet another indication of his avoidant patterning (Jolly 37–40). He became engaged to her on Boxing Day 1876, after escorting her home two miles on foot during a snowstorm from a party at his parents' house (Jolly

40). He wrote in his diary only that "she loves me," nothing about his feelings for her (as quoted in Jolly 40). Lodge's mother encouraged the engagement, as did his aunt, but he had to work diligently to improve his income to satisfy her parents. He commented that "I was rather annoyed at this, as showing a lack of faith in my earning capacity. A little help at that early stage would have been very welcome. I was already doing all I could, but I set to work at once to do more" (*Past* 129). They were married just eight months later, in August 1877, and then spent an ill-prepared honeymoon in Heidelberg, during which Lodge had to borrow money from their landlady (*Past* 126).

To a certain degree Lodge repeated the pattern of family life that he had experienced. He overworked from the time of his marriage, and the couple had a large number of children at frequent intervals, from 1878 to 1896 (Illustration 2.2). Six boys and then six girls survived into adulthood, but at least two infants did not survive childhood, although they reappear in the family narrative, suggesting their profound impact, as we shall see. He had received his DSc just two months before marrying, and attended the British Association meeting at Plymouth from 14 August to the day before he was married, on the morning of the 22nd (*Past* 140). He continued to teach at University College and Bedford College, to carry out a research program on heat and

Illustration 2.2 Oliver Lodge with his family; Raymond seated on floor at left

electricity, and to publish both his first book in 1879, as well as articles (Jolly 43–44). In 1881 he applied for and obtained a position at the new University College at Liverpool. The building was a former lunatic asylum, and Lodge had to begin from scratch to create a laboratory. He proposed touring laboratories in Europe for ideas, which he did on a "solitary pilgrimage" from June to September; once again he mentions that he "was very shy" and that it was "a profitable though lonely tour" (*Past* 153). Presumably his wife was left alone as well, with three children under the age of four.

This would be the first of numerous work-related travels, particularly after Lodge began his second career in psychical research, when the family was left behind. In this, too, Lodge repeated his father's pattern. During the first years in Liverpool, Lodge lectured to several levels of students in engineering and mathematics, claiming that "the work was getting beyond even my energy. I sometimes lectured five hours a day" (*Past* 159). Childrearing was left to Mary, Lodge admitting that "it is not good to be so busy that one cannot attend to the children, but roughly speaking that was my case" (*Past* 249). Lodge's main interaction with them was reading aloud books like *Treasure Island* and *The Prisoner of Zenda* (*Past* 249). Nevertheless, overwork took its toll and Lodge suffered from "awful headaches" and was "sometimes irritable" to the extent that his "children were somewhat afraid of me," as he recognized in retrospect (*Past* 253, 252). He also admitted that "truly I fear I did not get to know them properly when they were small," and that "my wife must have had many troubles" running the household since they lived in financially straitened circumstances (*Past* 253). In summary of this period, Lodge claims that "the elder children had rather a bad time. We were poor, and not able to give them a fair chance: the younger ones must've had a much better childhood" (*Past* 248). Although the family's financial circumstances improved as Lodge became more famous and patented various inventions, even after he became President of Birmingham University in 1900 "life was just as strenuous as at Liverpool" (*Past* 324). Lodge's ambitions merely increased when he had more time within his own control, and he "dictated a number of books and articles in my spare time, working all day long at one thing or another" (*Past* 324).

Although circumstances as a struggling academic with a growing family undoubtedly contributed to the insecurity and stress within Lodge's household, his fundamental approach to human relationships also played a significant role. To his credit, Lodge recognized this inclination to become absorbed in his inner world at the expense of the external world and relationships in particular. He notes that even as a child he had little appreciation for scenery, no artistic faculty, was not good at observation, and had no memory for people's names, as his father did (*Past* 110). He adds that:

> My instinct seemed to be more abstract, rejoicing in hidden forces, atomic occurrences, and other things which can never be seen – ultimately becoming more absorbed in the ether as a non-sensuous reality – than in the material objects around us. This is probably a confession, and should not be pressed to extremes. (*Past* 111)

From a young age Lodge transformed this inclination arising from his attachment pattern into a habit and an advantage in his scientific work, which he called "brooding." He claims that:

> I was not easily diverted from a course of brooding by transient happenings. I was not conscious of any of this at the time; it is only on looking back that I traced the beginnings of my life work in those still dormant instincts which enabled me to brood over such elementary phenomena as came my way. (*Past* 343)

Lodge's brooding lay at the root not only of his scientific work, but also of his growing interest in the "imponderables" of psychical research (*Past* 111).

Lodge had been introduced to psychical research by the work of fellow physicist William Barrett and by Edmund Gurney, who had attended Lodge's University College lectures on mechanics in the 1870s (*Conviction* 3). Gurney introduced him to Frederic Myers, who became "an intimate friend" during the last twenty years of Myers's life and then in his afterlife as well (*Conviction* 2). Although they were temperamental opposites, Myers being sensuous and Lodge not, both shared an avoidant-resistant patterning as well as obsessional drivenness. Lodge's first actual pursuit of psychical research occurred when Myers invited him to investigate a case of thought transference in Liverpool in 1883 (*Past* 273). He did so, and over several weeks gradually became convinced that thought transference or telepathy, as Myers was calling it, was genuine (*Past* 274). Not only were his experiments published in the proceedings of the SPR, but he also managed to get them published in the prestigious journal *Nature* in 1884 (*Past* 274). This would be the first of innumerable articles on psychical research that Lodge contributed both to reputable and more popular publications throughout the rest of his life. The key event which "thoroughly convinced" (*Past* 279) him of human survival and which committed him to a lifelong quest to demonstrate this, occurred during his "first experience with any trance medium – with F. W. H. Myers taking notes" in 1889, with the famous medium Mrs Piper (*Past* 277). He was astonished when his Aunt Anne who had died of cancer, "ostensibly took possession of the medium; and in her own energetic manner reminded me of her promise to come back if she could, and spoke a few sentences in her own well remembered voice" (*Past* 277). Lodge considers it significant that Aunt Anne was fulfilling her promise to him, but it is also significant that it was Aunt Anne, to whom Lodge had probably the strongest emotional and intellectual bond, even though his parents would also presumably have been candidates since his mother had died in 1879 and his father in 1884, both worn out by overwork according to Lodge (*Past* 33). He did subsequently contact through Mrs Piper "old deceased relatives of whose early youth I knew nothing whatever, and was told of incidents which were subsequently verified by their surviving elderly contemporaries" (*Past* 278). Lodge continued to investigate psychical phenomena through the 1890s, with a particular focus on what the SPR called physical phenomena. He had joined the committee on physical phenomena in 1887. By far the most extraordinary experiment he participated in occurred on physiologist Charles Richet's Mediterranean island, involving a medium called Eusapia Palladino. As a child she had suffered traumatic loss, her mother dying in childbirth and her father being murdered when she was twelve (Jolly 103). Now forty, she had developed the capacity to cause heavy furniture to move around the room, to cause the investigators to be grasped, presumably by her control John King, and to manifest ectoplasm. Claims by Lodge, Myers, and the other investigators that her powers were genuine were courageous and generated publicity and skepticism (Jolly 104–5). Lodge firmly believed, however, that the strength of her psychic ideation had directed the ether, allowing her to use energy to move physical objects or project forms. In 1899, Lodge had perhaps the first serious intimation of his own mortality when he "narrowly survived a bout of typhoid fever" (Rowlands), and it is tempting to speculate that this near-death incident spurred on his investigations for evidence of survival.

Certainly Lodge's increasing intimacy with and admiration for Frederic Myers during this entire period did have that effect. Lodge had "great talks" with Myers (220) and was particularly impressed by Myers's "portentous memory" (*Past* 279), his "remarkable interest in science" (*Past* 280), and his role in "laying the foundation for a cosmic philosophy" based on evidence (*Conviction* 46). In one letter he wrote that "it is difficult to exaggerate my admiration for him and his special form of genius" (Hill 220). At Cambridge, Myers introduced Lodge to the literati and intelligentsia, including Mark Twain, William James, and Charles Richet, the latter becoming a "great friend" of Lodge's (*Past* 291). Then in January of 1901 Myers died. Lodge was devastated, but his grief was ameliorated when several mediums began to pick up messages from Myers. Another blow occurred one month after Myers's death when Lodge's principal scientific friend and mentor G. F. Fitzgerald died (Jolly 144). Lodge wrote that "My friendship with [Myers] and Fitzgerald has been among the chief influences in my life" (*Past* 220).

In the afterlife Myers continued to play an important role in Lodge's life, since Lodge became preoccupied with communications from Myers. Lodge published extensively on this and other evidence for survival, which kept him in the forefront of debates and made him a controversial and famous figure. Myers's communications also played an important role in shaping his attitude towards war loss, particularly that of his son Raymond. Lodge first encountered Myers's control in a sitting with the medium Mrs Thompson on 19 February 1901, about a month after Myers died. Lodge recorded that the impersonation "was really a remarkably vivid and lifelike one" (*Survival* 294). The Myers control predicted that Lodge would succeed Myers as president of the SPR and in this he was correct, although the Society had been trying to get Lord Rayleigh to take up the position (*Survival* 293). Lodge remarked that the sitting was "the best of the Myers sittings in which I have been immediately concerned" (*Survival* 294). However, Myers's voice began to be channeled by several mediums in different countries. Similar statements were received from Myers about the same time, although unbeknown to each other. These extensive cross-correspondences, as they were called, enhanced Lodge's conviction that it was actually Myers communicating (*Conviction* 10–11). Lodge recollected that Myers "has taken the trouble to guide me in many ways since his departure from earth life. He has shown noteworthy signs of his continued affection, and I am grateful" (*Past* 288).

Not only did Lodge become the president of the SPR at this time, but he had just become President of the newly-established Birmingham University in June 1900. Furthermore, in June 1902 he was created knight bachelor, at the same time as fellow spiritualist seeker Arthur Conan Doyle, which further cemented their friendship. Lodge's position in society was well established, and his scientific and psychic investigations gave him extensive connections across the classes, including the aristocracy. For instance, he became the life-long friend of Arthur Balfour, who became Prime Minister in 1902 and who shared Lodge's interest in philosophy and science (Jolly 116). However, it was Lodge's books and articles on psychic matters (along with hundreds of speaking engagements) which brought him celebrity status. These he published frequently over the course of the rest of his life, 70 on psychical research generally, 73 more on survival, 170 on philosophy and religion, and 54 on the ether (37 of these after the First World War) (Besterman viii–ix). He thus clearly continued to overwork, which took its toll on his health, and he had to take leave from the University several times, including a six-week rest cure in 1906 (Jolly 187). Between 1907 and 1909 he published three enormously popular books, reprinted frequently in cheap editions: *The Substance of Faith*, *The Survival of Man*, and *Man and the Universe* (Jolly 175). In *The Survival of Man* (1909) he summarized Society for Psychical Research findings, including his sittings with the Myers control, and he clearly stated his "conviction of man's survival of bodily death" (Preface). Even so, biographical and critical work on Lodge continues erroneously to claim that Lodge turned to spiritualism after the death of his son Raymond in 1915.[1]

While Lodge's book *Raymond*, a compilation of family expressions of grief, letters from Raymond, his afterlife communications and Lodge's controversial interpretation of the significance of these, became the most famous of his books on the war, it is not often commented on that he produced another, earlier, almost as popular book, *The War and After*, and that his involvement in the war effort was extensive. This might not have been predicted from his initial stance on the war, which was avoidant, typical of Lodge. At the outbreak of war he and Lady Lodge found themselves in Adelaide, Australia for the annual meeting of the British Association, of which he had become President in 1913. Despite being surrounded by patriotic fervor there, Lodge advocated "that the British Association should ignore the war since science was above the conflict" (Jolly 189). On returning from Australia, Lodge had his first taste of the war as his ship was pursued by a German cruiser, although he treated this like an adventure (Jolly 189–91). Nevertheless, Lodge threw himself into the war effort, sitting on the War Committee of the Royal Society and later the Admiralty's Board of Invention and Research (Jolly 193). He also engaged in propaganda, penning an article, "The War: a British View" for *The North American Review*, and then developing the ideas into *The War and After*. The short book sold for only one shilling and was reprinted five times after it appeared in August 1915, and twice in 1916. It was obviously widely disseminated – my copy is *ex libris* from the

Royal Military Academy in Woolwich – and had considerable impact, Lodge being told that "it played a significant part in bringing the United States into the war" (Jolly 195). Although Lodge felt duty-bound to write it, to his credit he advocates preserving "mental balance" and states that his reader should bear in mind "the services to humanity" of "the majority of our present foes" (vii). Not surprisingly, Lodge views the conflict as fundamentally a war of ideas, specifically religious and philosophical ones. In their drive to power, the Germans revolted against Christianity and distorted philosophical teaching. Lodge quotes liberally from the "mad mystic" Nietzsche to make his point (*War* 41). Nevertheless, his emotion does emerge when he refers to the present state of Europe as "a ghastly nightmare" and claims:

> Nor is the suffering limited to the wounded alone. The links of affection which bind one human being to another afford further opportunity for exquisite torture. The premature breakage of such links, and the agonized fear of friends for those exposed to the danger, give scope and room enough for a cry to the heavens, of magnitude such as cannot have ascended in any previous epoch of the world's history. (*War* 84)

Lodge's spiritualist views do not appear except in the conclusion, where he states that "Seers and sensitives have known intuitively that great events were being foreshadowed, they felt the coming of the present time, and have heralded the advent of a new era. The conflict is not solely material, the whole psychic atmosphere is troubled ..." (*War* 228). Lodge's anxiety was that "the advance of humanity in a spiritual direction would have been set back for centuries" (*War* 229). One comment of Lodge's is sadly prescient: "Bereavement is widespread. The voice of weeping is heard through all the lands: soon in every family there must be one dead" (*War* 84).

Lodge's son Raymond was very much alive when Sir Oliver wrote these words, but he had been in the trenches for a couple of months. He would be killed on 14 September 1915, just over a month after *The War and After* was published. Interestingly, Raymond had signed up while his parents were in Australia and did not inform them until their return. Perhaps this was a rebellious act, although by this time Raymond was 24. The last of the Lodge's boys, he had been born in 1889 just as Lodge was embarking on his labor-intensive ether experiments at Liverpool University. Lodge admitted that he did not have as much contact with Raymond during his formative years as he should have: "being so desperately busy all my life I failed to see as much as I should like either of him [Raymond] or of the other boys, but there was always an instinctive sympathy between us" (*Raymond* 9). Lodge identified with the boy because of the resemblance to himself when a child, including "small mental traits," a similar speech impediment, a "dislike of children's parties," and later on similar ability and tastes for engineering and machinery (*Raymond* 8). He also idealized his son, claiming that he was "one of the best youths I have ever known" with "a brilliant career" ahead of him (*Raymond* 9).

That an instinctive sympathy existed between them is reinforced by events immediately preceding Raymond's death. Lodge began to receive messages from Myers through Mrs Piper two weeks before Raymond's death, the first involving a classical allusion to Faunus. After checking with several classical scholars, Lodge interpreted "that the meaning was that some blow was going to fall, or was likely to fall ... and that Myers would intervene, apparently to protect me from it" (*Raymond* 92). Then on the day of Raymond's death, Lodge fell into "an exceptional state of depression" and could not complete a round of golf (*Raymond* 35). Raymond's brother Alec had "an extraordinarily painful and vivid dream" the night before he received the news as well (*Raymond* 35). From this point on, Raymond communicated frequently through mediums and during table tilting sessions and family séances. Raymond told Lodge that in the afterlife "Myers was the first person he saw, and that Myers had practically adopted him" (*Past* 288), and Myers continued to facilitate the communication. By 1916 Lodge considered that he had enough evidential messages to make them public, with the aim of comforting mourners. He did this "not without hesitation," however, since he was obtruding into family affairs: "I should not have done so were it not that the amount of premature and unnatural bereavement at the present time is so appalling that the pain caused by exposing one's own sorrow and its alleviation, to possible scoffers, becomes almost negligible in view of the service which it is legitimate to hope may thus be rendered to mourners ..." (*Raymond* vii–viii). When published in November, *Raymond, or Life and Death* immediately tapped into the worldwide mass trauma and the book went through six impressions in a month even though not cheaply priced, and then six more until 1922 when Lodge addressed critics in a condensed version, *Raymond Revised*.[2]

Raymond certainly serves as a testament, a domestic monument to son and brother. Not often noted is the fact that it is truly a family effort, with reminiscences, laments, and séance scripts involving most family members, including the return of two Lodge children who died in infancy, most significantly Laura, called Lily in the scripts. These spiritual beings are described as reuniting with Raymond, strongly suggesting that the family was engaged in healing not just from the immediate trauma of Raymond's death, but also from these earlier painful traumas (*Raymond* 159). Raymond's older brother Oliver wrote that the family's homage to him was in "growing like him and by holding our lives lightly in our Country's service, so that if need be we may die like him. This is true honour and his best Memorial"[3] (*Raymond* 6). He even included a poem for his brother:

> Who shall remember him, who climb
> His all un-ripened fame to wake,
> Who dies an age before his time?
> But nobly, but for England's sake.
> Who will believe us when we cry
> He was as great as he was brave?
> His name that years had lifted high
> Lies buried in that Belgian grave.
> Oh strong and patient, kind and true,
> Valiant of heart, and clear of brain –
> They cannot know the man we knew,
> Our words go down the wind like rain. (*Raymond* 6)

Ironically, the publication of *Raymond* with its intimate details of Raymond's life and family connections ensured that the last line did not come to pass. The arc of the narrative consists in the family's overcoming their initial skepticism, which is referenced several times by Lodge (*Raymond* 84, 151, 162, 174, 279), and more importantly for present purposes, Lodge's increasing knowledge and understanding of, and emotional connection with, his son. On several occasions Lodge learns details of Raymond's life, for example about a motoring trip Raymond had taken with his brothers during which they sent home a telegram signed "Argonauts" (*Raymond* 154–55). He also learns about sheet music songs that Raymond had bought and sung (*Raymond* 215, 216). Raymond shows concern for his father, saying "you are doing too much" (*Raymond* 248), but he also says "that you will be doing the most wonderful work of your life through the war. People are ready to listen" (*Raymond* 249). There are poignant moments, as when Lady Lodge reveals that they have left a chair for Raymond at Christmas time, and when Oliver confesses "I speak to your photograph sometimes" (*Raymond* 188, 248). He also notes instances of Raymond's laughter and humor (*Raymond* 182, 224, 251). Raymond reveals that when he first arrived "he felt a little depression. But it didn't last long" because he was soon surrounded by relatives and friends (*Raymond* 203). Raymond does not want to return, not because he wants "to be away from you all. I have still got you, because I feel you so close, closer even" (*Raymond* 202). Lodge remarks that through their family sittings "Raymond remains as much a member of the family group as ever" (*Raymond* 275).

Another part of Lodge's therapy is the strength and comfort he derives from his increasing belief that it is his son who is contacting him. In one of the earliest sittings mention was made of a group photograph including Raymond holding a walking stick, but the family had no knowledge of such a photograph. Two months later the mother of a fellow officer of Raymond's sent the Lodges a photograph corresponding in its details to the one described by the control (*Raymond* 110). In another sitting, Feda, the control of Mrs Leonard, described a "sand boat," an unusual contraption that Raymond and his brothers had built in 1906, confirmed by a photograph (*Raymond* 251–53). Lodge's children even carried out a successful cross-correspondence test. At a spontaneous sitting in Birmingham, Alec asked his brother Raymond "to get Feda in London to say the word 'Honolulu'" at a simultaneous sitting there with two other siblings (*Raymond* 271). The chances of this word arising were slim, but Lodge considers that it could have been an example of telepathy (*Raymond* 275). There are other correspondences in personality between the Raymond conveyed through his letters from the front and the Raymond appearing in the séances. For example, Raymond's letters show him to have a lively sense of humor: he asks whether the family has seen the *Punch* joke "where the Aunt says: 'send me a postcard when you're safely in the trenches!'? Well, there is a great deal of truth in that ..." (*Raymond* 24). He takes pleasure in simple things like "a welcome shave" or "a glorious hot bath" (*Raymond* 18, 36), as well as in his work building dugouts and huts (*Raymond* 33, 34). He was keen on generating acrostics (*Raymond* 21, 25), and he continued to do so in the afterlife (*Raymond* 224). Lodge summarized that Raymond was "always acting in a manner consistent with his personality and memories and varying moods" (*Raymond* 375). The sense that Raymond's personality persisted provided a large amount of the appeal and comfort of the book.

Lodge concluded the communications from the Raymond section of the book by claiming that "every possible ground of suspicion or doubt seems to the family to be now removed" (*Raymond* 279). In the third section Lodge articulated his theory of "intercommunication between two grades of existence" with the possibility that additional grades of existence would be discovered (*Raymond* 288). He addressed the "repugnant" topic of "death and decay" by asserting that "everything removed from the emotional arena, and transplanted into the intellectual, becomes interesting and tractable and worthy of study" (*Raymond* 303). Lodge clearly did not believe that study of and focus on afterlife communications was maudlin or would lead to crippling grief, although he did not recommend that all bereaved persons should seek such communication. Instead he "recommend[ed] people in general to learn and realize that their loved ones are still active and useful and interested and happy – more alive than ever in one sense – and to make up their minds to live a useful life till they rejoin them" (*Raymond* 342). People "should not selfishly seek to lessen pain by discouraging all mention, and even hiding everything likely to remind them, of those they have lost; nor should they give themselves over to unavailing and prostrating grief" (*Raymond* 343). Clearly, the process of communicating with Raymond as well as communicating this publicly helped Lodge modify his characteristic avoidant-resistant response to attachment.

Lodge mentions that Raymond brought messages from deceased friends, which provided help and comfort to both parents and widows (*Raymond* 226, 279). The publication of *Raymond* spawned numerous other publications of spirit soldier communications, for several of which Lodge wrote prefaces,[4] including Claude H. Kelway Bamber's *Claude's Book*, edited by L. Kelway-Bamber. Also, *Raymond* caused a sensation and provoked a range of rapid critical responses, from academics, such as psychiatrist Charles Mercier, to religious leaders, including Viscount Halifax, President of the English Church Union.[5] Almost all of them attacked a passage in which Raymond describes recent arrivals to the afterlife desiring cigars and "whiskey sodas" and claiming that "they can manufacture even that" (*Raymond* 197–98). Lodge knew very well that this sort of "triviality" and "nonsense" (*Raymond* 269, 349) would provoke scorn, but to his credit he included this regardless, since he did not want to suppress any evidence (*Raymond* 172), and it countered conventional notions of the afterlife: "the idea that a departed friend ought to be occupied wholly and entirely with grave matters, and ought not to remember jokes and fun, is a gratuitous claim which has to be abandoned" (*Raymond* 349).[6] From an object-relations viewpoint, the disoriented new arrivals' desire for familiar objects and oral gratification in particular makes psychological sense. Another point frequently raised against Lodge was his naïveté in assuming that he could present himself to a medium anonymously when he had been involved in psychic investigations for such a long period of time and so frequently appeared in the media, including in photographs. Lodge's fame increased enormously after the publication of *Raymond*, and he dealt conscientiously with the correspondence, enlisting J. Arthur Hill, his secretary on psychical matters, to help. As late as 1930, Lodge wrote that, "Messages purporting to come from [Raymond] have reached me from all parts of the world" (*Conviction* 21), from Winnipeg, Canada to Russia.[7] Raymond entered into the popular culture as well in plays and novels. For instance, a highly successful play, Sutton Vane's *Outward Bound* (1923), was based on the whiskey and cigars episode, as Lodge acknowledged (Hill 184). Huxley's novels *Eyeless in Gaza* and *Time Must Have a Stop* also reference the book, as will be discussed in Chapter 7.

Much attention has been given to *Raymond*, but Lodge's sequel, or one might say, counterpoint, *Christopher* (1918), has been almost completely neglected, even though it demonstrates how Lodge continued to work through his trauma and it also provides yet another link with Myers in the afterlife. While working on this manuscript, Lodge suffered another loss when his son-in-law Lieutenant Langley was killed in May 1918 while flying, leaving his daughter Nora with a two-week-old child (Hill 153). The subject of *Christopher*, Christopher Tennant, was killed in battle on 3 September 1917. He was a friend of the Lodge family (and a nephew of Frederic Myers) and an opposite type to Raymond, being scholarly and artistic. Lodge very consciously memorializes this soldier, claiming that he will "try to raise an altar" to his memory in his volume (*Christopher* 3). It is an odd compilation of biography, including biography by Christopher's mother of his sister who died at an early age, editorializing commentary by Lodge, autobiographical fragment, representative letters, a long description by Mrs Tennant of Robert Louis Stevenson's garden and house at Hyères, where the family had visited, and even a sonnet attributed to Frederic Myers obtained through a medium (*Christopher* 73).

The book perfectly illustrates the impact of an earlier traumatic loss when a second one occurs. Christopher's sister Daphne, called The Darling, died at eighteen months in 1908 when Christopher was ten (*Christopher* 22). A memorial chapter in the book demonstrates that the impact on the family was profound. Her ashes were kept beside her teddy bear and her mother thereafter signed her intimate letters "Daphne's mother" (*Christopher* 25, 58). Although Christopher's uncle by marriage, Frederic Myers, had died when Christopher was three-and-a-half, Myers "became a living reality in the boy's life" (*Christopher* 84).

From the age of ten Christopher "read omnivorously," including Frederic Myers's prose and poetry. They shared a love of the classics, nature, and poetry. From age fifteen he read Myers's and then Lodge's psychical research material, becoming convinced "that life and love and memory survive the grave" (*Christopher* 85). After signing up for the military he even made a pact to communicate from the afterlife with his mother: "the aim was that each might feel secure of the other" (*Christopher* 54). When Christopher was killed within a month of going to the front, Mrs Tennant was consoled in her belief that Myers and others would take care of her boy, and she had "no agonies of mind as to where his dear young body lies" (*Christopher* 60). Although she does admit that there is "a side of me which is bleeding," Lodge claims that the comfort she finds in reunion with him before long and "the same absence of prostrating grief or unreasoning and uncontrolled emotion have continued to this day" (*Christopher* 60–61). He argues that she is much better off than those dominated by traditional religious belief who have anxieties about whether their loved one is saved or not (*Christopher* 61); this illustration of belief in survival as a strength against "undue mourning" justifies this book.

However, ironically there is evidence that Lodge's own early trauma was revived in the process of writing *Christopher*. Lodge compares the slaughter in war to "the less obtrusive moral and intellectual slaughter always going on in time of peace" (*Christopher* 9), by which he means destruction of promise and talent by the current school system. He returns to this point later, claiming "yet what a condemnation it is that such a nature [as Christopher's] could feel less out of place and homeless even amid the hardships and horrors of war than he felt while at school!" (*Christopher* 43–44). A chapter on "School Discipline" erupts into the narrative without much connection to Christopher's experience, Lodge asserting that "I feel bound to say something on the subject of school, as it not invariably but too often is" (*Christopher* 35). He lists various defects, including "suppression of natural emotional expression" (*Christopher* 36). With emotional force, he comments on bullying, claiming, "in the worst cases the thoughtless power of the stronger develops into an obscene brutality" (*Christopher* 38), and on vice, "including every kind of evil conduct" (*Christopher* 44). He hopes that the "wave of reality" engendered by the war will "emancipate us" through change to the school system (*Christopher* 36). When we finally get to Christopher's account of his schooling much further on in the narrative, we find that he was lonely, bullied, and not very happy at school, but unlike Lodge, Christopher conveyed his feelings to his mother (*Christopher* 159, 161, 175). Also, unlike Lodge's parents Mrs Tennant took action, writing to the housemaster who made efforts to stop the bullying (*Christopher* 161). As with Lodge's mother, Christopher's mother was obviously a dominating force in her son's life; at nineteen he claims in a letter to her that "I'm never completely happy except when you are with me" (*Christopher* 188). Lodge identified with Christopher as well because "he maintained a critical attitude towards the public school system as he had known it" and he was "a rebel" (*Christopher* 88). Just as Lodge had failed to get an exhibition at Cambridge, so too did Christopher (*Christopher* 168). Thus, in making the connection between school trauma and war trauma, and in conveying and editorializing on Christopher's experience in school, Lodge apparently continued to work through his own early trauma as revived by the loss of Raymond and then Christopher, with whom he identified in some significant ways. Lodge returned to the trauma of his schooling in his autobiography, *Past Years*, as we have seen.

Lodge's comment that "War came and spoilt everything" (*Past* 261) summarizes its impact, but his response was typical of him – he took on more work. From this point on much of his life would be dedicated to proselytizing about survival after death and, connected with this, his exploration of the spiritual dimension of the ether. This is why he retired from the Presidency of the University of Birmingham in February 1919. Three days after his retirement ceremony in January 1920, he embarked on a lecture tour of forty US towns, giving nearly one hundred lectures in four months (Jolly 217, 219). Both he and his wife continued to be in contact with Raymond and were significantly influenced by his communications. While his wife visited Vichy in France in July 1919, Lodge received a message from Raymond that he had found a retirement house for his parents. By coincidence Lodge visited his friend Lord Glenconner, who owned a house that fitted a description his wife had received from a professional clairvoyant in 1913, which had been copied out by Raymond while he was alive. Some of the features described in 1913 had only recently been added to Glenconner's house (*Why* 81–93). In due course the Lodges moved in, Lodge commenting that this was only one instance when Raymond "has shown knowledge of current events and been of service": he apparently expressed joy that they had got the house (*Why* 91).

Lodge increasingly viewed his life in mystical terms as he became more absorbed in pondering the omnipresence of the ether. In *Ether and Reality* (1925), he argued that the ether interpenetrated the physical and spiritual realms: "it fills all space in the most thorough manner: there is nothing so omnipresent and so efficient in the physical universe" (*Ether* 25–26). Towards the end of that volume Lodge starts to sound like a mystic, when he claims that "the ether of space is a theme of unknown and apparently infinite magnitude, and of a reality beyond the present conception of man. It is ... a consummate substance of overpowering grandeur. By a kind of instinct, one feels it to be the home of spiritual existence, the realm of the awe-inspiring and the supernal" (*Ether* 173). He concluded that "it is the primary instrument of mind, the vehicle of soul, the habitation of spirit. Truly it may be called the living garment of God" (*Ether* 179). In *Why I Believe*, he contrasts imperfect matter with the ether, which "has never shown any sign of the least imperfection; it is absolutely transparent, it dissipates no energy, and any structure composed of ether is likely to be permanent" (10). By 1933 in *My Philosophy*, he is referring to the ether of space as his "life study" and he admits an obsession with it: "when in my old age I came to write this book, I found that the ether pervaded all my ideas, both of this world and the next" ("Foreword"). In this book in which he quotes from poets throughout, especially the Romantics, and particularly Myers, he emphasizes that the ether is a medium of cohesion, and predicts that "the bringing in of the ether into the scheme of psychics, as it has already been partially brought into the scheme of physics, is the work which I feel sure is lying ahead for generations of men" (*Philosophy* 237). Like the traditional mystic, for whom unity with God is the object, for Lodge being immersed in the ether became his primary goal.

Ironically, during the years 1922 to 1932 when he published thirteen books, wrote numerous popular articles, and gave countless lectures, he became what his biographer Jolly refers to as a "prophet of the people" (223), often generating controversy, his name appearing in the press hundreds of times each year. In 1930 he was listed in a *Spectator* poll as one of the four best brains of Britain, along with Shaw, Birkenhead, and Churchill (Jolly 224). Throughout this period he met with leading lights in science and society, including Einstein in 1933 (Jolly 231). In 1927 he conducted a mass telepathy experiment on BBC radio, and subsequently disappeared into the ether himself, in the sense that he broadcast many talks on the ether, survival after death, and science, which generated a large amount of correspondence (Jolly 229). In February 1929 his wife died, but by May Lodge was communicating with her, reunited with Raymond and Myers, through Mrs Leonard's control Feda, on various topics, including "the extraordinary ties and links that exist where there is love" (*Conviction* 34).

In the final chapter of his autobiography Lodge confirmed that "a spiritual world is the greatest of realities, but we cannot fully apprehend it yet ... Infinite possibilities for progress lie ahead, yet it behooves us strenuously to make the most of the present possibilities of earth life" and he closed the work saying "Forward, then, into the unknown!" (352). Lodge moved into that realm on the day of his wedding anniversary, 22 August 1940. He had been driven in his work throughout his life, his psychic secretary Arthur Hill commenting that Lodge experienced "few and rare intervals for rest or recreation" (284), and he was diligent up to his passing and beyond. He had set up a posthumous experiment at the Society for Psychical Research consisting of seven envelopes with clues in each leading towards a final message. In December 1951, this was revealed to be a five finger piano exercise learned as a child that Lodge became obsessed with during his life; however, the experiment was inconclusive (Jolly 236). He had hoped "that when my time comes" he would be able to communicate messages as well as Myers had, and messages from Lodge did purportedly continue, again from various places around the world, including through Margaret Hamilton in Winnipeg and more recently to Robert Leichtman, a psychiatrist, through the medium D. Kendrick Johnson, published as *Sir Oliver Lodge Returns*.

3

From Parodist to Proselytizer: Arthur Conan Doyle's "Vital Message"

> Up in a dingy attic two little figures were seated on the side of the wretched straw-stuffed bed, their arms enlacing each other, their cheeks touching, their tears mingling. They had to cry in silence, for any sound might remind the ogre downstairs of their existence. Now and again one would break into an uncontrollable sob, and the other would whisper, "Hush! Hush! Oh hush!" Then suddenly they heard the slam of the outer door and that heavy tread booming over the wooden flap. They squeezed each other in their joy. Perhaps when he came back he might kill them, but for a few short hours at least they were safe from him. As to the woman, she was spiteful and vicious, but she did not seem so deadly as the man. (*Land* 193)

This scenario, depicting a brother and sister hiding and suppressing their emotion for fear of antagonizing their alcoholic father, "a man who grew more dangerous in his cups" (186), appears in Arthur Conan Doyle's last novel, *The Land of Mist*, a thinly disguised apologia of spiritualism. Although Doyle warned "that the created is not the creator," "the doll and its maker are never identical" (as quoted in Stashower 279–80), this passage, and in fact an entire self-contained chapter dealing with these abusive parents and their neglect of their children in poverty-stricken surroundings, erupts into an otherwise didactic narrative and, I would argue, captures something of the emotional devastation Doyle felt as a child living with an alcoholic father, despite differing details. (Doyle's mother was not abusive like this stepmother, and the fictional father meets a gruesome death by the end of the chapter.) A recent biographer, Douglas Kerr, admits that the chapter is "a strange interlude" but dismisses it as "melodrama, either remembered from the stage, or experienced afresh in the silent cinema" (229). This is typical of most Doyle biographers, who "have tended to walk gingerly around the subject of [Doyle's] psychology," as Jon Lellenberg claims in his survey of them (*Quest* 13), to say nothing of their confusion, embarrassment, or ambivalence towards Doyle's ardent championing of spiritualism in the latter part of his life.[1] During his lifetime he was harshly criticized for becoming a spiritualist after having created the logical machine Sherlock Holmes: "that is the central paradox of Arthur's life," claims Andrew Lycett (131). Daniel Stashower adds that:

> years later, when Conan Doyle's interest in the spirit realm had become a matter of public record, critics never tired of pointing out the contrast between the author's beliefs and those of the clear thinking, intensely logical Sherlock Holmes. The prevailing view at that time, which persists today, held that Conan Doyle underwent some softening of the brain in later life. In fact, the strange tension between the material and the spirit worlds is evident in all phases of Conan Doyle's career. (86)[2]

Stashower's last statement is closer to the truth, but the psychological roots of this tension and of Doyle's complicated personality need to be probed further.

On the surface Doyle epitomizes the English gentleman of his time: gregarious, clubbable, and thoroughly engaged in and even shaping cultural debates, yet his life contains as many puzzles and secrets as a volume of Sherlock Holmes stories. In his early years Doyle was traumatized not only by his severely unstable home life, exacerbated by his father's alcoholism, but also by the harsh discipline and punishment he experienced at the hands of Jesuit priests at Stonyhurst, where he was sent at age nine. By then he had adopted an avoidant-resistant pattern of attachment along with several of the significant symptoms of the child of an alcoholic, including fear and suppression of emotions, approval seeking, an addiction to excitement, an overdeveloped sense of responsibility, and obsessional drivenness (*Adult Children*).[3] Through his dominant mother's guidance he found solace in literature, although he trained in the more practical field of medicine with the aim of supporting his family. Doyle rebelled against the ardent Catholicism of his paternal side, but pursued questions of spirituality from an early age. When he began writing, spiritual and psychic themes engaged him, as well as escapist historical romance. He wrote the first Sherlock Holmes stories concurrently, and although these appear to depict a rationalist protagonist, a paragon of materialism, of the opposite type to Doyle, I will argue that Holmes displays Doyle's avoidant-resistant patterning as well as some of the characteristics of the medium and mystic. Doyle also gave Holmes at least one characteristic of his father's: his addiction. Holmes represented the shadow self of Doyle and his father, and this suggests a deeper reason than boredom for his indifference to Holmes's "death." Doyle abruptly killed off other protagonists in his early fiction as well. From a dismissive attitude towards death, Doyle's attitude evolved towards a more compassionate engagement with death and mourning, particularly after the loss in 1906 of his first wife, Louisa, following a lengthy battle with tuberculosis. Doyle's mourning was complicated by his guilt over having had a platonic relationship with a younger woman, Jean Leckie, for nine years while married to Louisa. During this time he also moved from a skeptical attitude towards psychical research to a more engaged embracing of spiritualism. Although he was an enthusiastic propagandist for the First World War, after he experienced multiple losses, particularly of his son Kingsley and his brother Innes, he became preoccupied with the suffering and losses caused by the conflict. Whereas in his earlier life he tended to renegotiate difficult relationships in his fiction, he now did so through mediums in séances where communication was made with lost loved ones. He also felt a responsibility to communicate details about the source of comfort in his bereavement. He became known as the St Paul of spiritualism, proselytizing about it throughout the world, both in person and in print (Stashower 344). As he proudly notes in his autobiography, he traveled 55,000 miles, spoke to a quarter of a million people (*Memories* 389), and wrote hundreds of thousands of words about spiritualism. Despite some blunders of judgment, Doyle maintained his high profile as a spiritualist, and his beliefs had an enormous impact on the spiritualist societies that sprang up in England after the war, as well as on thousands of families mourning their lost loved ones. As with Myers and Lodge, Doyle's communications continued beyond his death in 1930 up until the present day.

Doyle's autobiography, *Memories and Adventures*, is a masterpiece of evasion, matched only by his friends J. M. Barrie's and Kipling's autobiographies. It contains very little introspection and conceals a number of Doyle's secrets. He spends very little time on his childhood, and, as Richard Lancelyn Green observes, "He is factual and without sentiment, offering no psychological explanations" nor a glimpse into his emotional life. Green surmises that "It is as if Conan Doyle – whose character suggested kindliness and trust – had a fear of intimacy. When he describes his life he omits the inner man" (43). This is entirely consistent with the avoidant/dismissive style of reporting attachment history. Nevertheless, Doyle's selection of what to include as well as the omissions, which can be filled in from other sources, including his letters, are revealing, making it possible to construct a reasonably accurate portrait of his early family life. Doyle faced the challenges of insecurity, anxiety, and poverty. In his autobiography, Doyle proudly emphasizes the artistic accomplishments of his father's Anglo-Irish and Catholic family and the aristocratic connections and military prowess of his mother's also Irish family tree, "on which many of the great ones of the earth have roosted" (*Memories* 3). Despite his self-conscious emphasis on the "romance of ancestry," he does introduce themes of poverty, mental instability, and death. His mother's father, William Foley, "died

Illustration 3.1 Arthur Conan Doyle age 6, with his father Charles Altamont Doyle. Reprinted by permission of the Arthur Conan Doyle Collection – Lancelyn Green Bequest, Portsmouth City Council

young and left his family in relative poverty" (*Memories* 3). The deathbed of Foley's wife (Doyle's grandmother), "or rather the white waxen thing which lay upon that bed," constitutes Doyle's "very earliest recollection" (*Memories* 3). One of his mother's ancestors had part of his head shot off in battle, and this legend became "the family tradition that we lose our heads in action" (*Memories* 3). Although said humorously, Doyle directly links himself to this unfortunate man, claiming that he suffered "very bad fits of temper, which some of us have had with less excuse" (*Memories* 3).

When discussing his own father, Charles Doyle (1833–1893), Arthur acts as an apologist, asserting that Charles was thrown into a hard-drinking Edinburgh "at a dangerously early age, especially for one with his artistic temperament" (*Memories* 4). This displacement of the problem with the attachment figure onto the environment and idealization of this person is entirely congruent with the avoidant-attachment pattern (Crittenden *Assessing* 90). Doyle over-praises Charles as "a great and original artist," "the greatest" in his artistic family, "concerned not only with fairies and delicate themes of the kind, but with wild and fearsome subjects," subjects so misunderstood that he was forced to do book illustrations (*Memories* 4). Doyle paints his father (Illustration 3.1) as a preoccupied dreamer whose "thoughts were always in the clouds," who "had no appreciation of the realities of life," and who "was of little help" to Doyle's mother Mary Foley (*Memories* 5). He concludes his portrait by claiming that, "the world, not the family, gets the fruits of genius," ironically a claim that could be made about Arthur as well, as we shall see (*Memories* 5). What he does not say is that Charles's alcoholism wreaked havoc in this family with wide-ranging consequences, almost from the time his parents married in 1855 when his father was twenty-two and his mother was eighteen. Instead, Doyle puts a positive spin on the situation, claiming that "we lived in the hardy and bracing atmosphere of poverty," although he does admit that his mother "bore the long, sordid strain," without specifying what that comprised (*Memories* 5).

Doyle's parents had met when Charles came to Edinburgh in 1849 as a lonely seventeen-year-old. The daughter of his landlady, Mary, then just twelve, soon went off to school in France, not returning until 1854, so the couple only knew each other for a short period before they married. A year after they married they had a child, Annette (Illustration 3.2), the first of ten, seven of whom survived into adulthood. Their second child, also a daughter, Catherine, died from water on the brain in October 1858 at just six months old. Mary was depressed and pregnant with Arthur, born seven months later on 22 May 1859. By this time Charles, too, was depressed, and the family was living in straitened circumstances at 11 Picardy Place (Lycett 17). Doyle's maternal grandmother and aunt joined the family there in 1861 when Doyle's sister Mary was born. In 1862 they moved to a seaside suburb, and would make a total of seven moves by the time Arthur was ten (Stashower 22). This is where Doyle's grandmother died suddenly of cancer in May at the age of fifty-two when Arthur was just three. To compound this loss, by this time Doyle's father Charles was drinking and behaving erratically. Mary Doyle recalled in a letter to a physician that, in December 1862, Charles "had such a bad attack that for nearly a year he had to be on half pay and for months he could only crawl and was perfectly idiotic, could not tell his own name. Since then he has been from one fit of dipsomania to another." Charles traded valuable sketches for drink, would steal household items of worth, and "break open the children's money boxes. He even drank furniture varnish ..." (Lellenberg *Letters* 307–8).

In this chaotic, disruptive household, Mary turned to her eldest son, Arthur, for emotional support, particularly after Arthur's sister and Mary's namesake died at the age of two in June of 1863. Not only did Mary overinvest in him, but Arthur idealized her and sought her approval for the rest of his life, while at the same time resenting the

Illustration 3.2 Arthur Conan Doyle with his sister Annette. Reprinted by permission of the Arthur Conan Doyle Collection – Lancelyn Green Bequest, Portsmouth City Council

control she exerted over him and the intrusions into his adult life. He tended to avoid topics of disagreement in his extensive letters to the "Ma'am," as he referred to her (Stashower 22). However, in his early years, he fell under her spell, describing her as "my dear little mother with her gray Irish eyes and her vivacious Celtic ways – indeed, no one met her without being captivated by her" (*Memories* 6). Most significantly, Mary provided a lifeline that would influence the rest of his life: partly to manage her own anxiety, she told him stories, vivid and dramatically rendered. Doyle recalled that "as far back as I can remember anything at all, the vivid stories which she would tell me stand out so clearly that they obscure the real facts of my life" (as quoted in Stashower 22; see also Lycett 23, Lellenberg *Letters* 226). Doyle became a "rapid reader" of escapist adventure stories and also "wrote a little book and illustrated it myself in early days" (*Memories* 7). The story featured a man and a tiger "who amalgamated," and it is tempting to speculate that Doyle captured something of the ferociousness of a father out of control, without knowing how to get him out of this "scrape," as he put it (*Memories* 7).

Doyle may have been sent away briefly when his father's alcoholism was at his worst, but he very definitely was sent away to school at the Jesuit Hodder preparatory school and then Stonyhurst in England at the age of nine in 1868 (when his father suffered another bout of alcoholism and depression, Lycett 27). Given the family dysfunction and his intense bond with his mother, it is not surprising that he "felt very lonesome and wept bitterly upon the way" (*Memories* 8). Doyle struggles to be fair to the Jesuits, but he tends to damn with faint praise, commenting on the useless subjects studied, for instance, "which cost me so many weary hours" (*Memories* 9). He does become impassioned and quite detailed when he describes the methods of "severe" corporal punishment experienced, suggesting that his family trauma was compounded here. Priests using a large piece of India rubber beat senior boys nine times on each hand, and he asserts that "to take twice nine upon a cold day was about the extremity of human endurance" (*Memories* 10). Doyle claims resistance to, a preoccupation with, the punishment, claiming that:

> if I was more beaten than others it was not that I was in any way vicious, but it was that I had a nature which responded eagerly to affectionate kindness (which I never received), but which rebelled against threats and took a perverted pride in showing that it would not be cowed by violence. I went out of my way to do really

mischievous and outrageous things simply to show that my spirit was unbroken. (*Memories* 11)

Doyle seems to have been isolated there and made "no lasting friendship," but he learned two important lessons; that he had a "literary streak" in him and that he could not abide "the uncompromising bigotry of the Jesuit theology," which led to his rebellion against his faith (*Memories* 11, 15).

While Arthur went on in the fall of 1875 to a Jesuit school in Austria, Mary developed a relationship with Dr Bryan Waller, a twenty-two-year-old boarder in the Doyle home. One of the secrets concealed by Doyle, who never referred to Waller in print, his exact relationship with Doyle's mother remains unclear. He was fifteen years younger than Mary and only six years older than Doyle (Stashower 68–69), but he provided medical and financial support to the family, advice to Arthur about medical school, and a home for Mary on his estate, where she lived for three decades, even after Waller got married. Arthur's sister, born 2 March 1877, was christened Bryan Mary Julia Josephine, which might suggest that the child was Waller's, but biographer Andrew Lycett concludes that Mary merely wanted to honor Waller's "emotional and financial support" (Lycett 52). Still, being to some degree supplanted by Waller must have caused Arthur some anxiety if not resentment, especially when he learned that his mother would not be in Edinburgh to greet him on his return from Austria, but would be at Waller's family estate, Masongill (Lycett 43). Nevertheless, Doyle found compensation for his maternal dependency in several "second mothers" as he referred to them and addressed as "Mam" in his extensive correspondence with them. (They included Mrs Charlotte Drummond, Mrs Amy Hoare, and Mrs Margaret Ryan; Lellenberg *Letters* 7.)

During his time away, Doyle's father had been pensioned off from his job at the early age of forty-four, very likely because of alcoholism (Lellenberg *Letters* 79). Dr Waller apparently stepped into a fatherly role and advised Doyle on his choice of medicine at Edinburgh. While there, Doyle studied under Dr Joseph Bell and Dr William Rutherford, the main models for Sherlock Holmes, and Professor Challenger respectively, as has been well documented (Lycett 51; Stashower 76–77, 276). Just as Doyle was about to graduate, his father was institutionalized for his alcoholism at a "health resort in Aberdeenshire" as Doyle put it (Lellenberg *Letters* 136). In his autobiography Doyle finessed the truth, writing that, "my father's health had utterly broken," but he was more candid when he stated that "I, aged twenty, found myself practically the head of a large and struggling family" (*Memories* 25). Doyle's response to his father's deterioration was complex. On the one hand he did take more than his fair share of the responsibility for the family, becoming a second, or even third husband (if one includes Waller) for his mother Mary. He continuously sent funds to support "the Ma'am" as well as his siblings for the rest of his life. On the other hand he had the impulse to escape the situation, but was drawn to excitingly dangerous situations, also characteristic of the child of an alcoholic (*Adult Children*). His first major adventure was a voyage on a whaling ship in April of 1880, where as a reckless novice he repeatedly fell through the ice, once with near fatal consequences (*Memories* 36; Stashower 38). Although he refused a second voyage, he claimed that "the life is dangerously fascinating" (*Memories* 36). A third response was to seek isolation and channel his emotion into his writing.

An early story, "The Surgeon of Gaster Fell," evokes Doyle's avoidant response and also the therapeutic role of writing for Doyle. In 1885, protagonist James Alberton seeks seclusion in an isolated dwelling on the Yorkshire moors in order to immerse himself in "mystic studies" with only books as his "hundred companions" ("Surgeon" 1, 6). Against his will, he is drawn into a mystery involving the two adult Cameron children, one of them an exotic beauty and the other the surgeon of the title, who are attempting to deal with their mentally disturbed, violent father in order to keep him from the lunatic asylum. Alberton is alternately fascinated and repelled, especially after the father ransacks his rooms, a violation that enrages Alberton and may recall Charles's ransacking of his children's money boxes ("Surgeon" 11). Although the Camerons' attempt to suppress the truth, it is revealed, not in person but in a concluding letter from the "Kirkby Lunatic Asylum" mainly because the surgeon ironically fears Alberton's "very violent temper" ("Surgeon" 13). The solution – the father's incarceration – is achieved at a remove from Alberton, who makes no comment on the letter, but he has obviously been altered by the gruesome experience.

Doyle met a third person at Edinburgh University who exerted an enormous impact on him as a young man, a fellow student named George Budd. Doyle became embroiled in this mentally unstable man's life against the strong opposition of his mother, and he relived the chaos engendered by his father's condition when he entered into medical practice with this compulsive personality. Doyle's attraction to this brilliant, charismatic, yet "capricious creature" (*Stark* 151) who is ultimately vindictive makes perfect sense given that Arthur was the child of an alcoholic, but Arthur worked through his feelings about this destructive relationship in probably his most revealing autobiographical fiction, *The Stark Munro Letters* (1895), which opens in 1881. The novel is set up as a confessional (and it expresses Doyle's religious uncertainty as well) to the protagonist Stark Munro's friend Bertie, who has moved to America. Munro conveys his therapeutic strategy in the following passage:

> I have no one to whom I can talk upon such matters. I am all driven inwards, and thought turns sour when one lets it stagnate like that. It is a grand thing to be able to tell it all to a sympathetic listener – and the more so perhaps when he looks at it all from another standpoint. It steadies and sobers one.
> Those whom I love best are those who have least sympathy with my struggles. (*Stark* 83)

Writing to a conventional friend "steadies and sobers" Munro, a revealing metaphor given Doyle's need for steadiness in dealing with his father's alcoholism. Budd, who is thinly fictionalized as Cullingworth, had the opposite effect on Munro/Doyle. Munro opens the novel by analyzing the "many-sided" Cullingworth in considerable detail, claiming that "His temper was nothing less than infernal" (*Stark* 6). He also had more than a touch of Charles Doyle about him. Munro claims that, "He was not a man who drank hard, but a little drink would have a very great effect upon him. Then it was that the ideas would surge from his brain, each more fantastic and ingenious than the last" (*Stark* 7).

Cullingworth first summons Munro for advice when he has got himself into debt in his medical practice by extravagant spending. Cullingworth then evades his debtors and sets up a new practice in Bradfield (a fictionalized Plymouth), where he commands Munro to come with the promise of work, since his practice has been a "colossal success" (*Stark* 105). Cullingworth continuously makes extravagant claims, but he succeeds in his practice by luring patients with free examinations and then charging them exorbitantly for drugs (*Stark* 138). Munro becomes complicit in this enterprise until Cullingworth paranoically believes that Munro is causing the practice to go downhill, at which time he offers him a pound a month to set up on his own. Munro chooses a place where he knows no one, which is what Doyle did when he chose to set up a practice in the Portsmouth suburb of Southsea. This seems like a move guaranteed to thwart success, but it was a city "large enough for solitude" (*Stark* 209), as Munro puts it, and for anonymity, where Charles Doyles's reputation could not haunt the young Doyle. Earlier in the novel Doyle had fictionalized something of his father's mental deterioration when Munro takes a position looking after the Hon. James Saltire, deranged son of Lord Saltire, and a distant relation of Munro's. His behavior is erratic, and he occasionally breaks into a "violent mania" which Munro describes as bringing excitement into his life (*Stark* 68, 74). Throughout the novel, Munro continually rescues people from drunks, or rescues drunks themselves, such as Captain Whitehall, who similarly to Cullingworth imposes himself on Munro and behaves erratically (*Stark* 229, 250), or escapes the deceit of drunks, such as his boarder Mrs Wotton (*Stark* 302). At one point Munro exclaims "beware of drink! Above everything, beware of drink!" as a principal piece of advice for succeeding as a doctor (*Stark* 309). Despite his efforts to make connections in the city, Munro lives in poverty with few patients. When he is in most desperate need he is vengefully betrayed by Cullingworth, who withdraws his promised monthly remittance, claiming to have found a letter critical of Cullingworth from Munro's mother (*Stark* 262). Munro discovers that Cullingworth has violated his privacy by reading his letters from his mother all along, and that Cullingworth has "used me atrociously" (*Stark* 339). Although Munro has defied his mother throughout the narrative, causing a "serious breach" in their relationship, her insight that Cullingworth is a bankrupt swindler and unscrupulous proves to be true (*Stark* 180). Doyle wrote in his autobiography that his "mother had greatly resented my association with Cullingworth" (that is, Budd) and even more so his "resistance" against her advice (*Memories* 55–56).

The Stark Munro Letters also provides insight into Doyle's spiritual leanings during this period, as well as his resistance against his Catholic upbringing and his paternal Catholic relatives. Munro writes extensively about his religious beliefs, the gist of which is that he cannot accept the dogmas of any religions (*Stark* 16), but that his observations of Nature confirm his belief in a Maker and in the evolution of faith (*Stark* 46–48). He also acknowledges that he was "miserable and plunged in utter spiritual darkness" after losing his faith (*Stark* 45) and that his religious opinions annoyed his father, leading to his separation from him (*Stark* 15). We know from Doyle's autobiography that he rejected his father's relatives' offer of introductions to the Bishop with the aim of setting him up as the Catholic doctor in Portsmouth. Doyle recalls that "I had so entirely broken away from the old faith that I could not possibly use it for material ends. I therefore burned the letter of introduction" (*Memories* 61). This cost Doyle financially and also led to a permanent breach with his father's family (Nordon 29–30). Doyle dramatizes this decision well in *The Stark Munro Letters* (288), after Munro has struggled with loneliness, melancholy, and even thoughts of suicide, writing one moonlit night that "life is a deadly, lonely thing when a man has no one on his side but himself" (*Stark* 171). Nevertheless, Munro has the outlet of writing to his friend Bertie in America, and he also begins writing a novel (*Stark* 187). At one point he experiences a moment of mystical awakening while standing in an empty room of his new lodging and gazing through grimy panes. "A sudden sense of my own individuality and of my responsibility to some higher power" comes upon him and "all the world, the street, the cabs, the houses, seemed to fall away, and the mite of a figure and the unspeakable Guide of the Universe were for an instant face to face. I was on my knees – hurled down all against my own will, as it were" (*Stark* 235).

He cannot speak, and has "only vague yearnings and emotions," but eventually he attempts a prayer and feels "soothed and happier" afterwards (*Stark* 235). Although Munro continues to feel loneliness after this, he embraces the beliefs that "religion is a vital living thing" and that "true science must be synonymous with religion" (*Stark* 258, 281), beliefs that Doyle held remarkably consistently up to the time of his public avowal of spiritualism. Doyle addressed his loneliness first, by asking that his nine-year-old brother Innes join him (*Stark* 61), and in *Stark Munro* the mother suggests this (248).

Doyle found a more significant and permanent solution to his loneliness when he developed a relationship with the sister of a patient of his named Jack Hawkins, who had contracted cerebral meningitis and died under Doyle's roof and in his care. Doyle had had other dalliances with women, one even coming close to an engagement, and in fact he at one time claimed that he fell in love frequently and loved five at once (Stashower 44; Lellenberg *Letters* 140–41). However, this relationship was different, partly because it began under stressful circumstances, including loss and grieving. In *Memories*, Doyle claims that, "the family were naturally grieved at the worry to which they had quite innocently exposed me, and so our relations became intimate and sympathetic," as though his relationship was with the entire family, not only with Louisa, the daughter (*Memories* 65). Doyle's description of the entire relationship is brief and circumspect, giving the impression that companionship rather than passion brought them together: "we were married on August 6, 1885, and no man could have had a more gentle and amiable life's companion" (*Memories* 65). As Stashower claims, "her plight aroused protective feelings in Conan Doyle" (67), and in fact with Louisa (or "Touie" as he called her) Doyle performed yet another rescue mission, concordant with the behavior of the child of an alcoholic. The fact that Doyle's Ma'am approved and noted in Louisa a resemblance to herself only served to seal the deal (Stashower 67).

In *The Stark Munro Letters* Louisa is called Winnie and Munro's Ma'am's approval is dramatized, as well as the fact that Winnie brought £100 a year of her own money to the marriage, also biographically accurate (*Stark* 332–33). Soon after this episode Doyle brings the novel to a close, but not before dispatching Cullingworth to South America and also rather bizarrely killing off Stark Munro and his wife in a train accident. Earlier in the novel Munro expresses his views on death: "death, as I've seen it, has not been a painful or terrible process," although it seems "terrible to the onlooker" (*Stark* 155). When Munro and Winnie die simultaneously, "neither was left to mourn the other" (*Stark* 346). Undoubtedly this attitude stems partly from Doyle's experience as a doctor, but the abruptness and lack of reason for these deaths seem bizarre, until we realize that Doyle's stance towards death has been characteristically dismissive. He also has Munro express the opinion that Nature takes care of "the drunkard and the debauchee" by killing them off so that the race can advance (*Stark* 101–2). Throughout the novel we have seen that Doyle has been preoccupied with working through his feelings about Charles Doyle's alcoholism and consequent behavior, as well as defining his spiritual beliefs against those of his family.

During the early years of his medical practice Doyle also pursued spiritual questions by investigating psychical and spiritualist ideas. In 1881, at twenty-one years of age Doyle attended a lecture in Birmingham entitled "Does Death End All?" by a spiritualist from Boston (Nordon 33; Stashower 92). He also attended some meetings on psychic phenomena with a friend named Ball (Nordon 33). At this point Doyle was skeptical, but, like Oliver Lodge, the study of telepathy made him reconsider his position. In experiments with Ball, Doyle "showed beyond any doubt whatever that I could convey my thoughts without words" ("Early" 204). Thereafter, with typical obsessional thoroughness he read over seventy titles on the subject over a period of about two years (Nordon 149). Probably before his marriage in 1885 one of his patients, General Drayson, invited him to attend a table turning session, during which he took notes that he kept for many years ("Early" 204; Lellenberg *Letters* 210). Doyle claimed that he was too poor to employ professional mediums, but he did have an audience with a psychic whom Doyle was convinced had read his mind, and so he submitted an account of it to *Light*, the psychic weekly paper, in 1887 ("Early" 205). Frederic Myers immediately wrote to him to enlist his help in "weighing evidence" (Nordon 150), and this initiated a friendship with the psychical researcher that would last until his death. Doyle claimed that Myers's *Human Personality* would "take a permanent place in human literature" along with Darwin's *The Descent of Man* ("Early" 204). By 1888 he had read everything essential on psychical research, and plunged into a study of Theosophy because it seemed to present a more organized philosophy than spiritualism. He mentions reading A. P. Sinnett's books, including *The Occult World* and *Esoteric Buddhism* (*Memories* 80–81). However, his confidence in Theosophy was shaken by the psychical researchers' investigation of Mme Blavatsky (*Memories* 81).

During these years Doyle turned his hand to writing, so it is not surprising that a number of his early published works broach this subject of overwhelming fascination to him. Several of his earliest stories, including "The Silver Hatchet" (1883), "The Winning Shot" (1883), "Selecting a Ghost" (1883), "The Great Keinplatz Experiment" (1885), and "John Barrington Cowles" (1886) treat fantastic and gothic elements, including mesmerism, for sensational effect, occasionally with humor. His second novel, *The Mystery of Cloomber* (1889), deals more fully with the occult. A tale of revenge and paranoiac isolation, the novel concludes with a factual addendum in which Doyle, through one of his characters, explains Eastern occult philosophy. In one passage he asserts that, "the real value of their system lies, they declare, in its metaphysical or religious aspect, and there they claim to have cast a flood of light upon the destiny of the soul which will change religion from a mere speculation or aspiration to one of the exact sciences as demonstrable and as certain as geometry" (*Mystery* 203). He also cites A. P. Sinnett's *The Occult World* on "sounds produced at a distance by an adept" which had "haunted" the father in the story (*Mystery* 205).

Concurrently, Doyle penned the first Sherlock Holmes stories, "A Study in Scarlet" (1887), "The Sign of Four" (1890), and "A Scandal in Bohemia" (1891). In "A Study," Doyle quickly established the "coldbloodedness" of his detective and his "passion for definite and exact knowledge" (*Complete* 5), and he repeatedly claimed that Professor Joseph Bell was the model for Holmes (*Memories* 69). Early in his career he denied that Sherlock had any root in his own psyche, claiming that "he is not evolved out of anyone's inner consciousness" and concluded his description by asserting that, "Sherlock is utterly inhuman, no heart, but with a beautifully logical intellect" (Lellenberg *Letters* 243–44). However, in his autobiography, Doyle finally lets down his guard a little and answers the question of whether he himself had the qualities of Holmes or whether he was merely the Watson that he looked.

He admits that, "a man cannot spin a character out of his own inner consciousness and make it really life-like unless he has some possibilities of that character within him" (*Memories* 94). Doyle considered this a "dangerous admission for one who has drawn so many villains as I," but Sherlock Holmes is not a villain (*Memories* 94); rather the admission is dangerous because Sherlock Holmes does reveal Doyle's shadow-self. Holmes's character epitomizes Doyle's own avoidant-resistant attachment pattern, which has not been recognized, but Holmes is more complex than this in that he also captures Doyle's impulse towards mysticism and has some qualities of a medium. Furthermore, Holmes's behavior reflects something of Charles Doyle. The clearest statement of Holmes's avoidant stance towards attachment occurs in the opening of "A Scandal in Bohemia" where Watson explains Holmes's attitude towards his antagonist:

> it was not that he felt any emotion akin to love for Irene Adler. All emotions, and that one particularly, were abhorrent to his cold, precise, but admirably balanced mind. He was, I take it, the most perfect reasoning and observing machine that the world has seen, but as a lover he would have placed himself in a false position. He never spoke of the softer passions, save with a jibe and a sneer. (*Complete* 177)

Strong emotion is most disturbing for Holmes, and yet he becomes obsessed with her and preoccupied, demanding Irene's photograph from the King instead of lucrative payment. Watson claims that whenever he refers to this memento, "it is always under the honorable title of *the* woman" (*Complete* 194). She represents the archetype of woman, split between the idealized mother figure, brilliant and engaging, and the sexual adventurer associated with desire, and yet elusive, dangerous, and off-limits. Holmes reports that "she is the daintiest thing under a bonnet on this planet," glowing terms similar to those Doyle used to describe his mother. Yet Holmes must approach Irene in disguise, as she does towards him as well (*Complete* 193). He even becomes the unwilling witness to her marriage, being "half dragged up to the altar" by her "remarkably handsome" fiancé (*Complete* 186, 187). In having Holmes defeated by a woman, Doyle revealed a chink in Holmes's armor, a vulnerability, and this is a particularly unusual strategy given that this was only the third Holmes story and the first short story, but in penning it Doyle surreptitiously paid homage to and revealed ambivalence towards *the* woman, the Ma'am.

In these first stories, Holmes's mystic qualities underlie and even subvert his role as reasoning machine. In describing Cullingworth's character in *The Stark Munro Letters*, Munro says that he does not pretend to know what genius is, but he adds, "far from its being an infinite capacity for taking pains, its leading characteristic, as far as I have been able to observe it, has been that it allows the possessor of it to attain results by a sort of instinct which other men could only reach by hard work" (3). Sherlock Holmes certainly fulfills this definition, and in "A Study in Scarlet," he admits that, "I have a kind of intuition." He adds that "from a long habit the train of thoughts ran so swiftly through my mind that I arrived at the conclusion without being conscious of intermediate steps" (*Complete* 14). In "The Sign of Four" it is "the Celtic power of intuition" (*Complete* 93), linking this quality with Doyle's own heritage. Similarly to the mystic, and perhaps even the medium, Holmes frequently enters into a trance-like state, with a "dreamy, vacant expression in his eyes" or "vacant lackluster expression which showed mental abstraction" (*Complete* 9, 16; cf. also 109). He attends to unseen phenomena and appears to be telepathic. Watson asks whether, "without leaving your [Holmes's] room you can unravel some knot which other men can make nothing of, although they have seen every detail for themselves?" (*Complete* 14). He possesses arcane, esoteric knowledge, as Watson reveals: "his zeal for certain studies was remarkable, and within eccentric limits his knowledge was so extraordinarily ample and minute that his observations have fairly astounded me" (*Complete* 10).

Furthermore, he seems to resemble a medium, or at least a false medium or "conjuror" (*Complete* 25) with "a touch of charlatanism" about him (*Complete* 95). Daniel Stashower observes that "the detective's seemingly magical ability to conjure case histories from apparent trifles became his trademark, and remains the most engaging aspect of the stories" (77). Holmes has written an article in which he claims "by a momentary expression, a twitch of a muscle or a glance of an eye, to fathom a man's inmost thoughts" (*Complete* 12), a technique akin to muscle reading used by charlatans. Holmes's methods make him appear to be "a necromancer," his observations appearing "chimerical" (*Complete* 13). His difficulty in communicating his visions causes him to seem possessed and to speak in fragments, riddles, and puzzles, also similar to a medium.

Several of these qualities derive from Doyle's father Charles, whom he had described as "a man of sensitive genius" (*Memories* 25) and from the strategies Doyle adopted in order to cope with his father. Holmes is certainly a sensitive, swinging from ennui and black depression when lacking a case to impassioned monomania when pursuing one. When in the former state he is prey to addiction, and Doyle drew on his knowledge of the addict's behavior from his father, merely changing Holmes's addiction to cocaine, and from his medical experience, where he had seen "how drugs or alcohol would turn on fleeting phases of virtue or vice" (*Memories* 78). Although the addictive properties of cocaine were not as well understood as they are today, and the stigma attached to users not as great, Doyle again took a risk in opening his second Holmes story with a graphic description of Holmes's injecting himself with his "seven-percent solution" (*Complete* 91). Doyle captured something of his father's erratic, even violent behavior in Holmes as well. In "A Study in Scarlet," Watson reveals that Holmes's behavior can be excessive: "when it comes to beating the subjects in the dissecting rooms with a stick, it is certainly taking rather a bizarre shape" (*Complete* 5). Doyle had learned to be hyper-vigilant, constantly scanning his surroundings as a survival strategy in order to anticipate his father's next irrational behavior. Despite Doyle's disclaimer that "in ordinary life I am by no means observant," he obviously had immense skill at conveying intense and minute observation on the page, skills he gave to Holmes, along with Doyle's disparagement of irrational behavior (*Memories* 95). Doyle delighted in adopting disguises, on one occasion wearing a false beard, tricking, and thoroughly offending his brother-in-law Willie Hornung (Nordon 182–83), on another posing as Professor Challenger from his novel *The Lost World* (Lellenberg *Letters* 582–83), and he had a special uniform made when he toured the front lines during the First World War (Lellenberg *Letters* 618). This propensity for disguise he also gave to his detective. Since some of the deepest and most complex aspects of Doyle's personality emerged in the creation of Sherlock Holmes, it is not surprising that readers right from the beginning to the present day have been "perfectly convinced that he is a living human being" and written to him for help and advice, as a bemused and bewildered Doyle reported (as quoted in Stashower 437; cf. *Memories* 94, 103).

The success of the Sherlock Holmes stories brought Doyle to "a crossroads of [his] life" in 1891, but once again it was his response to death, or this time to his own near-death from influenza, from which his older sister Annette had died three years earlier, which provoked a momentous decision: "as weak as a child and as emotional but with a mind as clear as crystal," he determined to be a writer (*Memories* 91). He certainly was a driven, obsessional writer, at times writing 3,000 words a day (Stashower 128). Daniel Stashower claims that ruthless self-discipline marked his entire career (31). Doyle himself wrote that "my life has been too busy and too preoccupied to allow me to stray far from my beaten path," but Doyle toiled obsessively at whatever task he set himself or cause he championed (*Memories* 258). This drivenness would take its toll on his relationships, particularly with his children. Louisa and Arthur's first child Mary was born 28 January 1889. Doyle's mother decided that she should be named after her (and it is tempting to speculate whether she might also have been named after her child who died aged two), and thereafter "the Ma'am" continued to exert control, naming all of Doyle's children (G. Doyle 116). In August of 1890 Doyle impulsively decided to travel to Berlin to learn about a new cure for tuberculosis. This would be the first of numerous occasions when Mary was left behind while Arthur pursued a passion. When Mary was not yet two, in January of 1891 the Doyles traveled to Vienna so that Arthur could specialize in ophthalmology, leaving Mary with her maternal grandmother for just over two months. She recalled that "switching me off as a child was good for him but not good for me" (G. Doyle 101). The Doyle's first son, Kingsley, was born on 15 November 1892 (Lycett 181). In August of 1893 the Doyles traveled to Davos in Switzerland, and again in November of 1893, once again leaving the children with their grandmother. As Martin Booth remarks, it was not uncommon to leave children in the care of nannies or relatives during the Victorian period (189), but the length and frequency of Doyle's absences were undoubtedly extreme, especially after the nature of his relations with his wife Touie irrevocably altered.

In *Memories*, Doyle describes "the great misfortune which darkened and deflected our lives," the discovery on returning from Switzerland in the fall of 1893 that his wife had the advanced symptoms of tuberculosis, which he claimed was a "surprise" (*Memories* 114). He wondered whether she had overtaxed herself while on their excursion, or whether she had "encountered microbes in some bedroom," but this is disingenuous since as a doctor he should have recognized the early symptoms. Biographer Martin Booth confirms that it was once again his preoccupation that accounted for this oversight: "it was more a case of his being overly busy, living the life of the writer, working away at his serious books, meeting deadlines for Sherlock Holmes stories and not paying her the attention she was due as his wife" (189). Doyle claims that "I then set all my energy to work to save the situation" and that "we succeeded" by taking measures such as traveling to the Alps so that, despite the dire prognosis, Louisa's life was prolonged to 1906 (*Memories* 114–15). He assumed a familiar rescuing role, but that became difficult to maintain over the years as his frustration, sexual and otherwise, mounted. Whilst in Switzerland he describes being "able to devote myself to doing a good deal of work" and to winter sports, not mentioning anything about caring for Louisa (*Memories* 115).

Doyle omits mentioning another event with profound consequences that occurred at this time: the death of his father Charles, on 10 October 1893. In May 1885 Charles had been incarcerated in the Royal Lunatic Asylum after he had got drunk, become violent, and smashed a window to escape from his former residence, a nursing facility (Booth 185; Lellenberg *Letters* 263). He had then been moved to two other asylums as his condition worsened. In December 1892 his wife Mary wrote in anger a detailed history of his condition to the institutions' superintendent with the express purpose of keeping him incarcerated for fear that if free "he would kill himself in a few weeks," and she claimed Arthur would agree (Lellenberg *Letters* 306). Clearly Charles was becoming even more of a financial and emotional burden, and his deteriorating condition suggests that his death did not come as a complete shock. Doyle's response was typically avoidant, and his grieving must have been complicated by his ambivalent feelings towards his father. Doyle chose not to travel to Dumfries for the funeral (Lycett 194). More fascinatingly, when Charles was gravely ill, in the months leading up to his death, Doyle made the decision to kill off Holmes. Doyle gave the ostensible reason that he was weary of his detective, and there is certainly truth to this. A contemporary recorded him saying in Switzerland, where he decided to do away with Holmes, that "he is becoming such a burden to me that it makes my life unbearable" (as quoted in Lycett 191). These sentiments could have been expressed about his father as well and his response to the death of both was similar. Doyle wrote about Sherlock's death that "I fear I was utterly callous myself" (*Memories* 94). Nevertheless, Charles's death left unresolved feelings of embarrassment, resentment, and admiration. As Richard Green puts it, Charles "had cast a shadow for nearly forty years over his son's life," and Doyle "never wrote openly about his feelings" (40). Possibly in reviving Sherlock after his apparent death at Reichenbach Falls Doyle indirectly continued to probe his complex feelings towards his father.

Instead of organizing his father's funeral, Doyle attended a local lecture by Frederic Myers on "Recent Evidences as to Man's Survival of Death" (Lycett 194). Doyle recalled that "yet as year-by-year I read the wonderful literature of psychic science and experience, I became more and more impressed by the strength of the spiritualist position" (*Memories* 111). He appeared to channel any feelings of loss, including fears about the potential loss of his wife, into the intellectual pursuit of psychical research and into his much more emotional fictional writing about it. He joined the Society for Psychical Research one month after Charles's death, in November of 1893 (*Letters* 330), a momentous event that Stashower claims "marked a turning point of his life" (161). He also began to correspond with Oliver Lodge, who became a considerable influence on his life (Lellenberg *Letters* 331). Doyle had a significant psychic experience around this time when he investigated a haunted house at Norwood with skeptical psychical researcher Frank Podmore ("Early" 207). In his *Memories* he claims that he experienced "a fearsome uproar" in the middle of the night, and that "what occasioned it we never knew," but his friend the writer Jerome K. Jerome claimed that Doyle told him there was a natural explanation for the ghost, that it was concocted by the daughter of the owner, although strangely no motivation was given (Stashower 167). In *Memories* Doyle claimed that after the house burned down a child's skeleton was discovered in the garden, and a relative claimed the child had been killed there (143). Doyle's commentary takes on the tone of the mystic:

> the unknown and the marvelous press upon us from all sides. They loomed above us and around us in undefined and fluctuating shapes, some dark, some shimmering, but all warning us of the limitations of what we call matter, and of the need for spirituality if we are to keep in touch with the true inner facts of life. (*Memories* 143)

Doyle kept in touch with or at least broached the inner facts of life indirectly through two atypical works written around this time: an introspective poem, "The Inner Room," and a sensational tale of mesmerism and possession called "The Parasite." In the poem, "a most motley company ... one and all claim" the speaker as their own: among them in the shadows a soldier "conscience-clean," a priest with "leanings to the mystic," an "anxious-eyed" doubter, and "'mid them all" a cowed, "stark-faced fellow," possessed of "thoughts he dare not say / Half avowed" ("Inner"). The last-mentioned seems central, since his suppression of a crime or guilt or inexpressible emotions might "win" and then "All is o'er!" ("Inner"). Stashower speculates that this might allude to Doyle's conflicted feelings about his wife, perhaps an impulse to divorce her (210), but these lines may just as well express an anxiety that if he cannot find an outlet for stark emotion in his writing then he will fail, both as a human being and as a writer. More likely, the speaker concludes "if each shall have his day, / I shall swing and sway / In the same old weary way / As before" ("Inner"). Albeit with resignation, Doyle seems to admit of his complexity, of conflicting impulses and shadow selves, but it is all very oblique.

Although Doyle dashed off "The Parasite" just as he was finishing *The Stark Munro Letters* in 1894, this novella may also reveal an avoidant reaction to anxiety about being possessed by conflicting impulses. Admittedly both the subject matter and the form were topical. George du Maurier published the more famous tale of mesmerism, *Trilby*, in 1894, and fictionalized psychical case studies were also becoming popular – I have identified over fifty of them beginning in the mid-1880s (Johnson "Apparition"). However, Doyle made his story into a confessional using diary entries by his detached materialist protagonist Professor Austin Gilroy, a skeptic but "highly psychic man" whose "horizon of scientific possibilities has suddenly been enormously extended" by becoming the victim of possession by a demonic female medium ("Parasite" 2, 8). He undergoes a conversion, coming to believe that "hypnotic suggestion was finally established" ("Parasite" 7). Both Lycett and Stashower have sensed an autobiographical dimension in the tale but have been reluctant to pursue this on a literal level (Lycett 202; Stashower 172). I would argue that Doyle channeled the trauma of his wife's illness and his father's death into this passionate tale of love and hate and life on the brink of death, and the fantasy that underpins it. As in "A Scandal in Bohemia," Doyle splits the female into the exotic, dangerous, and threatening temptress, in this case Miss Penclosa, the demonic medium, "a monstrous parasite" ("Parasite" 15), and the idealized fiancée of Gilroy, Miss Agatha Marden. When Miss Penclosa invades Gilroy's mind and primitive instincts, just as bacteria had invaded Doyle's wife's body, Gilroy expresses anxiety and "suffer[s] that odious feeling which urges me to throw away my honor, my career, everything, for the sake of this creature ... She rouses something in me, something evil, something I had rather not think of. She paralyzes my better nature, too" ("Parasite" 13). This surely reflects something of Doyle's anxiety about the negative impact of his wife's illness on his own career, his mental and physical health, and his honor, since in all likelihood sexual relations between him and his wife had been advised against (Lycett 232). Penclosa disparages Agatha, introducing doubts into Gilroy's mind, and eventually provokes fierce ambivalence in Gilroy: "my soul was filled with a hatred as bestial as the love against which it was a reaction" ("Parasite" 18). Penclosa transforms Gilroy into "as desperate and dangerous a man as walks the earth" who beats up a colleague, appears to him as "a madman," and who comes to believe "my life is not worth living" ("Parasite" 25), perhaps reflecting Doyle's anxiety about becoming like his father, under the wrong influences. At the dénouement Gilroy determines to destroy the temptation that Penclosa represents in order to protect his fiancée, who has been oblivious to his trials and offers to take him away to the idyllic countryside for "rest and quiet" ("Parasite" 27). Strangely, Gilroy does not get a chance to do this, since Penclosa has suddenly died, a dreamlike incident that suggests she was a projection of the fear and anxiety in Doyle's psyche.

Doyle himself was not whisked away to the countryside, but entered a period of restless travel, initially without Louisa. On 1 November 1893 he had shipped Louisa off to Switzerland with her sister while he embarked on a lecture tour through England and Scotland before joining her in December (Lycett 196), and in the fall of 1894 he lectured in the United States, taking his brother Innes (Lycett 204). As Lycett notes, he also began to spend more time in London, partially to escape the atmosphere of illness at home (Lycett 203). He did, however, take Louisa to Egypt for her health in the winter of 1895, and again traveled up the Nile to Sudan in 1896.

Another momentous event occurred in 1897, omitted by Doyle from his autobiography: he met and fell in love with Jean Leckie (Lellenberg *Letters* 404). She was twenty-three and he was thirty-seven, a middle-aged married man with two children. Doyle kept the relationship, which he claimed was platonic, from his wife, although Georgina Doyle, the daughter of Mary, claims that Louisa knew about the affair which carried on for nine years until Louisa died in 1906. Perhaps the most unusual aspect of this relationship is that Doyle almost immediately sought the approval of his Ma'am, but once again it demonstrates the dominance of her in his life. As Stashower claims, "Conan Doyle took all of his problems to his mother" (207). Nevertheless, Doyle must have realized that his mother would likely be sympathetic since she had been in a similarly ambiguous situation, with a chronically ill spouse and another man paying her attention. Also characteristically, Doyle channeled his suppressed emotions into fiction, this time a wish-fulfillment novel titled *A Duet* (1899), a story of the early days of a marriage. Doyle claims that he "did not set out to write a fairy tale" but to describe a living couple "with all the weaknesses, temptations, and sorrows" which might overshadow their lives (as quoted in Stashower 203). The most controversial aspect was that Doyle showed the husband Frank to have had a "pre-matrimonial experience" with a woman called Violet, who contacts him again after his marriage, but Frank does not succumb. In a preface to a later edition Doyle claimed that it captured the "golden-tinted atmosphere of love" (Stashower 204); however, in his autobiography Doyle calls it merely "a domestic study," "partly founded upon early experiences of my own and of friends" (*Memories* 141). Nevertheless, he presented the manuscript to Jean, his new love (Lycett 243).

Ironically, Doyle had greater trouble in obtaining the approval from his Ma'am for his impulse to volunteer for the Boer War when it began in 1899. As mentioned, Doyle was frequently attracted to major crises, most recently the Egyptian crisis between British and dervishes, where he acted as war correspondent in 1896. On Christmas Day 1899, the Ma'am wrote that his loss at war would mean that "your family would be *ruined*, your Mother heart-broken – your children left without a father to bring them up, the greatest woe a child can have" (*Letters* 433). Doyle responded, "I have lived for six years in the sickroom and oh how weary of it I am!" (Lellenberg *Letters* 438). He volunteered, but was turned down and so participated in the Boer War as a medical officer. He also wrote extensively about the conflict, claiming in his autobiography that, "wonderful is the atmosphere of war" and that it is the world's "greatest thrill" (*Memories* 155–56). His patriotic, propagandist history of the war netted him a knighthood, which opened another breach between himself and his mother, since his "ambitious Mammie" wanted him to accept it and he had no interest (Lellenberg *Letters* 494). However, after having sat beside the King at a dinner he did not feel he could turn down the honor, but spent most of his time during the ceremony "plunged into psychic talk" with Oliver Lodge who also received his knighthood (*Memories* 205).

By this time Doyle, who had run for election while continuing to write at a frantic pace (up to sixteen hours a day), was experiencing various nervous states and insomnia, claiming that he felt "wrenched in two all the time" by his "difficult" position (*Memories* 187; Lellenberg *Letters* 442, 473, 476). Jean was experiencing "fits of depression" which Doyle put down to her artistic nature, when really she had been placed in an impossible situation, living a duplicitous life, since Doyle had told her he would not divorce Louisa (Lellenberg *Letters* 462). Despite their situation, Doyle continued to impose a grueling work schedule on himself, escaping again into writing a full-length historical fiction, *Sir Nigel*, as well as fighting, again unsuccessfully, for election in 1905 (Lellenberg *Letters* 528–30). During this time Touie, who was steadily losing weight, was neglected, but by the spring of 1906 she forced herself into the center of his consciousness when it was apparent that she was dying. After she passed away on 4 July 1906 at the age of forty-nine, Doyle was tortured by insomnia and depression, entering what he called "days of darkness" and claiming that he was unable to work, until he took up his next cause in late 1906, a case of injustice against an Indian man (*Memories* 209). Although Doyle's grieving was undoubtedly complicated, his letters suggest that he returned to writing another historical novel, *Rodney Stone*, by early September, and a play in October (Lellenberg *Letters* 536–37). He also sought the approval of his Ma'am for getting married to Jean "just a little over the proper period of mourning" of a year, although eventually the wedding was postponed to 3 September 1907 (Lellenberg *Letters* 540, 543).

Doyle's children by Louisa were now eighteen and sixteen, and Doyle and Jean expanded the family with sons born in 1909 and 1910, and a daughter, Jean, born in 1912 when Doyle was fifty-three. Jeffrey Meyers claims that "Conan Doyle was the most devoted of husbands and fathers" (xii), but the record suggests otherwise. He was preoccupied with work and, after 1897, with Jean, so was often absent. When he was home he could be quick-tempered, and even frightening, according to his daughter Mary (G. Doyle 96, 120). Following Arthur's marriage to Jean, he appears to have shut Mary and Kingsley out emotionally (G. Doyle 154, 200). Mary repeatedly refers to his behavior as changeable and unreliable (G. Doyle 159, 175), and she wrote to Kingsley that, "I am sure Daddy was born to be a Public Man and a husband, but not to be a Father. He just doesn't understand that side of things, because it simply isn't in him ..." (G. Doyle 178). A more likely explanation is that Doyle had suffered from inconsistent fathering himself, and so had no role model from which to develop as a father himself.

Doyle continued to investigate psychic matters during the first decade of the twentieth century, but he claimed that, "I cannot say that I increased my grasp of the religious or spiritual side of the subject" (*Memories* 232). Significantly, he did not attempt to communicate with Louisa in the afterlife, and in fact was discouraged from doing so by Jean, who considered the practice "uncanny and dangerous" (as quoted in Lycett 299). According to Andrew Lycett, Doyle never contacted Louisa through a medium (Lycett 299).

Doyle's avoidant attachment pattern strongly informs another fantasy written a year and a half before the outbreak of the First World War. "The Poison Belt," a sequel to the dinosaur discovery tale *The Lost World* (1912), strangely combines apocalypse with comedy. The threat of war was in the air and Doyle capitalized on that anxiety, as well as discussion of the ether, which he would have known about from Myers's *Human Personality* as well as very likely from his friend Lodge's experiments and publications on the ether, including *The Ether of Space* (1909).

In the sequel, Edward Malone, an everyman akin to Watson, narrates the story about a belt of poisonous ether that is apparently enveloping the world and killing off everyone, except the band of adventurers gathered together again by Professor George Challenger, as well as his wife. He has insisted they bring oxygen tanks to his home, where they seal themselves off from the poison (without bothering to save the servants). Like Sherlock Holmes, Challenger's predominant feature is his single-minded preoccupation, in this case with scientific observation of the unfolding catastrophe. His behavior is similarly unpredictable, as when he bites his housekeeper's leg in order to discover how the tainted ether has affected her ("Poison" 379). Challenger characteristically laughs at the impending disaster and argues that universal, painless death "is not, in my judgment, a matter for apprehension" ("Poison" 385), a stance reminiscent of Stark Munro. Challenger's behavior prompts Malone to expostulate, "surely, I thought, there are limits to mental detachment" ("Poison" 381). Malone provides a counterbalance in that he erupts with emotion in the stressful situation:

> Like a wave, the memory of the past swept over me, the good comradeship, the happy, adventurous days – all that we had suffered and worked for and won. That it should have come to this – to insults and abuse! Suddenly I was sobbing – sobbing in loud, gulping, uncontrollable sobs which refused to be concealed. ("Poison" 371)

His tears, strikingly, are considered "purely alcoholic" by another detached Professor in the party, Summerlee ("Poison" 372). After the poison belt clears and they believe that they are the only survivors, "Challenger with an abstracted face" advocates acceptance without saying more ("Poison" 413). On traveling to London, they are confronted by the "grinning faces" of the dead, but Challenger's repeated comment is "Pretty doin's! What!" ("Poison" 420). Doyle subverted a potentially powerful exploration of response to mass trauma by having humanity revive after the poison passes, as strong a denial of death as one finds in his fiction.

Doyle similarly denied the possibility of war "for a long time," believing contrary to popular opinion that the "German menace" "was non-existent – or at worst greatly exaggerated" (*Memories* 304). He then treated its approach as an opportunity to experiment with new military inventions, including the submarine and the airship, and publicly proposed innovations, from a channel tunnel to life belts to badges for wounded soldiers (Stashower 298–99; *Memories* 316, 371–72). It would be another adventure, but his application for service was rejected (after all, by now he was 55), so he turned his hand to propaganda, such as "England and the Next War" and "Danger!" (Stashower 298–301). However, he could not resist participating and initially formed a Civilian Reserve (*Memories* 323). In 1916 he inveigled his way to the front lines, ostensibly to report on the Italian front, although he wound up visiting all three fronts, a great adventure "in what was surely the most wonderful spot in the world – the front firing trench" (*Memories* 340). There he obtained special permission to meet up with his brother Innes, whom he had encouraged to enter the military, and his son Kingsley, who soon after was wounded in the battle of the Somme (*Memories* 351). He did experience something of the carnage of the war, especially on his last excursion, to the Australian front in late September 1918, but he described what he saw with detachment. After witnessing a shell explode on some men and horses, and a "shattered man, drenched crimson from head to foot," he comments, "The image of that dead driver might well haunt one in one's dreams" (*Memories* 384). By this time Doyle was obsessively working on a full history of the war, *The British Campaign in France and Flanders*, published in six volumes beginning in 1915. As late as September 1918, Doyle could write to his Ma'am "what a wonderful war year we have had! I think it will take two of my volumes," suggesting a certain detachment and narrowness of focus, as well as pride in his productivity on his "huge task" (Lellenberg *Letters* 645). Nevertheless, by this time Doyle had suffered a number of losses in the war beginning with his brother-in-law, Malcolm Leckie, reported missing after the battle of Mons in 1914 and confirmed as dead in December 1914. Other relatives were killed in rapid succession.

Doyle turned to spiritualism, initially as a means of contacting his brother-in-law. A friend of Jean's, Lily Loder-Symonds, developed the power of automatic writing, and she and the Doyles held séances beginning in the spring of 1915. Lily had lost two brothers by then and lost another in May (Lycett 359). Doyle became convinced of Lily's powers when information that only Malcolm Leckie could have known was conveyed to him. In July Doyle lost two nephews, Oscar Hornung and Alec Forbes, and another brother-in-law, Leslie Oldham, and soon messages were received from them as well. Doyle advised his mother, "You must not mourn, dear. It comes to all and how can it possibly come so well or so easily as to them [Oscar Hornung and Leslie Oldham]" (Lellenberg *Letters* 614). He did not inform her of his spiritualist activities, as she did not approve, and in fact never approved of this dimension of her son's life. Then Lily died on 28 January 1916, and Doyle wrote that it was a "'dies neganda,' a day to be denied" (Lycett 362). From this point on he relied on professional mediums. By late 1916 he had read and reviewed Oliver Lodge's *Raymond*, claiming about the whiskey and tobacco episode that "the incident proves to me [...] the unflinching courage and honesty of the man who chronicled it, knowing well the handle that he was giving to his enemies" (*New* 79). This evidence, coming from a man whom Doyle held in such high regard, affirmed his belief in spiritualism, which he announced in a letter to *Light* on 4 November 1916 (Lycett 367). By 22 November 1916 Doyle was writing to Lodge that a medium had correctly identified that Doyle had written on a slip of paper the name Raymond and she offered some not very convincing statements from Raymond (MS letter, University of Texas). Thereafter Doyle and Lodge corresponded regularly, exchanging evidence and notes about various mediums. On one occasion Lodge expressed his gratitude for Doyle's support against "the long-standing entrenchments of prejudice" (Lodge MS letter, May 1917, University of Texas).

Doyle's public confirmation of his conviction at a public meeting of the London Spiritualist Alliance on 25 October 1917, chaired by Sir Oliver Lodge, was the first of hundreds of such speeches that he gave around the world (Stashower 333). Doyle repeatedly claimed that he arrived at his conclusion over a long period of time and that the war served to bring "earnestness into all our souls and made us look more closely at our own beliefs and reassess their values" (*New* 39). Doyle's spiritualist conviction gave him a sense of security and comfort, but it also provided him with another cause, the biggest cause and purpose of his life (Stashower 347). In embracing this cause, he also adopted a rebellious stance, claiming that "I brought into it a combative and aggressive spirit which it lacked before, and which has now so forced it upon public attention that one can hardly pick up a paper without reading some comment upon it" (*Memories* 390). For him, the attack on "apathy, ignorance and materialism" was "a challenge to our manhood to attack and ever attack in the same bulldog spirit with which Foch faced the German lines" (*Memories* 390). On an unconscious level, it was his final rebellion against his mother. Although he rarely mentioned spiritualism to her, on one occasion he defended his beliefs to her: "I have had most undoubted messages from beyond both from paid & from unpaid mediums, so of that I cannot doubt, and I speak from 32 years' experience. Mediums are occasionally rogues, as you say, and I would test their results very severely – and do" (Lellenberg *Letters* 648). His embrace of it also caused disagreement with other members of his family, notably his son Kingsley, who developed a sincere Christian faith under his mother's influence (Lycett 372). Despite Jean's initial aversion to spiritualism, Doyle managed to convert her (*Memories* 388). Doyle's adoption of spiritualism also played into his overdeveloped sense of responsibility and his need to rescue others. This he would do on vast scale for the war bereaved. In almost prophetic, mystical terms, Doyle wrote that:

> In the days of universal sorrow and loss, when the voice of Rachel was heard throughout the land, it was borne in upon me that the knowledge which had come to me thus was not for my own consolation alone, but that God had placed me in a very special position for conveying it to that world which needed it so badly. (*Memories* 387)

No wonder that Doyle became known as "the St Paul of Spiritualism" (Stashower 344). The first of his numerous spiritualist tracts, *The New Revelation*, appeared early in 1918, and this "vital message" as Doyle put it, provided comfort to the many who read it, although reviewers accused him of naïveté, and one headline even asked, "Is Conan Doyle mad?" (Stashower 343). Nevertheless, in the book he sounded reasonable, advocating moderation in contacting those in the beyond:

> having got in touch, be moderate in your demands. Do not be satisfied with any evidence short of the best, but having got that, it seems to me, wait for that short period when we shall all be reunited. (*New* 98)

Not only did Doyle offer support and solace to grieving mothers and widows through his books and articles and by corresponding with them, but he directed so-called rescue circles, the purpose of which was to provide comfort and guidance to spirits confused about their condition after death (*New* 98–99; Kerr 229).

When Doyle's son Kingsley, weakened by his war wounds, unexpectedly died of influenza on 28 October 1918, Doyle only became more preoccupied with making a connection with him and others in the spirit realm (Illustration 3.3). Nevertheless, his attitude towards the death was characteristically avoidant. He decided not to cancel a lecture he was giving in Nottingham, asserting that "my duty is to other sufferers" (as quoted in Stashower 345). According to Lycett, Doyle had said a year earlier that Kingsley's nature was secretive and that "his son remained a closed book to him" (375). Within a few hours of Kingsley's death Doyle had contacted him and begun the process of renegotiating their relations (Booth 316). In September 1919, Kingsley asked, through a medium, "forgive me!" and Doyle responded "there was never anything to forgive. You were the best son a man ever had" (Lellenberg *Arthur* 654). Doyle's brother Innes, also "worn out with his war duties," died of influenza just four months later, and again Doyle's grieving must have been complicated since he had encouraged Innes to enter the military and had pulled strings for him, just as Kipling had done for his son John (Nordon 172–73; *Pheneas* 16). He too eventually communicated with Doyle, encouraging him with "you did better work than you realise" at his lectures (*Pheneas* 25).

Doyle hardly needed encouraging, and took up his new vocation with a vengeance. In 1918 and 1919 he lectured on spiritualism throughout the United Kingdom (Booth 315); in 1920 in Australia; in 1922 and 1923 in North America; in 1928 in parts of Africa; and in 1929 in

Illustration 3.3 Arthur Conan Doyle with a spirit manifestation of his son Kingsley. Reprinted by permission of the Arthur Conan Doyle Collection – Lancelyn Green Bequest, Portsmouth City Council

Scandinavia and Holland. He became heavily involved in organizing the spiritualist movement, for example becoming the first President of the International Spiritualist Federation in 1923 (an organization that continues to this day) and the Chairman of the International Spiritualist Congress in Paris in 1925. He also distributed about two hundred and fifty thousand pounds of his fortune to the cause, opened a Psychic Bookshop and Press in London, managed by his daughter Mary, and offset the costs of publishing books on spiritualism, including his own two-volume *History of Spiritualism*, published in 1926 and dedicated to Oliver Lodge (Stashower 399–400). Nor was he afraid of engaging with his opponents, as he did with Joseph McCabe of the Rationalist Press organization at London's Queen's Hall in 1920. When McCabe demanded the names of ten university professors who believed in spiritualism, Doyle gave him forty, but had a list of 160 people of high distinction at his fingertips and triumphed at the meeting (Stashower 349–50). He also developed an ambivalent relationship with the famous conjurer Houdini, who initially claimed to be a seeker and was open to obtaining messages from the beyond through mediums, at least according to Conan Doyle (*Edge* 33). Interestingly, both men had similar family backgrounds, as Daniel Stashower notes: "As children, both had weak, absent fathers, and later compensated for the privations of childhood by showering wealth on their strong-willed mothers" (Stashower 380). When Houdini began to publicly denounce mediums, Doyle became frustrated with him, claiming that his public stance differed from his private beliefs, and after Houdini's death Doyle suggested that the mystery of whether Houdini possessed abnormal powers remained to be solved (*Edge* 47).

By the time Doyle's second apologia for spiritualism, *The Vital Message*, appeared in November 1919, just one year after the Armistice, Doyle had fully adopted the prophetic role. He rationalizes why the war was "forced upon mankind" (*Vital* 16), asserting rather dramatically that "the inner reason" was that it was "needful to shake mankind loose from gossip and pink teas, and sword-worship, Saturday night drunks, and self-seeking politics and theological quibbles – to wake them up to make them realize that they stand upon a narrow knife-edge between two awful eternities" (*Vital* 20–21). Wickedness and materialism, in particular that of Germany, had brought about the war (*Vital* 19, 193). "The shock of the war," he adds, was "to force the human race to realise and use the vast new revelation" of spiritualism, "the movement which is destined to bring vitality to the dead and cold religions" (*Vital* 17, 42). Doyle notes the numerous accounts of the beyond that emanated from the trauma of the war, claiming *Raymond* was "most deserving of study" (*Vital* 104). However, he offers a critique of it, suggesting that Sir Oliver's "Weighty thoughts get in the way of the clear utterances of his son," and he advocates an edition with "nothing but the words of Raymond and his spirit friends" in order to reach more people (*Vital* 106). In a chapter titled "The Coming World," Doyle presents a picture of the afterlife as a world where individuals have the opportunity to develop those gifts they possess (*Vital* 130). He emphasizes union and reunion, restoration and repair, claiming that "every man or woman finds a soul mate sooner or later. The child grows up to the normal, so that the mother who lost a babe of two years old, and dies herself twenty years later finds a grown-up daughter of twenty-two awaiting her coming" (*Vital* 131). Doyle went on to examine the New Testament in light of the new psychic knowledge, concluding that "Christ's teaching is not to blame" but that Men in particular have ceased to take it seriously (*Vital* 192). He makes some good (and prescient) points that when religion loses its grip on people materialism becomes dominant and that religion must evolve in order to maintain its vitality and act as a compelling force ensuring morality (*Vital* 192–94). Doyle's afterlife, a beautiful, classless, "world of sympathy" (*Vital* 133), was considered naïve by critics, but no one could doubt Doyle's sincerity.

Andrew S. Malec claims that Doyle's conviction about the afterlife enabled him to leave his mother in precarious health to travel to Australia and then to carry on proselytizing there when she died (71), but this is the avoidant pattern we have seen with Doyle all along, despite his idealizing her as a "world-mother mourning over everything which was weak or oppressed" after her death (Lellenberg *Letters* 679). Pierre Nordon observes that Doyle was always in command of his feelings and that "after losing someone he loved – his first wife, his brother, his oldest son, his mother – there is no evidence that he mourned for them for a long time" (182, 189). As with Kingsley, a distance had opened up between Doyle and his mother because of his spiritualism. Doyle wrote that, "for my own psychic work she had, I fear, neither sympathy nor understanding, but she had an innate faith and spirituality ..." (as quoted in Stashower 369). As with other relatives, messages from the Ma'am were communicated in due course after Doyle's wife Jean began her automatic writing in 1921.

Doyle published excerpts from these in *Pheneas Speaks* (1926), Pheneas being Doyle's long-deceased Arabian guide. Pheneas spoke about a range of topics from large to small, including prophesying that "when the great change comes to humanity then all creeds and churches will cease to exist" (*Pheneas* 73). However, many of the communications focused on family relations. When Doyle was told that the Ma'am "understands all about this great truth now, and only regrets she didn't when with you," he replied "poor dear Mammie" (*Pheneas* 23), again evidence of his renegotiating a relationship in the beyond. Nor was Pheneas always flattering, on one occasion claiming that the problem in communicating occurred because Doyle "would not show interest enough in the other world, but only in the future of this world," which hurt Doyle (*Pheneas* 209). Although disparaging, H. G. Wells demonstrated considerable insight when he reviewed *Pheneas Speaks* and claimed, "this Pheneas, I venture to think, is an imposter, wrought of self-deception, as pathetic as a ragdoll which some lonely child has made for its own comfort" (as quoted in Stashower 401). As does a ragdoll for a child, these communications do appear to have acted as transitional experiences for Doyle, but they seem to have been therapeutic, enabling him to transcend his avoidant behavior, express feelings, and be more compassionate.

Similarly to Lodge, Doyle based some fairly significant decisions on communications from the beyond, for instance when Pheneas found them a place for "soul refreshment," and Doyle bought the recommended cottage in the New Forest (*Pheneas* 106). More so than Lodge, however, Doyle could be quite gullible, especially about spirit photography, which had long interested him. He was famously taken in by the fairy photographs faked by sisters at Cottingley (Cox 223–25). Nevertheless, Doyle may have been vulnerable about these because his family and specifically his father had believed in fairies. As Stashower insightfully suggests, if the fairies existed Doyle would be able to redeem his father as a visionary rather than merely a drunkard (361), and so his belief may have had an unconsciously reparative motive.

During the period when Pheneas communicated with Doyle, he worked on a new novel, *The Land of Mist*, which came "so fast" that it practically wrote itself. This "big psychic novel" as Doyle called it, was his first in ten years, and was most often harshly criticized when it first appeared in February 1925, a trend that has continued to the present. In it Doyle turned to the novel of ideas, as Huxley was to do, and developed a utopian vision based on spiritualism. I would argue that part of the reason the novel was so harshly treated was because it did not fall within the horizon of expectations for the readership of Doyle's detective adventures and historical romances, or particularly for the Professor Challenger series of which this is the final and atypical one. The novel undoubtedly has a didactic quality to it, but it does have its merits, including some trenchant satire as well as dramatic and humorous scenes. Most important for present purposes, it contains a number of fantasies and insights revealing of Doyle's personality and particularly of the therapeutic roles of the novel and of spiritualism. Doyle splits himself into several of the characters, including Algernon Mailey, the solidly grounded spiritualist, the open-minded Edward Malone, the adventure-seeking turned psychic quester Lord Roxton, and particularly Professor George Challenger, the combative materialist eventually transformed by personal experience. Among the subjects satirized are the materialists like Challenger who refuse to examine the evidence for spiritualism, underhanded provocateurs, perhaps with a touch of Houdini about them, determined to trick the spiritualists and capitalize on them in the press (*Land* 60), fake mediums driven by financial gain, notably Silas Linden, and the injustices perpetrated by the police and legal system. In the last-mentioned, we see the sense of responsibility that Doyle felt in the face of injustice throughout his life. A genuine medium, Tom Linden, a victim of blackmail by his brother, is targeted by two police plants and then arrested. The court case against him is described as "a disgrace" since the charges are based on the outdated witchcraft and vagrancy acts (*Land* 119–20). The defense lawyer makes the point that these acts would condemn any sacred or holy person, and the Magistrate replies sharply that the Apostolic Age is past (*Land* 125). Nor does Doyle limit his satire to those opposing spiritualism, since he condemns wealthy patrons who benefit from spiritualist communication but neglect to support mediums, either when they are brought before the court or when in financial distress (*Land* 120).

Stashower harshly criticizes *The Land of Mist*, claiming that "the novel managed to be instructive and scientific without any regard whatever to storytelling" (Stashower 404). However, Doyle peppered the novel with dramatic scenes, such as Tom Linden's trumped-up trial (*Land* 121–26) and Lord Roxton and Padre Mason's battle with the evil spirit of Dr Tremayne in a haunted house (*Land* 147–53). Comic touches include some messages conveyed through mediums, and the recipients' responses to them. For example, a soldier receives a message from a corporal with the initials J. H. When asked whether he knows him, the soldier replies "Yes – but he's dead," not realizing that he is in a spiritualistic church (*Land* 30). Challenger himself also maintains his gruffly humorous side, as when he describes human beings as "Four buckets of water and a bagful of salts" (*Land* 19), or when he labels Malone's enthusiasm for spiritualism *"microbus spiritualensis"* (*Land* 228).

At the heart of this novel is an engaging story, and not surprisingly given the pattern of Doyle's fiction writing, it is a story of loss and reparation. As the novel opens, the narrator tells us that Challenger is "losing something of his fire" and that the "definite date for the change" was the death of his wife (*Land* 11–12). A few pages on, Challenger reveals that he had received a sign from her on the night after her cremation, a "peculiar way of knocking" at the door, but he dismisses it as deception by his own emotions (*Land* 19). Perhaps caught up in the anger stage of the grieving process, Challenger combats his daughter Enid and fiancé Malone's gradual conversion to spiritualism throughout the novel as well as spiritualism in general, but he is converted when his daughter Enid while in a trance conveys that his wife had indeed communicated by knocking on the night after her death. More impressively, Enid names two patients that Challenger believed he had long ago killed with experimental drugs, and she assures him that their deaths have been the result of pneumonia. Since Challenger has never spoken of this incident to anyone, he becomes convinced of Enid's powers, and reconciled to her and her plans to marry Edward, as well as feeling closer to his dead wife and relieved of guilt from the past. Initially in shock, Challenger has the moral courage to change his beliefs and becomes "a gentler, humbler, and more spiritual man" (*Land* 275).

Although Challenger is idealized as a convert to spiritualism, it could be argued that Doyle's embrace of spiritualism had some similarly positive effects on him, and also met some more ambiguous needs in him. In *The Land of Mist*, Doyle shows compassion for purportedly genuine mediums, more often than not scorned and treated unjustly or as freaks, and he suggests that their occupational hazard is alcoholism, since they cannot handle the visions that come to them (*Land* 100). Doyle himself also treated mediums with respect and admiration, realizing that they were prone to temptations because of the tremendous pressure of expectation on them to produce results. Instead of collecting fees for his spiritualist lectures, he had organizers contribute to a fund for needy spiritualists that he had established (Lycett 380). More broadly, Doyle's spiritualist quest brought him into closer communion with fellow seekers, as he expresses in *The Land of Mist*: "Nothing draws people together into such intimate soul-to-soul relationship as psychic quest ... This close vital comradeship is one of the outstanding features of such communion" (*Land* 166). Contrary to Kerr's statement that "almost nobody was able to take seriously" his teaching (Kerr 254), Doyle brought consolation to thousands through his spiritualist crusade, claiming in a newsreel that, "I'm quite sure that I could fill a room of my house with the letters that I've received from people telling me of the consolation which my writings on the subject – and my lectures on the subject – have given to them. How they would have once more heard the sound of a vanished voice, and felt the touch of a vanished hand" (Doyle as quoted in Stashower 438). He showed compassion to those who wrote to him about psychic experiences, conscientiously replying to them with sympathy (*Edge* 63). His shift in focus might even be glimpsed in a late Sherlock Holmes story, "The Adventure of the Three Garridebs" (1924), when Sherlock has a rare burst of emotion demonstrating genuine concern in reaction to his fear that Watson might die from a gunshot wound (*Complete* 1241). In pursuing spiritualism Doyle rebelled against the dominant materialist culture, as well as the dogmatic Jesuit religious tradition in which he was educated. He became an advocate for tolerance, suggesting that in the afterlife "All religions would be equal, for all alike produce gentle, unselfish souls who are God's elect" (*Memories* 398). His prophesying in fact brought him into the radical tradition of idealist mystics, including William Blake, as Kerr notes, but also looking forward to Aldous Huxley, as we shall see. He also anticipates liberal theology of the later twentieth and twenty-first centuries. At the close of *Pheneas Speaks*, he reveals that Pheneas:

> proclaims that the world must prepare itself for great change, physical and spiritual, all leading to a higher level of human existence, which would seem, so far as we can trace it, to imply a more equal distribution of wealth, greater simplicity of life, far greater humanity both to fellow creatures and to animals, abstinence from flesh diet, and the end of all dogmatic religions, forms, and rituals, inspiration coming direct from constant contact with the spirit world, so that the two spheres will act in close harmony and cooperation. (*Pheneas* 214–15)

If Doyle could be intolerant of those who refused to examine psychical evidence as he saw it, sound self-important (Lycett 381), or bring an overly "combative and aggressive spirit" to spiritualism (*Memories* 390), these flaws only prove his humanity, and his complexity.[4] For him, spiritualism fed his life-long craving for adventure, his need to rescue, and his over-developed sense of responsibility. If a mystic, he was certainly not detached from the world around him. As Nordon notes of Doyle's spiritualist leadership, "No other writer of his time can claim to be more committed than he was, and his moral prestige among them all has never been questioned. His sense of responsibility and of human solidarity was clearly the dominant note of his character, at everything he undertook for the impress of his exacting moral standard" (Nordon 172).

After Doyle's death on Monday, 7 July 1930 at seventy-one years old, hundreds of people attended his funeral service on the lawn at his home, Windlesham, where few mourning emblems were in evidence and the mood was more upbeat than at a traditional service. Doyle had requested a "happier burial service – something that might start a new epoch in the history of funerals," according to wife Jean, and in fact prescient of the "celebration of life" ceremonies more common today (as quoted in Lycett 432). At a memorial service two days later at the Albert Hall, 6,000 people attended, and a medium claimed to see Doyle on the stage and conveyed a purported private message from him to Jean (Lycett 433). Tributes to Doyle appeared around the world, testifying to his cultural impact. J. M. Barrie wrote that, "I have always thought him one of the best men I have ever known, there can never have been a straighter nor a more honorable" (as quoted in Stashower 441). A telegram from Oliver Lodge praising Doyle was read at the Memorial service: "'our great hearted champion will soon be continuing his campaign on the other side with added wisdom and knowledge,' adding, 'sursum corda!' – Lift up your hearts" (as quoted in Stashower 12). Lodge's words were soon borne out, as Doyle purportedly began sending messages soon after the service to his wife Jean, then the family, and subsequently through famous mediums such as Eileen Garrett (Stashower 443). One medium, Grace Cooke, known as Minesta, channeled a spirit called "White Eagle," and purportedly conveyed Doyle's revised views on life and the after-life, a script of 84 printed pages conveyed over two years, and approved by Lady Conan Doyle (Cooke). As with Myers and Lodge, messages continue to be received from Doyle up to the present. *A Study in Survival* (2009) by Dr Roger Straughan, who claims to have received messages from Doyle through randomly selected passages from his books, represents one of the most recent accounts of this phenomenon.

Doyle's vital message, though it diverted him from writing fiction, was arguably vital to his well-being. In his childhood, Doyle had suffered multiple losses, including his father to alcoholism and a mother to preoccupation with surviving poverty and later to the attentions of a man just slightly older than Doyle. Nevertheless, she overinvested in her eldest son, had high expectations of him and placed heavy demands on him, continuing to be overinvolved in his life when he was an adult. Doyle developed an avoidant-resistant pattern of attachment in response to these challenges, taking on the responsibilities of his father and excusing his behavior, and idealizing, flattering, and seeking the approval of the Ma'am. However, his moniker for her also reveals his distancing from her, typical of the avoidant strategy (Crittenden 89), and he demonstrated his ambivalence towards her by rebelling against her through various acts throughout his life, from participating in the Boer War to taking up spiritualism. His avoidant patterning extended into his other adult relationships as well, particularly with his first wife, Louisa, after he belatedly diagnosed her illness and used travel as an escape before he became surreptitiously preoccupied with his new love, Jean Leckie. Doyle was even avoidant to the extent that he disliked people being overfamiliar with him by calling him by his first name or expressing physical closeness, such as handshakes (a characteristic of avoidance described by Howe 108). Doyle wrote that, "I take a liberty with no man, and there is something in me which rises up in anger if any man takes a liberty with me" (*Memories* 202; Austin 107). More significant demands on his intimacy could also arouse his anger, as the children of his first marriage, Mary and Kinglsey, rued. Nevertheless, Doyle learned at an early stage from his mother that inadmissible emotion could be displaced and expressed through storytelling, and he accomplished this from his earliest fiction onwards.

After Doyle experienced multiple losses during the First World War, his initial dismissive attitude became one of preoccupation. Through communications with lost loved ones he renegotiated fraught relationships, prominently with his son and mother. Daniel Stashower considers that, if the messages were fraudulent, then the possibility is that they were "a conscious deception on Jean's part, a calculated effort to bolster her husband's flagging resolve," and he notes that "nearly every communication told Conan Doyle precisely what he most wanted to hear" (366). In this case, it could be argued that Jean at least was not respecting the integrity of the lost loved ones by having them apologize for their doubts about spiritualism (Stashower 370), and she might even have fostered Doyle's sense of his omnipotence. If the messages are considered genuine, then they can be seen to bring about reconciliation. Regardless, though, Doyle resisted reducing lost loved ones to monuments, to epigraphs on a tombstone, but kept their memory and his emotion regarding them alive. He continued to probe his curiosity about the greatest mysteries faced by mankind in a public and creative way. Biographers and critics have castigated Doyle for diverting his energies into spiritualism to the detriment of his fiction writing, but Doyle channeled his energy into a different kind of narrative, one vital to him and one that engaged the emotions of his contemporary audience; it continues to challenge students of his complex life and work today.

4
"Well-Remembered Voices": Mourning and Spirit Communication in Barrie's and Kipling's First World War Narratives

"In the silence something happens. A well-remembered voice says, 'Father.' Mr. Don looks into the greyness from which this voice comes and he sees his son. We see no one, but we are to understand that, to Mr. Don, Dick is standing there in his habit as he lived. He goes to his boy."
Barrie, "A Well-Remembered Voice" (1918)

"My name, my speech, my self I had forgot.
My wife and children came – I knew them not.
I died. My Mother followed. At her call
And on her bosom I remembered all."
Kipling, "Shock" from *Epitaphs of the War* (1919)

The sun glints on the ice of a pond as two strapping lads skate, or rather one skates while the other critiques the performance, as they have only one pair of skates between them. When the second boy, dark-haired and flush, dons the skates, his hands fumble with the buckles. In a flash he is up and off at high speed, careening around and returning to the first, named David, who laughs at his friend's antics, until he bears down on him, unable to stop, and knocks David to the ice.

The mother, her face set, gazes down at the little white christening robe she cradles and presses it to her breast. Later she takes it to bed, absently fingering its pathetic frills. At the bedroom door, a slight boy of six peeps in, scrutinizes his mother, winces, and disappears for a time. Then he peeps in again, turns to his sister, out of sight, and she whispers intensely for him to go in and "tell her she's still got you." She gives him a push, and he is in the darkened room, the door shut behind him. He remembers:

I was afraid. And I stood still. I suppose I was breathing hard, or perhaps I was crying, for after a time I heard this listless voice that had never been this listless before say, 'Is that you?' ... I thought it was the dead boy she was speaking to, and I said in a little lonely voice, 'No, it's no (*sic*) him, it's just me.' Then I heard a cry, and my mother turned in bed, and though it was dark I knew that she was holding out her arms.

After that I sat a great deal in her bed trying to make her forget him, which was my crafty way of playing physician, and if I saw anyone out of doors do something that made the others laugh I immediately hastened to that dark room and did it before her. I suppose I was an odd little figure; I have been told that my anxiety to brighten her gave my face a strained look and put a tremor into the joke ... (*Margaret* 12–13)

A few years later and many miles south in the United Kingdom, another six-year-old boy, also small for his age, feels abandoned by his mother and father. This is how he re-created the moment of parting:

... they roused Punch and Judy in the chill dawn of a February morning to say Good-bye; and of all people in the wide earth to Papa and Mamma – both crying this time. Punch was very sleepy and Judy was cross.

'Don't forget us,' pleaded Mamma. 'Oh my little son, don't forget us, and see that Judy remembers too.'

'I've told Judy to bemember,' said Punch wriggling, for his father's beard tickled his neck. I've told Judy – 10 – 40 – 'leven thousand times. But Ju's so young – quite a baby – isn't she?'

'Yes,' said Papa, quite a baby, and you must be good to Judy, and make haste to learn to write and – and – and'...

Punch was back in his bed again. Judy was fast asleep, and there was the rattle of a cab below. Papa and Mamma had gone away. Not to Nassick; that was across the sea. To someplace much nearer, of course, and equally of course they would return. They came back after dinner parties ... Assuredly they would come back again. So Punch fell asleep till the true morning, when the black-haired boy met him with the information that Papa and Mamma had gone to Bombay, and that he and Judy were to stay at Downe Lodge forever. Auntie Rosa, tearfully appealed to for a contradiction, said that Harry had spoken the truth, and that it behoved Punch to fold up his clothes neatly on going to bed. Punch went out and wept bitterly with Judy, into whose fair head he had driven some ideas of the meaning of separation. ("Baa Baa" 142–43)

The six-year-old in the first scenario is J. M. Barrie (Illustration 4.1), while "Punch" in the second scenario is Rudyard Kipling's fictionalized version of himself at six. Both experienced the trauma of abandonment and both of these lost boys learned to respond by renegotiating the turbulent emotions attached to this experience in storytelling. In some of their work these emotions erupt in a manner disproportionate to the subject matter and they obtrude. Both writers recounted being plagued by a triumvirate of them, Barrie's being "three murderers, Rejection, Despair ... and Silence" (*Greenwood* 27), and Kipling's "Hate, Suspicion and Despair" ("Baa Baa" 164). Although their losses were partial, in that Barrie's mother lived another twenty-nine years after the death of Barrie's brother David, just two days before his thirteenth birthday, and

Illustration 4.1 J. M. Barrie at age 6

Kipling's parents suddenly returned after six years' absence in India, their lives were irrevocably altered, as well as being complicated by other consequent issues. Given the similarities in their emotional patterning and response to loss, it is surprising that they are so rarely compared. Barrie and Kipling share a great deal in common besides the fact that their reputations now rest, at least in the popular mind, on their classic children's stories *Peter Pan* and *The Jungle Book* respectively. Both wrote prolifically, achieved high acclaim and financial success during their lifetimes, and suffered a decline in their reputations – perhaps reflected in the return to their earliest years in elusive yet melancholy memoirs written when each was seventy years of age. Their sensitivity to early loss made it a real challenge to deal with the loss of their sons (or surrogate sons) in the First World War. They were shattered by these deaths and became preoccupied for many years with them in their writing. Further, both engaged in complex, ambivalent ways with supernatural or psychical phenomena, including uncanny or spirit communication with dead soldiers, as a means of coping with the trauma of loss. While a spate of relatively recent critiques and biographies, including Sandra Kemp's *Kipling's Hidden Narratives* (1988), Martin Seymour-Smith's *Rudyard Kipling* (1989), Harry Ricketts' Kipling biography *The Unforgiving Minute* (1999), and Lisa Chaney's Barrie biography *Hide-and-Seek With Angels* (2005)[1] have acknowledged the complexity (akin to the modernists) of Barrie's and Kipling's writing as well of their elusive personalities, more needs to be said about the relationship between their responses to loss and their probing of the uncanny – absolutely key to understanding their personalities and some of their writing. Drawing on object-relations and attachment theory, this chapter demonstrates how responses to war loss, particularly as manifested in Barrie's plays *Dear Brutus* and "A Well-Remembered Voice," and Rudyard Kipling's short stories "Mary Postgate" (1915), "A Madonna of the Trenches" (1924), and "The Gardener" (1926), have been at least partially shaped by Barrie's and Kipling's responses to separations and loss in early life.

Several striking similarities can be seen in the trajectories of their emotional lives, beginning with severe disruptions to their early object relations and in their responses to these ruptures. J. M. Barrie, born in 1860, was literally lost in the crowd as the third and youngest son, and ninth of ten children born to David Barrie, a weaver, and Margaret Ogilvy (Illustration 4.2). David seems to have been a distant figure, whereas Mary was a strong-willed, manipulative woman, and the driving force of the family. Unlike J. M.'s two older brothers who were physically strong, ambitious, and talented, Barrie was slight and,

Illustration 4.2 Barrie with his mother, Margaret Ogilvy

as his biographer Lisa Chaney puts it, "unexceptional" (15). Most of Barrie's biographers agree that the key event in his early life is the one described above, when brother David, who was his mother's favorite, died from a skating accident. Margaret, who had experienced early loss herself, at age eight when the father she idolized died, became crippled by grief and remained preoccupied with her son David for the rest of her life (*Margaret* 27). Chaney argues that David's death did not, as Barrie believed, wrest Margaret's attention away from J. M., but that "it had always been absent" (21). After David's death, seven-year-old J. M., considered the runt of the family, attempted to replace his brother by becoming, as Barrie put it, "so like him that even my mother should not see the difference" (*Margaret* 16).[2] He went to the lengths of learning David's whistle and wearing his clothes (*Margaret* 16). In this way he claimed his mother's attention and consoled her, but it was a desperate and anxiety-provoking strategy, as mentioned above. Barrie wrote that, "I kept a record of her laughs on a piece of paper," surely as clear an example of an obsessional attempt to manage anxiety as one is likely to find (*Margaret* 14). In Barrie's "anxious solicitude," as Cynthia Asquith described it (54), lay the very origins of his creativity, since as a young teenager he began to write stories to entertain his mother, and his first published successes were stories of his mother's childhood, collected in *Auld Licht Idylls* (1888). Nevertheless, his attempts to connect with his preoccupied mother left him frustrated and harboring a strong sense of rejection and inferiority (Birkin 6).

Barrie had become a replacement child, one who cannot form an identity separate from the dead child because the bereaved parent, typically predisposed to depression (Sabbadini 531), denies loss and retains "intense emotional ties to the dead child" (Grout and Romanoff; Anisfeld 313). Barrie could have only a pseudo-identity since his mother imposed her idealized version of David onto Barrie. Psychologists Cain and Cain claim that "the parents of replacement children 'compelled them to be like their dead siblings, to be identical with them, yet made it clear that they would never be accepted as "the same," and could never really be as good'" (as quoted in Anisfeld 313). Barrie experienced all of the typical consequences, including a sense of inferiority, low self-esteem, guilt, and, mingled with this, the sense of being an opportunist, of having triumphed (Anisfeld 314). The replacement child not only feels haunted by the ghost of the dead child, but becomes a ghost himself, feeling insubstantial, unreal, and an impostor, and this certainly fits with Barrie's haunted sensibility. Anisfeld articulates the thought process involved: "If someone else had to die so that I could live, I must have caused that person's death, and I will then be haunted by the ghost of the rival I have slain, who becomes my double ... Triumph and guilt are inextricably fused" (314).

Barrie's first novel, *Better Dead* (1888), with its confused tone of mockery towards suicide and violence, captures his consequent anger, depression, and impulse to take his own life. In it the orphan protagonist, Andrew Riach, fails to achieve recognition as a writer when he travels from Scotland to London, and so joins the "Society For Doing Without Some People." Their goal is to murder the eminent, especially those who are past their prime (*Better* 21). Physically Andrew is the opposite of Barrie – in fact resembling David in being "fair and somewhat heavily built" – except that Andrew demonstrates the avoidant pattern of attachment, "with a face as inexpressive as book-covers" and rationalizes that "love is folly" (*Better* 6, 7). In the essay on which this bizarre satire was based, Barrie wrote, "I am no apologist for murder; indeed, it is my deep regard for the sanctity of life, and a torturing sense of the way in which it is adulterated, so to speak, by thousands of Spurious Existences, that suggest the foundation of this Society" (*Greenwood* 25). Could one of these spurious existences be the ghost of David, which haunted Barrie as well as his mother? In the novel, Andrew tells the stranger who introduces him to the Society that at times he has "felt tempted to take [his] life" (*Better* 21), and significantly Andrew (unsuccessfully) proposes an increase in the Society's activity: "My proposal is that everybody should have to die on reaching the age of forty-five years" (*Better* 52–53). Barrie's brother David had died when his mother was forty-seven, and it is tempting to speculate that Barrie unconsciously wishes his mother had died before that tragedy happened in order to spare her and him its consequences. Certainly the intensity of emotion expressed in this work does not match the subject matter, and I would argue that he sublimated his not being noticed by his mother into not being noticed as a writer. Andrew's fate veers away from Barrie's in that Andrew returns to Scotland to marry his ignorant girlfriend "for solace," the narrator commenting that "Once [a man] settles down it does not much matter whom he marries" (*Better* 56). This is the road back to Scotland not taken by Barrie, but it does reveal his ambivalence towards women and foreshadows his marital troubles. Barrie felt ambivalent about this story too, in the Introduction to the 1896 Author's Edition revealing that it, along with his other early works "were written mainly to please one woman who is now dead," his mother, and stopping its publication in Great Britain perhaps because he realized that he had exposed too much: "This juvenile effort is a field of prickles into which none may be advised to penetrate" (*Better* 3, 4). Yet in his autobiography he reprints the article on which *Better Dead* was based and devotes a chapter to it, revealing that "from no other book of his had he such a lively rush of blood to the head as when 'Better Dead' was first placed into his hands" and that he carried it with him wherever he went (*Greenwood* 30).

He also confessed that at this lonely time in his life he shrank "even from expressing an opinion" (*Greenwood* 29), conveying a lack of a sense of self. His insecurity and frustration were exacerbated by his slight physique and short stature of barely five feet. In a 1931 letter he reflected that if he had grown to six feet three inches "it would have made a great difference in my life. I would not have bothered turning out reels of printed matter. My one aim would have been to become a favourite of the ladies which between you and me has always been my sorrowful ambition" (as quoted in Birkin 21). As Barrie's stature as a writer increased, and his plays were produced, he did attempt to become a favorite of the ladies, becoming infatuated with a number of his leading actresses. In 1894 he married one of them, Mary Ansell, despite realizing how temperamentally unsuited he was to marriage (Birkin 26).

In the following year his sister, Jane Ann, who had been their mother's main caretaker, died suddenly of cancer, followed by Barrie's mother herself two days later, just twelve hours before Barrie arrived home.[3] Deeply shocked, Barrie returned to London, writing that "now I sit thinking and thinking" about her (as quoted in Birkin 36). Note that his response was cerebral and not emotive. According to Chaney, his friends noticed how reserved he was and his wife realized "that Barrie's attachment to his mother was impregnable" (127–28). Barrie was driven to write an unusually intimate and yet possibly unreliable memoir of his relations with his mother, who was otherwise completely unknown, published in December of 1896, just over a year after her death. In *Margaret Ogilvy* (his mother's maiden name),[4] he describes his sister's sacrifice as revealing "The fierce joy of loving too much, it is a terrible thing," but this comment could well be applied to Barrie himself (*Margaret* 203). The book demonstrates Barrie's intense ambivalence towards his mother. On the one hand he idealizes her, claiming that his only worthwhile writing ideas "almost certainly" came from her (*Margaret* 113), and that the one thousand letters he wrote her "are the only writing of mine of which I shall ever boast" (*Margaret* 158). On the other hand, he conveys – only partially with a self-conscious, playful sarcasm – a portrait of a self-involved, ambitious, manipulative woman, who was mothered by her children, typical of the avoidant pattern of attachment. The book opens dramatically with a description of his mother's preoccupation with the arrival of six new chairs – a triumph of her thrift – on the day of J. M.'s birth, as though, being outnumbered by them, Barrie didn't stand a chance of gaining his mother's attention right from the beginning (*Margaret* 1).[5] Barrie states outright that his mother "was a very ambitious woman" (*Margaret* 51) and declares that her ambition for him to become a writer became his, using the metaphor of weaving (his father's actual profession): "I weaved sufficiently well to please her, which has been my only steadfast ambition since I was a boy" (*Margaret* 55). Margaret became totally enmeshed in Barrie's success, to the extent of preserving the envelopes containing his first cheques, taking inordinate pride in her frequent fictional representation in Barrie's books, and critiquing his work when the details varied from her life (*Margaret* 82, 163, 174–75). For his part, Barrie (along with Jane

Ann) attended to his mother's needs, making sure that she ate and did what she was supposed to, claiming that "It is a terrible thing to have a mother who prevaricates" (*Margaret* 93). Their routine turned into a kind of lover's game, Barrie stating that "my object is to fire her with the spirit of the game, so that she eats unwittingly" (*Margaret* 112). Perhaps most revealingly, when Barrie confided his reluctance to give up childhood games, she relayed her own similar feeling (being herself preoccupied with her childhood), "which convinced us both that we were very like each other inside" (*Margaret* 29).

Barrie's deep split in his attitude to his mother complicated and prolonged his response to her loss. His pattern of attachment to Margaret and his longer-term response to her loss can be seen in his attachment beginning in 1897 to the Llewelyn-Davies family – Sylvia, Arthur, and their sons, George, Jack, Peter, Michael, and Nico. Barrie's extraordinarily close relations with the boys, who formed the basis for Peter Pan and the lost boys, has been extensively analyzed, notably in Birkin's *J. M. Barrie and the Lost Boys* (1979) and by Piers Dudgeon in *Captivated: J. M. Barrie, the du Mauriers and the Dark Side of Neverland* (2008). Barrie was just as intensely attached to Sylvia. He fascinated her, entrancing her with his fictionalizing of her and the boys (Dudgeon 16) and causing her to become more distant from her husband. However, Barrie also played a nursing role to Arthur during his illness from cancer. The deaths from cancer of Arthur, in 1907, and Sylvia in 1910, along with the affair of Barrie's wife Mary with Gilbert Canaan and her subsequent divorce from Barrie in 1909 radically undermined Barrie's psychological equilibrium.

By this point in his adult life the pattern of Barrie's attachments was clearly avoidant-resistant. Barrie became renowned for being "remote" and "exceedingly reserved" (Asquith 7, 55; Birkin 178; Chaney 103); he provides the clearest example of his suppression of feeling and retreat into an inner world of thwarted attachments in *The Greenwood Hat*, a memoir written when he was seventy. In it he splits himself into two characters, his present seventy-year-old self and his self as a young man, named Mr Anon. He writes:

> In short, Mr Anon, that man of secret sorrows, found it useless to love, because, after a look at the length and breadth of him, none would listen. Unable to get a hearing in person, which is probably the more satisfactory way when feasible, he discussed the tender passion with them [the ladies], as you might say, by deputy or in a mask; in other words, he wrote many articles on the subject of love ... (214)

Adult love could only be expressed indirectly, in intellectual form. As his adult relationships were thwarted or severed, Barrie directed his need for attachment with increasing intensity to a series of boys, including the Llewelyn-Davies's, with whom he became over-involved and preoccupied. Peter Llewelyn-Davies commented on "the peculiar" form which J. M. B.'s affection for George and Michael took: "a dash of the paternal, a lot of the maternal, and much, too, of the lover ..." (Birkin 235). Nico, the youngest son, wrote that Barrie's influence was "oppressive maybe and over-constant" (Birkin 283); it could be manipulative, possibly involved pedophilic fantasies (Dudgeon 23), and was certainly obsessive. Barrie had written a letter a week to George while he was at Eton, but in the wake of Sylvia's death he wrote a letter a day to Michael, which amounted to over two thousand letters by the time Michael graduated. He sometimes self-consciously wrote "quite as if I was a young lady" and as a "mother" (as quoted in Birkin 239). When Peter and George signed up in the war and were shipped overseas, Barrie was filled with a mother's anxiety, wrote to them constantly, and sent boxes of goods and supplies. After George told him about a man killed next to him, Barrie wrote that he was "sadder today than ever" and that he wished George was "a girl of 21 instead of a boy, so that I could say the things to you that are now always in my heart. For four years I have been waiting for you to become 21 & a little more, so that we could get closer and closer to each other, without any words needed." He concluded, "I have lost all sense I ever had of war being glorious, it is just unspeakably monstrous to me" (as quoted in Birkin 242). George was killed four days later, on 15 March 1915. Barrie was devastated. Peter summarized the cumulative impact of the losses on his "poor little devil" of an "Uncle":

> Oh, miserable Jimmie ... Shaken to the core – whatever dark fancies may have lurked at the back of his queer fond mind – by the death of Arthur; tortured a year later by the ordeal of his own divorce; then so soon afterwards prostrated, ravaged and utterly undone when Sylvia pursued Arthur to the grave; and after only four and a half years, George; George, whom he had loved with such a deep, strange, complicated, increasing love, and who as he knew well would have been such a pillar to him to lean on in the difficult job of guiding the destinies of Sylvia and Arthur Llewelyn-Davies's boys – "my boys." (as quoted in Birkin 244)

Barrie's grieving was long, complicated, and never resolved. During the war he also lost two nephews and his close friend Bron Herbert among others (Chaney 314–15). Two years later, Cynthia Asquith, who became Barrie's secretary, confidante, and mother-substitute, observed that, "I at once felt Barrie's immensely strong personality, but could find no crack in what seemed an impenetrable shell of sadness and preoccupation" (1–2). In 1921, Barrie was once again shattered, this time by the drowning of Michael and a friend, possibly in a suicide pact (Birkin 293). Barrie lived alone until his death in 1937, and biographers frequently comment on his loneliness (Asquith 56; Birkin 258, 278; Chaney 39, 329; Dunbar 9).

Asquith in her memoir of Barrie also comments frequently on the variableness of his moods, on one occasion claiming that "He's a queer mixture – an extraordinarily plural personality" (22; cf. also 16, 54–55, 150, 199). When she accompanied him, at age seventy-three, to his boyhood neighborhood, she noted that his "alternations between gloom and glory were difficult to keep up with" (Asquith 189). From this point on, his depressions increased in frequency and intensity, making him physically ill (Asquith 199, 205, 214, 223). Near the end of his life he took daily doses of heroin, initially prescribed to help him sleep and making him "blissfully exhilarated," as Cynthia Asquith put it, but later used to achieve a dramatic rush (Asquith 103–4; Dudgeon 10).

Rudyard Kipling similarly suffered from a key traumatic event in childhood with long-term destabilizing effects, contributing for example to his developing an avoidant-resistant pattern of attachment. Five years younger than Barrie, Kipling was born in 1865, only nine and a half months after his parents, Alice and Lockwood, were married in Bombay. Both parents were artistic and ambitious. Kipling biographer Martin Seymour-Smith (1989) describes Alice as defiant and impetuous and as possessing "reserves of malice"; she broke three engagements before marrying Lockwood (14–15). From a very early age Rudyard was described by family members as a "noisy," "angry" baby, "a power" who manipulated his mother and acted spoiled (Seymour-Smith 17). The photograph of Rudyard at the age of one with his mother hints at this as she chides him with her finger (Illustration 4.3). When he was two and a half, he was taken back to England for a brief time by his pregnant mother, where she bore his sister, Trix. His parents returned again to England in 1871, but this time they left both children with an evangelical couple who took in children for pay. Since Kipling's parents did not inform Rudyard and Trix of their departure nor of its impermanent nature, the children felt completely abandoned. If any justification is needed for emphasizing this childhood trauma, it can be found in Kipling's own words, since he mythologized this six-year period

Illustration 4.3 Rudyard Kipling on his mother Alice's knee in 1866

of his life at what he called "The House of Desolation" (*Something* 7) (Illustration 4.4), and he devoted a disproportionate amount of space to it in that otherwise evasive autobiography, *Something of Myself* (Pinney xxii). His rage at his parents was directed towards his caretaker, Rosa, who caned him and kept him in solitary confinement (*Something* 6). Kipling referred to her son, slightly older than himself, as "The Devil Boy" (*Something* 7). Their treatment of him Kipling called "calculated torture" (*Something* 6), and his sister Trix, who admittedly was only three when their parents left, later recounted that "Ruddy was systematically bullied day and night" (Fleming 3). The horror of the situation was magnified by its contrast to the paradise of Kipling's earlier life in India, where he soaked up the sights, sounds, and smells, comforted by servants, listening to his mother's piano-playing, and playing with clay in his father's studio (*Something* 1–4). Furthermore, during his six years in the House of Desolation Kipling's eyesight began to fail, and there was no one to diagnose it, a predicament Aldous Huxley was to experience, also during a stressful period, as we shall see. Kipling's school

Illustration 4.4 Kipling, nearly 6, at the time of his stay at "The House of Desolation," Lorne Lodge

performance suffered, he concealed this, was exposed and beaten, "and sent to school through the streets of Southsea with the placard 'Liar' between my shoulders" (*Something* 16).

Nevertheless, Kipling insightfully considered that his impulse to write originated from this unbearable situation. Initially, Rosa made reading a punishment for Ruddy, but he discovered that reading "was a means to everything that would make me happy. So I read everything that came within my reach. As soon as my pleasure in this was known, deprivation from reading was added to my punishments. I then read by stealth and the more earnestly" (*Something* 7). In order to avoid punishment he had to construct careful fabrications: "Yet it made me give attention to the lies I soon found it necessary to tell: and this, I presume, is the foundation of literary effort" (*Something* 6). Typical of the avoidant type, Kipling learned to observe closely in order to anticipate erratic behavior, and this also served him well as a writer: He wrote that his life "Demanded constant wariness, the habit of observation, and attendance on moods and tempers; the noting of discrepancies between speech and action; a certain reserve of demeanour; and automatic suspicion of sudden favours" (*Something* 15–16). Kipling's "certain reserve" is dramatically illustrated by his response to his mother's sudden return after six years: "She told me afterwards that when she first came up to my room to kiss me goodnight, I flung up an arm to guard off the cuff that I had been trained to expect" (*Something* 17). He also expressed avoidance in his referring to his mother as "the Mother" on this occasion (*Something* 17). Although Seymour-Smith speculates that Kipling may have embellished the horrors of his abuse, Rudyard did experience the first of several breakdowns while there (26, 71; *Something* 12, 40). Also, he wrote about this period of abandonment repeatedly in his fiction, notably in *The Light That Failed* (1901) and most closely in his early story "Baa Baa, Black Sheep" (1888). Although some of the autobiographical details have been changed, some perhaps for dramatic purposes, the emotion lines up with that expressed in Kipling's autobiography. As an example of alteration, Kipling made himself and his sister into "Punch and Judy" in the story, a puzzling decision, but possibly he wanted to suggest their helplessness as puppets being manipulated by unseen hands. The best example in which genuine emotion seems to be expressed occurs after the separation scene from "Baa Baa, Black Sheep" quoted at the beginning of this chapter. The narrator erupts with:

> When a matured man discovers that he has been deserted by Providence, deprived of his God, and cast without help, comfort or sympathy upon a world which is new and strange to him, his despair, which may find expression in evil-living, the writing of his experiences, or the more satisfactory diversion of suicide, is generally supposed to be impressive. A child, under exactly similar circumstances as far as its knowledge goes, cannot very well curse God and die. It calls till its nose is red, its eyes are sore, and its head aches. Punch and Judy, through no fault of their own, had lost all their world. They sat in the hall and cried; the black-haired boy looking on from afar. ("Baa Baa" 143)

Notice that the narrator intrudes, claiming that the consequence of abandonment for the matured man is despair, which can be expressed in three very different ways: evil-living, writing, and, more satisfactorily, suicide. These options appear before the choice open to the child, of crying, but in effect Kipling has expressed the consequences of the child's traumatic loss in adulthood, and he obviously chose to manage his despair through writing, although like Barrie, Kipling seems to have considered suicide. At the close of "Baa Baa, Black Sheep," Punch claims that now that his Mamma has returned it is "as if she had never gone," but again the narrator intrudes, contradicting this, with the last, insightful words of experience: "Not altogether, O Punch, for when young lips have drunk deep of the bitter waters of Hate, Suspicion and Despair, all the Love in the world will not wholly take away that knowledge" ("Baa Baa" 164). Sudden loss accompanied by rejection and bullying and humiliation, against which he felt helpless, caused Kipling to channel his roiling emotions into his inner world, and eventually into his writing.

The bullying continued at school until Kipling was fourteen when he became strong enough to fight back (*Something* 25). He also learned to use words as weapons, writing personal limericks against opponents and creating an imitation of the Inferno in a notebook "into which I put, under appropriate torture, all my friends and most of the masters" (*Something* 33–34).

By this time Kipling had become quite secretive, as a means of self-protection. Avoidant behavior and a "morbid lust for privacy" run as motifs through his biography up to the years when he moved to his estate at Burwash, and virtually became a recluse (Seymour-Smith 328). As a young man, for instance, Kipling shrank from intimacy with women and yet characteristically attached himself to women unattainable because they were already married. When one of these women, Mrs Edmonia Hill, was to depart from him to live in India, Kipling's fear of abandonment precipitated him into engaging himself to her sister. "The engagement quickly broke down," claims Thomas Pinney (xii). A somewhat similar pattern occurred when Kipling became attracted to someone of his own gender, Wolcott Balestier, an American with whom he collaborated on a novel. Upon Balestier's sudden death of typhoid, Kipling broke off a world tour, returned to London, and proposed to and married Balestier's sister within a month of the death. This woman, Caroline (known as Carrie), appears to have fulfilled a mothering role for Kipling, although she was also a depressive, as well as controlling, jealous, and possessive (Seymour-Smith 199, 203, 204, 298). Kipling himself experienced severe depressions throughout his life, but to a greater degree than with Barrie these alternated with spurts of mania (Seymour-Smith 162, 265, 295). Similarly to Barrie, however, Kipling was deeply shaken by two significant losses in the few years prior to the First World War: his mother, Alice, died late in 1910, and his father Lockwood two months later in 1911. Kipling overworked, suffered a bout of influenza, and had a breakdown (*Something* 56).

Also like Barrie, Kipling over-invested in his children, particularly his son John, whose birth in 1897 he described as the launching of a ship: "The vessel at present needs at least 15 yrs [sic] for full completion but at the end of that time may be an efficient addition to the Navy, for which service it is intended. Date of launch Aug. 17th, 1:50 a.m. No casualties. Christened John" (as quoted in Ricketts *Unforgiving* 238). Despite the tongue-in-cheek tone here, Kipling was determined that his son should carry out his own desire, thwarted because of weak eyesight, of joining the military. To that end he enrolled his son in a militaristic school. At the outbreak of the First World War, John was, ironically, rejected for service because of his weak eyesight, a trait he had likely inherited from his father, and the consequences of which Kipling should have understood very well and sympathized with. Nevertheless, Kipling pulled strings to get him enlisted and was emotionally devastated after his son was lost in action in October 1915. The letters he wrote afterwards were typically avoidant; he put on a brave face and even encouraged his cousin to let his son enlist at seventeen (*Letters* 348). In one, dated 12 November 1915 he wrote that John's "was a short life. I'm sorry that all the years' work ended in that one afternoon but – lots of people are in our position and it's something to have bred a man ... We're pounding on in our insanely English fashion" (*Letters* 345). Though circumspect, his emotion does erupt periodically. On his fiftieth birthday, 30 December 1915, he admitted that, "I have gone through several very dark moments, and no doubt I will go through worse," and "I am filled with an entirely personal sadness, not at all public" (*Letters* 352, 354). In June of 1916 we get a glimpse of his preoccupation when he says, "Meantime my personal heart is heavy for as the year turns round and days and dates repeat themselves one is dragged back to the past of last year and that is not pleasant" and, a few sentences later, his anger, projected on a large scale: "Never believe again, that the English do not know how to hate: It was a long lesson and we were slow learners but we have our teaching by heart at last." (He was writing to a Frenchman; *Letters* 379–80.) Not only was Kipling's mourning complicated because of his role in getting John enlisted, but also because, of his three children, John was the apple of his mother's eye (Seymour-Smith 336), and because John's body was never recovered. Illustration 4.5 shows an apprehensive Rudyard and Carrie Kipling, not having given up the ghost as late as 1930 when they visited Dud Corner Cemetery, Loos where John Kipling's name is inscribed on the Memorial Wall. Through these long years of frustrated and futile inquiries and trips to gravesites in France neither parent recovered their physical health.

Illustration 4.5 Rudyard and Carrie Kipling visiting Dud Corner Cemetery, Loos, in 1930 where John Kipling's name is inscribed on the Memorial Wall. Reprinted by permission of the Mary Evans Picture Library

Lord Birkenhead writes that "Ill health overshadowed [Kipling's] entire later life. He was driven in upon himself ..." (323). Kipling suffered increasingly from "gastritis," evidently an undiagnosed duodenal ulcer, the condition that according to Pinney provoked "an overflowing measure of disabling pain, anxiety, depression and general wretchedness" (xvii), before eventually killing him in 1936. The couple became emotionally estranged from one another: Carrie was inconsolable over the loss of her son, and Kipling, increasingly isolated and lonely, brooded over the location of his son's body. That preoccupation was the driving force behind his obsessive work for the Imperial War Graves Commission (Seymour-Smith 349).

Thus, from these brief sketches of the emotional patterning in Barrie's and Kipling's lives, we can see that neither one typically negotiated well the inevitable losses of loved ones, and that from an early age both responded in an avoidant-resistant pattern to separation and loss. However, they differ of course from most on similar trajectories in that both discovered early on the mixed blessings of writing. From an object-relations perspective, writing filled several roles: it served as an extension of early symbolic play, an adaptation to absence or, in the case of Barrie, to an intensely preoccupied mother; it served to contain anxious and obsessional ideas, such as fear of abandonment, within the enclosed, ordered, and safe space of story; it enabled both writers to adopt various roles and to renegotiate severed or thwarted relationships; but in a negative sense writing proved only temporarily therapeutic, and seemed to have promoted preoccupation with psychic scars. Intense feelings without objective correlatives in the stories sometimes obtrude and mar the artistic effect of certain works.

Most commentators on Barrie and Kipling have noted their genius at game playing from an early age and in their adult lives as well. Barrie, famous as "the boy who could not grow up" (Birkin 40), arranged and participated in elaborate games with the Llewelyn-Davies boys and others. Seymour-Smith says of Kipling that he was able to open himself up completely only to children (235) and that part of him never grew up (272). Barrie, especially, saw writing as a kind of game, claiming that "literature was my game" (*Margaret* 50) and reflecting "What is genius? It is the power to be a boy again at will" (as quoted in Birkin 43). In his plays Barrie frequently introduced an element of fantasy, often expressed through non-verbal theatrical effects, as Hollingdale notes (xvii). About Kipling, Pinney claims that "Games and the idea of playing are, in fact, quite prominent among the figures that run through Kipling's work" (xxxii).

Their symbolic play in writing provided an essential outlet for reconfiguring damaged and frustrating relationships, and thus had a driven quality to it. Perhaps reflecting a need to enter into that intermediate area of experience described by Winnicott, Barrie wrote his books "on the old chair on which [he] was nursed" (*Margaret* 25). Asquith repeatedly remarks on Barrie's extraordinary capacity to adopt the roles and feelings of others (26, 52, 54, 195), to become, as Barrie himself put it, "a dozen persons within the hour" (*Margaret* 117). That he was compelled to do so he suggested in the following: "The most precious possession I ever had was my joy in hard work ... Hard work, more than any woman in the world, is the one who stands up best for her man" (as quoted in Birkin 16). Barrie could not always manage his intense emotions in a way appropriate to the artistic form in which he worked, and he has been severely criticized for both an excess of sentimentality and for excessive cruelty, especially with regards to suffering and death. Novelist and critic George Blake wrote:

> It is perhaps the most puzzling thing about Barrie from first to last that the expert toucher of emotions, the weaver of charmingly

whimsical webs, the delight of the nurseries, had in all his dealings as a writer with such topics as death and sepulture and grief and suffering the way of a sadist. (as quoted in Birkin 16, 18)

As we have seen, Kipling too discovered early on the consolations of literature and was obsessionally driven to contain his anxiety and anger through writing, again not always successfully. He strongly identified with Browning's Fra Lippo Lippi, who has the lines: "I was a baby when my mother died / And father died and left me in the street" (as quoted in Pinney xxx). In one of many references to Fra Lippo in his autobiography, Kipling said that he was "a not too remote – I dare to think – ancestor of mine" (*Something* 22). Kipling manifested intense ambivalence towards women in his writing; his first novel, *The Light That Failed*, has been called an anti-feminist tract (Seymour-Smith 161), and yet he also idealized motherhood, notably in his story "The Brushwood Boy." As Seymour-Smith details, Kipling directed his inner rage at society through his fiction, one of his most dominant recurring themes, for instance, being hatred (29). He has been criticized for his knee-jerk, reactionary, and even jingoistic responses to various enemies, including the Germans in the First World War.

One of the most significant ways both writers discovered of renegotiating relational issues, recovering loss and seeking reparation was in their engagement with the psychical, the uncanny, or supernatural. Most biographers have not probed the psychological dimension of Barrie's and Kipling's tentative forays into the spiritual realm, Chaney, for example, writing rather dismissively that "Barrie was neither Christian nor anti-Christian" (40). Barrie and Kipling were of their age in that they viewed with skepticism the conventional tenets of the Christian faith and in that they sought out alternative forms of belief. Some of these, including the spiritualist and theosophical movements, Barrie and Kipling also approached skeptically, even derisively. However, they took the findings of the Society for Psychical Research more seriously, although still demonstrating some ambivalence. I would argue, however, that Barrie and Kipling's probing of the supernatural fulfilled a profound psychological need in both writers. The possibility of the survival of loved ones touched them at the deepest core of their beings, where they were ambivalently attached to it. Symbolic play with this possibility allowed them to move beyond the closed world of permanent loss, despite their skepticism on an intellectual level.

Barrie's first experience with the supernatural began in childhood and had a profound impact on him. Essentially he grew up with a ghost in the house since his mother frequently spoke to his dead brother David (*Margaret* 18–19), a disturbing experience for Barrie, and he himself felt ghostlike as the replacement child for David. He recounted that on one occasion "I thought it was the dead boy she was speaking to" when she was actually addressing Barrie (*Margaret* 12). Barrie's recurring nightmare captures the complexity of his feeling of being haunted. He had to fight off the ghost David, but also the ghost of his mother, with whom he was too closely enmeshed: he "would fling [his] arms about wildly as if fighting a ghost" (as quoted in Birkin 27), a ghost that over time resolved into a woman who beckoned him to a church to be married. The nightmare persisted into early adulthood, Barrie claiming in 1887 that "My weird dream never varies now. Always I see myself being married, and then I wake up with the scream of a lost soul, clammy and shivering" (as quoted in Birkin 27). Yet at the same time he feared abandonment by his preoccupied mother, which he projected into a universal claim in his 1902 novel *The Little White Bird*. The narrator (a thinly disguised Barrie) states that "The only ghosts, I believe, who creep into this world, are dead young mothers, returned to see how their children fare. There is no other inducement great enough to bring the departed back" (40). He adds, "What is saddest about ghosts is that they may not know their child," since he has grown and "they hate the unknown boy he has become" (*Little* 41).[6] This is the fate of Peter Pan, introduced in this novel, since he escapes from his mother to play with the fairies, self-absorbed and reluctant to return. When he decides "to be his mother's boy" he discovers to his horror that he has been replaced with "another little boy," the narrator claiming that "there is no second chance" (*Little* 187). Living an otherworldly existence has cost him his attachment to his mother, and in Barrie's subsequent, obsessive reworkings of the story Peter Pan remains a lost boy, suspended in time in the Never Land, a transitional space as substitute for the mother after he has been barred from his nursery.

Kipling as well was early on in his life exposed to the supernatural through a connection with the female and maternal. Both his sister Trix and his mother took theosophy quite seriously. Kipling wrote that "At one time our little world was full of the aftermaths of Theosophy" (*Something* 35). His father actually knew Madame Blavatsky, although according to Kipling he considered her "one of the most interesting and unscrupulous imposters he had ever met" (*Something* 35). Trix became a medium and attained some fame, at least in psychical research circles, under the pseudonym "Mrs Holland" by channeling messages from prominent psychical researcher Frederic Myers (Haynes 61).

Seymour-Smith cautiously claims that theosophy and the occult in general had an impact on Kipling (331), and Sandra Kemp demonstrates that Kipling's equivocal response to the uncanny enhances the complexity of his psychological ghost stories.[7] I would go further than both and argue that his psychological patterning made him preoccupied with these beliefs, if skeptical towards some of them. He believed himself dependent in his writing on his Daemon, who wrote the stories through him (Pinney xxx), and yet he claimed in *Something of Myself* that "I am in no way 'psychic'" (*Something* 125). Nevertheless, just before this assertion he recounted an uncanny event. In the summer before the First World War he was invited to watch military maneuvers on a field at Aldershot, which provoked a hallucination of Boer War dead as ghosts: "I conceived the whole pressure of our dead of the Boer War flickering and re-forming as the horizon flickered in the heat" (*Something* 125). This suggests his preoccupation with the war he had championed, and the cost in lost lives, and perhaps also anxiety about the distinct possibility of another war. As well, immediately following his disclaimer about being a psychic he related a prescient dream which convinced him "that I had 'passed beyond the bounds of ordinance'" (*Something* 125–26). Significantly, this "perfectly clear dream" predicted events during his attendance "six weeks or more later" at a ceremony to unveil a memorial to "The Million Dead" when a neighbor in the crowd "barred my vision" and another man wanted a word with him (*Something* 126). Did this premonition express his anxiety about facing up to the huge war losses, including that of his son, and his guilt about not being able to foresee this tragedy (his vision was barred) and about being taken to task for this by the man who wanted a word? Kipling dismisses the latter, claiming that the word "was about some utterly trivial matter that I have forgotten," but perhaps his unconscious had more powerful motives (*Something* 126).

A large number of his stories similarly reach beyond the fringes of the known into the unexplained. "The Sending of Dana Da" (1888), for instance, satirizes the gullibility of believers in occult gurus and their practices, "including spiritualism, palmistry, fortune-telling by cards, hot chestnuts, double-kernelled nuts and tallow-droppings" (146). "Wireless" (1902) ironically shows a psychic transmission or telepathic invasion to be far more significant than a concurrent experiment with a wireless telegraphic transmission. Several ghost stories develop the theme that life is not worth living after the loss of the loved one (Stableford 438). In "They" (1904), the narrator discovers at a "House Beautiful" deep in the countryside several ghost children, among them his own dead child. After she takes his hand, his immediate reaction is intellectual, as he says, "I knew," but he then experiences both sorrow and joy ("They" 308). His resolve to leave this house of spirits appears to reflect Kipling's reconciliation to his daughter Josephine's death in 1899, although the story leaves the narrator sitting "a little longer," perhaps hinting at a reluctance to part ("They" 310).

Thus, by the outset of the war both writers had produced a substantial body of fantasy and supernatural work. In the early stages of the war they turned their hands to another kind of fantasy, penning propaganda glorifying the war (Birkin 223, 239; Gray 194). For Kipling this was merely a continuation of his intense propaganda efforts on behalf of the British in the Boer War, "a reaction to his devastation at the loss of his daughter" Josephine, according to Ricketts (261). As the casualties mounted in the so-called Great War, however, Barrie in particular experienced doubts about it and separation anxiety as George Llewelyn-Davies departed for the front. His play *The New Word* (produced 22 March 1915, a week after George's death) expresses and attempts to control that anxiety in its focus on the revelation of emotional truths between a father and a son that brings them closer together just prior to the son's departure for the front. It is also his first play to connect separation owing to the circumstances of war with the arousal of feelings about earlier loss, in this case, of the soldier son's brother, who died as a child. Birkin observes that "an older theme had found its way into the play – a memory that had been in the author's mind since the age of six" (239). A dialogue between the departing soldier, Roger, and his mother captures this:

> Mrs Torrence, sweetly, '... I'll tell you something. You know your brother Harry died when he was seven. To you, I suppose, it is as if he had never been. You were barely five.'
>
> Roger. 'I don't remember him, mater.'
>
> Mrs Torrence. 'No – no. But I do Rogie. He would be twenty-one now; but though you and Emma grew up I have always gone on seeing him as just seven. Always till the war broke out. And now I see him a man of twenty-one, dressed in khaki, fighting for his country, same as you ...' ("New" 76)

Significantly, although Roger makes no response to this, immediately afterward his mother leaves the room. Roger and his father speak "new" words to one another, ostensibly words pertaining to the military but in reality a new vocabulary of emotional intimacy ("New" 88).

Kipling's early war stories similarly probe beneath simple patriotism, containing subtexts involving attachment issues, although this aspect has not always been recognized. Donald Gray, for instance, argues that Kipling's three early war stories "express a simple morality about the war" (194); however, one of them is much more complex than a simple outburst of anger and hatred towards the Germans. In "Mary Postgate" (published September 1915), Kipling intuitively links childhood loss and its complications with a reaction to war loss, just as Barrie had done. Much of the criticism of "Mary Postgate" focuses on the shock of the ending, as Mary Postgate vengefully and with pleasure watches a man she assumes to be a German parachutist die. Nevertheless, the complexity arises from the great pains Kipling took to set the stage for this, detailing the relationship between an orphaned boy, Wyndham, and Mary Postgate, his caretaker. And it is a painful read, a too vivid account of Wyndham's abuse of the colorless, convenient, and slave-like Mary. On arriving at his aunt's at age eleven, Wyndham quickly adopts a series of derogatory nicknames for Mary, and "Later on he filled the house with clamour, argument, and harangues as to his personal needs, likes and dislikes, and the limitations of 'you women,' reducing Mary to tears of physical fatigue ..." ("Mary" 421). After signing up, Wyndham becomes even more demanding and demeaning; he wields the technical language of warfare as a weapon against Mary, dehumanizing her in his taunt about her ignorance of war machines: "'You *look* more or less like a human being,' he said in his new Service voice. 'You *must* have had a brain at some time in your past'" ("Mary" 422). Wyndham is killed before seeing action and, not surprisingly, both his aunt, Miss Fowler and Mary have difficulty mourning:

> 'It can't be natural not to cry,' Mary said at last. 'I'm so afraid you'll have a reaction.'
>
> 'As I told you, we old people slip from under the stroke. It's you I'm afraid for. Have you cried yet?'
>
> 'I can't. It only makes me angry with the Germans.' ("Mary" 428)

The remainder of the story deals with Mary's "Deadly methodical" disposal of Wyndham's effects, her reaction to the death of a little girl, Edna, in the village, which she mistakenly believes to have been perpetrated by a gun from a plane, and her treatment of the helpless soldier. Her intense ambivalence towards Wyndham is subtly suggested. She seems to have been passionately attached to her tormentor, since we are told when she lights the match to his effects that it "would burn her heart to ashes" ("Mary" 436). On the other hand, she has an uncanny experience of hearing the propeller of Wyndham's plane before Edna is killed, suggesting that in her unconscious there may be a connection between Wyndham and the death of the girl, though consciously she blames the Germans. (The reader, by the way, is made aware that the girl most likely dies from an accident unrelated to the war.) Furthermore, she treats the dying soldier, whom she assumes to be German although he speaks both French and English to her, as she has been treated: she calls him "a bloody pagan" using Wyndham's own words ("Mary" 438); she refers to him as a "thing" and an "it," dehumanizing him just as she had been dehumanized; and she fetches Wyndham's gun to torment the man. Not only does she seek vengeance against Wyndham, however, but also she redeems all of the deaths, "under the most distressing circumstances," within her family:

> She would stay where she was till she was entirely satisfied that It was dead – dead as dear papa in the late 'eighties; aunt Mary in 'eighty-nine; mamma in 'ninety-one; cousin Dick in 'ninety-five; Lady McCausland's housemaid in 'ninety-nine; Lady McCausland's sister in nineteen hundred and one; Wynn buried five days ago; and Edna Gerritt still waiting for decent earth to hide her. ("Mary" 439)

Seymour-Smith claims that Kipling "mirrors exactly" the relationship between his son John and his wife Carrie in this story (343), but the emotional patterning certainly reflects what we have seen of Kipling's earliest attachments. On the one hand he seems to have projected his anger and rage at his early caretaker Rosa through Wyndham's abuse of Mary. He also exacts revenge against her by describing her cruelty and animalistic behavior, "her underlip caught up by one faded canine, brows knit and nostrils wide" ("Mary" 439) as she carries out her vengeance. She is the one who uses "the destructor," an outdoor furnace, to burn all of Wyndham's effects, including books and toys; the obsessive listing of these transitional objects obtrudes awkwardly into the narrative ("Mary" 431). On the other hand, Kipling seems to identify with Mary on some level as a victim of abuse and as someone whose only reaction to loss is vengeful anger; her response mirrors Kipling's avoidant-resistant response, down to the preoccupation with losses in the past.

After the "sons" of Barrie and Kipling actually died, their already fragile equilibriums were radically destabilized, and the tragedies only exacerbated their earliest anxieties about loss. In the play *Dear Brutus*

(1917), Barrie returned to one of his earliest and most prevalent themes: regrets over not having second chances. The shattering of Barrie's sense of self is reflected in his splitting of his various regrets into eight characters' voices. The supernatural element enters through one of Barrie's "voices" – Lob, a Puck-like figure, who is lonely but "does not allow his secret sorrow to embitter him or darken the house" (*Dear* 24). Recall that Barrie applied the phrase "man of secret sorrows" to himself (*Greenwood* 214). Lob brings together his guests on Midsummer Night's Eve and tells them that a strange woodland appears on this night from which people never return. When the others lose interest in finding the woods, Lob acts out a childish temper-tantrum, claiming that "Nobody cares for me – nobody loves me. And I need to be loved" (*Dear* 29). In order to placate him, the others seek the woods, where, Lob finally tells them, they will receive a second chance in life. Almost all of the characters discover that they wouldn't have been any better off, one of them lamenting: "Too late – never-forever-forever-never. They are the saddest words in the English tongue" (*Dear* 70). Only one, Dearth, discovers fulfillment with a daughter, Margaret (recall, the name of Barrie's mother), before this "might-have-been" ghost is lost to him (*Dear* 77, 98).[8]

Barrie's fantasy of reuniting with a lost love is more directly and hopefully portrayed in "A Well-Remembered Voice" (1918). In this one-act play, Barrie manifests typical ambivalence towards spiritualism. A mother grieves openly for her soldier son Dick's death that occurred five months previously; she attempts to contact him in the beyond at a séance with several of her friends. Her husband, Mr Don, who avoids participating, has isolated himself in his inglenook (or fireplace alcove, similar to where Barrie spent much of his time), and hears the voices of the others "only as empty sounds" (*Well* 145). The charismatic Mrs Don assumes that his detached response has arisen because "a son is so much more to a mother than to a father" (*Well* 156). We are told that "All the lovely things which happened in that house in the days when Dick was alive were between him and [his mother]; those two shut the door softly on old Don, always anxious not to hurt his feelings, and then ran into each other's arms" (*Well* 148). Ironically, however, this Oedipal scenario is overcome when out of the "silence" "A well-remembered voice says, 'Father,'" and Dick manifests as a ghost solely to Mr Don, although Barrie made the ghost's presence somewhat ambiguous since the stage directions state that "We see no one, but we are to understand that, to Mr Don, Dick is standing there in his habit as he lived" (*Well* 139). Also ironically, Dick has no knowledge of the messages supposedly sent and returned through table turning. The two discuss incidents that they had never broached when alive, and they express regret at not having been more intimate (*Well* 63). The fantasy here is that the son now has a greater appreciation of his father, is more loyal to him than the mother, and has achieved greater wisdom than he possessed formerly. Dick consoles his father, claiming that the veil between the living and the dead becomes very thin in wartime (*Well* 166) and that death is such "a little thing" (*Well* 165); he presents the beyond in a very favorable light, claiming that he and his friends still joke and have fun there (*Well* 170), but that this is dependent on the mood of loved ones in the land of the living. When Dick's fiancée enters the room, Don ironically acts as the medium through which Dick expresses his desire for her to "be bright" (*Well* 183). In effect, Dick takes on a fatherly role to Mr Don, consoling him and admonishing him to return to his routines and to "be bright" as well (*Well* 188). Only one moment of doubt about the other world enters when Mr Don asks Dick whether he would rather be living than in the beyond, and he replies "Not always" (*Well* 186). Barrie leaves open the effectiveness of the séance, since the password Dick has used to gain access to the realm of the living is the message "Love Bade Me Welcome" that has been spelled out on the table earlier in the evening. At the denouement, after Dick's departure, Mr Don's emotions are not revealed, but instead he will "think it out" (*Well* 188), clearly an avoidant-resistant response to loss.

Similarly to Barrie, Kipling also manifested an avoidant-resistant response and demonstrated ambivalence towards reunion through spiritualist practices. One of his first responses was the poem "My Boy Jack" (published in October 1916), although not specifically written about his son John, as is commonly thought, but about a mother who has lost her Jack Tar in the naval battle of Jutland (Southam). Still, in its repetition with variations of the question "Have you news of my boy Jack?" and the italicized, disembodied, mystical negative responses, "*Not this tide,*" and "*None this tide, / Nor any tide*" Kipling drew on his own anxiety and endless longing. The faint consolation that Jack "did not shame his kind" and that the parent "gave" him does not compensate for his loss. This poem demonstrates emotional reserve, but the "Epitaphs of the War" (1918) take that reserve even further in their intense compression, and yet they reveal preoccupation with death, considering it from so many different stances in the thirty-three epitaphs of two to sixteen lines each. Despite the fact that Kipling claimed they were not personal (as quoted in Holberton, "Epitaphs"), several poems bear on his and his wife Carrie's relationship with John, especially "An Only Son": "I have slain none except my Mother. She, / (Blessing her slayer) died of grief for me" (as quoted in Holberton, "Epitaphs"). The poem stabs at the ironies that a soldier like John who was killed in his first action may not have killed any enemy but only his mother by grief, and that she dies blessing her son the slayer; it is also prescient, since Carrie and Kipling died a long, drawn-out death from grief. In "Common Form," Kipling imagines how any soldier, even his son, might have answered the question of why he had died: "If any question why we died / Tell them, because our fathers lied" (Kipling "Common") Here Kipling takes on the anger and judgment of the sons and implies his guilt and immorality, a recipe for complicated mourning. In "Shock," used as the epigraph to this chapter, only when the soldier's mother, not his wife or children, joins him in the afterlife does he "on her bosom" remember all (Kipling "Shock"). Kipling drew on a deeper, earlier response to loss here, as Kipling regained his identity when his mother returned from India when he was a child, and the sentiment expressed here aligns with "Kipling's many tributes to mother-love" (Holberton "Epitaphs"). In the same volume appeared "En-dor," "a direct attack on the present mania of 'Spiritualism' among such as have lost men during the war," as Kipling claimed in a letter (as quoted in Radcliffe). Yet Kipling's main target is the fraudulent mediums who extract "a wage" from exploiting the bereaved, even though he never names them as mediums, referring instead to their "alien lips" and "stranger's speech" (Kipling "En-dor"). When asked whether there was any basis to spiritualism he replied, "There is; I know. Have nothing to do with it" (as quoted in Radcliffe). John Radcliffe suggests that Kipling's hostility may have come from his perception that spiritualism had had a negative impact on his sister Trix, who suffered from bouts of mental illness. Kipling also had to withstand the pressure of his wife Carrie's desperate desire to try and contact John through a medium.

Nevertheless, Kipling was compelled to probe further the possibility of spirit connections between soldiers and their loved ones in two critically acclaimed stories written after John's death. In "A Madonna of the Trenches," a hysteric ex-soldier reveals to his doctor the uncanny vision, a crisis apparition, that has destabilized him. Strangwick believes that his Auntie Armine appeared on the battlefield on the day of her death in England and called her lover "Uncle" John Godsoe, a soldier, into a dugout where he gassed himself in order to be with her for "Eternity" ("Madonna" 259). The relationship has been illicit, and the young Strangwick's shock at the intensity of their desire has Oedipal overtones; nevertheless, the intensity of the relationship in death is privileged over those in the real world. Strangwick reacts with anger that he will never be able to achieve such a desire: "'And I'm damned if it's goin' to be even once for me!' he went on with sudden insane fury" ("Madonna" 259). Out of his confused rambling it emerges that Strangwick has recently been implicated in a breach of promise action ("Madonna" 260), his claim being that his fiancée "ain't his ideal" ("Madonna" 261). "The Gardener" deals more directly with a "parent's" dealing with loss of a soldier son, and potentially demonstrates greater acceptance of the death. Most of the commentary on the story has focused on the ambiguously supernatural or at least mystical denouement. Helen Turrell is aided in her search for her nephew's gravesite by a man whom she supposes to be the gardener, but who seems to be Christ-like and who might have an uncanny knowledge of her true maternal feelings for her ward, or her possible status as his biological mother. From a psychological viewpoint, however, the interest in the story lies in the way that Kipling once again links a childhood loss with the death of a soldier in wartime. As in "Mary Postgate," an orphaned child enters into a household and has a stormy relationship with his caretaker. Helen Turrell takes in her brother's child and has him christened Michael. Once he discovers that Helen is not his mother, he rages, and is even more enraged when she tells others of their true relationship. He screams, "You've hurted me in my insides and I'll hurt you back. I'll hurt you as long as I live!" ("Gardener" 401). He later adds: "And when I'm dead I'll hurt you worse" ("Gardener" 402). The intensity of the outburst is not fully supported in the context of the story, and only makes complete sense in the light of Kipling's emotional patterning. Despite Michael's anger, "his interest in Helen was constant and increasing throughout" his growing years ("Gardener" 403). Kipling apparently also projected something of himself into Helen. After Michael is killed and buried by a shell, Helen does not seem to be able genuinely to mourn: we are told that, "then she took her place in the dreary procession that was impelled to go through an inevitable series of unprofitable emotions" ("Gardener" 405). She reflects that "I'm being manufactured into a bereaved next of kin" ("Gardener" 406). Her avoidant response is brought into relief through her contact with a woman, Mrs Scarsworth, who searches out grave sites on commission. This woman finally reveals with intense passion that she has had an unconventional love relationship, reminiscent of Auntie Armine's in "A Madonna of the Trenches," and that she does this work in order to visit the site of her lover's grave. Helen's limpid response of "Oh, my dear! My dear!" offends the woman, who departs ("Gardener" 412). Even after visiting Michael's grave, Helen never shows any emotional response.

Thus, both Kipling's and Barrie's earliest responses to separation and loss were avoidant-resistant. Kipling surmounted the challenges of losing both his parents for an unknown amount of time, and suffering systematic bullying, by escaping into reading and then reworking his trauma in fiction. As a replacement child Barrie grappled with the ghost of his brother David and his mother's preoccupation with the loss by repeatedly reworking both of their stories in his fiction. The loss of those dearest to them in the First World War revived their relational anxiety and transformed their attitude towards the war. Barrie and Kipling worked through their preoccupation with those lost, and their well-remembered voices that haunted them, in highly compressed, often subtle and highly imaginative wartime and post-war poetry, short stories, and plays. Supernatural and mystical occurrences provided an intermediate area of experience necessary for re-examining and even renegotiating earlier less than satisfactory relationships. Some of this work, such as Barrie's *Dear Brutus* – considered "one of the outstanding theatrical successes of the war" (Mackail 531) – served to buoy up their sinking reputations. One reason at least for this seems clear. In a culture preoccupied with loss and mourning, a new psychoclass of group fantasies emerged, including a greater need to accept the supernatural and to connect with lost loved ones. Bestselling works such as prominent psychical researcher Oliver Lodge's *Raymond* (1916), a vivid account of his son's communications while living and also from beyond the grave, helped to create a new horizon of expectations in readers, as we have seen. Barrie and Kipling mediated those fantasies, capturing the spirit of the age. When the wave of culture moved on, Barrie and Kipling were left in its wake, isolated and preoccupied with psychically crippling losses until their own deaths in 1937 and 1933 respectively.[9]

5
Mourning, the War, and the "New Mysticism" in May Sinclair and Virginia Woolf

> "I don't think our literature was at all affected by the war, though I am not prepared to say this positively."
> May Sinclair, interview, *NYT Book Review*, 1924

> "We do not like the war in fiction, and we do not like the supernatural."
> Virginia Woolf, "Before Midnight" 1917 *Essays* II 87

A compact woman stands gazing at the fire in the drawing-room grate, a fixed expression on her face. Her dark brown hair tightly plaited in a coronet gives her a regal composure, although she stands barely five feet tall. In her black dress, she might be mourning, but the hazy room, filled mostly with earnest young pipe-smoking men, indiscriminately dressed, belies this. They speak in intense, yet inaudible voices that ebb and flow around her. Here and there a peacock woman struts among them. One of these bears down on the prim woman, a tall, beaky-featured Amazon with a mass of copper-colored hair, Lady Ottoline Morrell. Her white shawl with great scarlet flowers on it flows behind her. In tow she has a slim young woman, hair swept back above her ears to an untidy bun, dark shadows around her melancholy eyes. Round shouldered, she is faun-like and furtive. The gargantuan woman plunges into conversation, gushing that the compact woman, May Sinclair (Illustration 5.1), has recently published, not one but two novels, both about men's disrespectful treatment of women. Miss Sinclair's steely dark brown eyes note the faun's eyes widen in fear and admiration, quickly overlaid with, what is it, anxiety, or perhaps jealousy? Prompted by the gargantuan, the young woman, whose name is Virginia Stephen, apologetically says that she has been reviewing for the *Cornhill Magazine*, a name which makes Miss Sinclair's

Illustration 5.1 May Sinclair in 1898. Reprinted by permission of The Rare Book and Manuscript Library, The University of Pennsylvania Libraries

eyebrows rise, but that she is not sure about writing. Her voice has a soft bell-like quality to it, as if heard in the distance through a fog. The conversation falters until, in pity, Miss Sinclair offers in a clear, high-pitched voice that she is writing a novel about the struggles of writers and their mystic moments of inspiration, to be called The Creators. Again Miss Sinclair notes that mingled admiration and anxiety, but also a flash of real interest. The intensity with which Miss Stephen scrutinizes her causes Miss Sinclair to avert her eyes. Lady Ottoline says, "how fascinating!" and explains her absorption with all matters psychical, prompting Miss Sinclair to describe the uncanny and transcendent moments that she, and also her friend Evelyn Underhill, have experienced. Her eyes flash and the skin alongside them creases, the closest movement to a smile she permits herself as she recollects these moments. Virginia Stephen cannot help being drawn in, and nods with understanding. However, later she will write to her friend Nelly Cecil (Lady), acerbically (a characteristic of her descriptions, particularly of women) that Miss Sinclair, possessed of "medicinal morality," "talked very seriously of her 'work'; and ecstatic moods in which she swings (like a spider again) halfway to heaven, detached from Earth. This was at Mrs Protheros" (*Letters* I 390).

I have here attempted a glimpse of what might have transpired during the only known meeting of two remarkable women; what is even more remarkable is that they discussed mystical moments, integral to both of their lives and their fiction. This meeting occurred in April 1909, when May Sinclair, forty-six, was at the height of her fame, with friends the likes of Thomas Hardy and protégés the likes of Ezra Pound, while Virginia Woolf at twenty-seven was struggling to write her first novel, "Melymbrosia," not published until 1915 as *The Voyage Out*. A few days earlier yet another relative of Virginia Stephen's had died, her Aunt Caroline Stephen (nicknamed "the Quaker"), also a woman of strict morality, yet compassionate. Aunt Caroline had offered her home to Virginia when she was recovering from a breakdown in late 1904; now she was writing "the Quaker's" obituary when she met Sinclair (Palmer 159; *Letters* I 390).

Both May Sinclair and Virginia Woolf struggled with loss, beginning early in their lives and complicated by other issues, such as Sinclair's father's alcoholism and bankruptcy and her mother's oppressive manipulations, and Virginia Woolf's father's severe depression, her own manic-depression, and the sexual abuse she suffered at the hands of her half-brothers. Both discovered early on the consolations of literature, and as writers developed creative reparative strategies with incredible fortitude and insights (enhanced by their extensive knowledge of the formal psychology of the day, as I have detailed in *Dynamic Psychology*). These strategies enabled them to manage their mourning and resist conventional attitudes, particularly expectations of women regarding grieving. They shared mysticism as a significant response to loss. The advent of the war triggered their sensitivity to loss, although they responded differently to the conflict. May Sinclair took a patriotic stance, participating briefly in a Red Cross volunteer medical unit sent to Belgium in September 1914, despite anxieties and misgivings before embarking. Virginia Woolf was a pacifist. Nevertheless, both suffered anxiety about the war and they encountered great difficulty in dealing directly in their fiction with battlefront trauma. A number of reasons can account for this, including their position as non-combatant women in a patriarchally-driven conflict.[1] Yet the war profoundly altered their writing, overtly and covertly. Both wrote repeatedly about it: May

Sinclair serialized her brief Belgian experience in the *English Review*, elaborated on it in *A Journal of Impressions in Belgium* (1915), and treated aspects of the war in four novels, notably *The Tree of Heaven* (1917). In the revisionist collection of essays, *Virginia Woolf and War*, Nancy Bazin and Jane Lauter show how frequently and deeply Woolf responded to war, beginning with *Jacob's Room* (1921), that they are able convincingly to re-frame her as a war novelist. Bazin and Lauter broach the issue of the impact of early losses and abuse on her sensitivity to the conflagration, but they do not develop this link significantly. I intend to do so by focusing on Sinclair's and Woolf's early trauma, their avoidant-resistant pattern of attachment, and their response to war loss, primarily in Sinclair's *The Tree of Heaven*, and Woolf's *Mrs. Dalloway*, though touching on Woolf's *Jacob's Room*. The few critics, including Laura Stempel Mumford, Sharon Ouditt, and Dorothy Goldman, who have attended to *The Tree of Heaven* have emphasized Sinclair's "prowar stance" in showing war as the highest form of communal behavior that makes civilization possible (Goldman 40; Mumford 169, 175, 179; Ouditt, 103). Sinclair certainly conveys this attitude on an intellectual level, and in her Belgian *Journal* she does report experiencing a curious, almost mystical ecstasy (along with a variety of less positive feelings) in the face of danger; however, analysis using insights from object relations and attachment theory shows that *The Tree of Heaven*, along with Woolf's *Mrs. Dalloway* more deeply and ambivalently engage with the war, contain a strong anti-war subtext, and depict mysticism as an integral response. Despite their public statements disliking and denying the impact of war in fiction, captured in the above epigraphs and suggestive of their avoidant attachment pattern, writing through the trauma of war loss freed them up to renegotiate childhood trauma in closely autobiographical novels: Sinclair did this in *Mary Olivier*, written during the last year of the war, and Woolf accomplished this in *To the Lighthouse*, although with varying results.

Both May Sinclair and Virginia Woolf experienced over-engaged or impinging caretaking and severe disruptions in early object relations, both adopted an avoidant-resistant attachment pattern, and both manifested intense sensitivity to threats of loss or actual losses later in life. Born in 1863, May Sinclair was the youngest child and only girl of six children brought up by a strictly religious, over-controlling mother and a frequently absent, alcoholic father who was made bankrupt in 1870 (Boll 27). Sinclair graphically portrays her parents William and Amelia in *Mary Olivier*, which she claimed was autobiographical (Boll 244). In the novel, the protagonist's Mary's "little holy Mamma" (*Mary* 69), starved for affection by her husband, invests her love in her sons. Mary is only too aware of this and feels excluded, as this poignant passage reveals:

> Mamma and Mark were happy together; their happiness tingled, you could feel it tingling, like the happiness of lovers. They didn't want anybody but each other. You existed for them as an object in some unintelligible time and in a space outside their space. The only difference was that Mark knew you were there and Mamma didn't. (*Mary* 241)

Mrs Olivier perceives Mary as a rival, her ambivalence appearing in that she both withholds love from Mary and attempts to keep her dependent by controlling her (*Mary* 69–70, 145). Notably, she tries to prevent Mary from educating herself and to force Mary to adopt her orthodox religious beliefs (*Mary* 114). Typical of the avoidant pattern, she tolerates Mary only when she is "a good girl and keep[s] quiet," as on one occasion when Mamma, "a wounded bird," has sought solitude, interrupted by Mary (*Mary* 162). Mary's father is established early on as a drunken bully as when he holds a very young Mary on his knee against her will and, saying "Drinky-winky," "he put his glass to her shaking mouth. She turned her head away, and he took it between his thumb and finger and turned it back again ... The smell and the sour, burning taste of the wine made her cry" (*Mary* 5). Only mildly chastised by Mamma, he denies coercion, claiming "I never tease anybody" (*Mary* 6). As a teenager, Mary finally confronts her father for bullying his sister, and again his response is dismissive: he orders her up to bed (*Mary* 107). Despite his negative impact on Mary, when he is dying Mary responds with "a rising hysteria of pity" (*Mary* 189).

In all likelihood, Sinclair's parents separated when May was about seven, after her father's shipping business failed. May was dispatched to an uncle's in Liverpool, but when she returned her mother's attempts to stave off poverty precipitated frequent moves (Boll 27; Raitt 27), although as with her biography in general Sinclair was "evasive and contradictory," as Raitt puts it, about the family's moves (22). To one interviewer she claimed that "she had 'lived a very quiet life in the country' until she moved to London in 1896" (as quoted in Raitt 22). On another occasion, she claimed that "we were all over – that is, we were constantly moving" (as quoted in Steell 513). Exacerbating this instability, Sinclair suffered a series of losses, including the death of her father by alcohol-related disease when May was eighteen, and the premature deaths of four brothers from heart disease with disturbing regularity when she was twenty-four, twenty-five, twenty-eight, and thirty-three (Boll 25). All of these had occurred by the time May published her first novel at age thirty-four.[2] She remained preoccupied with these deaths, expressing her anxiety in her intellectual preoccupation with heredity, since she feared inheriting her father's alcoholism and her brothers' heart conditions (Boll 29). She herself was a teetaler, and believed that those with a hereditary taint should remain celibate (Raitt 225). Nevertheless, as a child of an alcoholic she also developed an intense obsessive capacity for observing and scrutinizing emotional states. One interviewer remarked that "her power – indefinable, all observant, analytic – is to be found in her eyes; what those eyes miss isn't worth hiding or trying to hide" (Tante 374).

Apparently, just prior to May's father's death her mother Amelia had permitted May to attend Cheltenham Ladies' College, perhaps one last attempt on Amelia's part to give the pretense of living a middle-class life. May's father William died during the school year, on 19 November 1881 and Amelia evidently needed May at home so she left at the end of the academic year (Raitt 28). She continued to live with and care for her mother until her death in 1901, when May was thirty-eight. The struggle between them continued as well, her mother attempting to prevent May from developing herself intellectually and venturing beyond religious orthodoxy, and May rebelling against this by educating herself, learning several languages and reading voraciously, particularly in philosophy, to the point of exhaustion (Boll 26, 27). A comment of G. B. Stern, a friend of Sinclair's, about Sinclair's autobiographical novel *Mary Olivier* (1919) suggests the intensity of the struggle. Stern claimed that she hated the character of little Mamma because "I remembered you [Sinclair] told me once you had a nervous break-down because you tried to write in the same room with your own mother" (as quoted in Boll 27). The year after her mother's death, Sinclair suffered a nervous breakdown, and she deliberately isolated herself, her reclusiveness remarked on by friends (Raitt 84).

Sinclair also suffered breakdowns from overwork and exhaustion in 1899 and 1904, when she feared madness, as well as periods of depression which brought her to the brink of despair.[3] In her adult years, her shyness, intensity, and chronic anxiety to be fair to people were frequently noted (Boll 117). "A shy, remote creature," was how her novelist friend Ida Wylie described her (as quoted in Raitt 29). Her live-in companion, Florence Bartrop, commented repeatedly on her "reserve" and that she did not see Sinclair laugh much (Boll 118; Raitt 264).

Nevertheless, she was not above making fun of her obsessive need for isolation, as in a brief comic sketch in which she described herself as an animal: "Its habit is to hide itself in an outer burrow, or studio, during the forenoon, when the little creature applies itself, with comic fury, to building up a heap of manuscripts wh. wd. seem to serve it for purposes of protection & indeed nutrition" (1907–1908, as quoted in Raitt 269).

Sinclair's response to the onset of the First World War was paradoxical. Like most of the other writers under study, she was initially enthusiastic and patriotic. On 18 September 1914 she signed an Authors' Declaration in *The Times*, "stating that 'Great Britain could not without dishonour have refused to take part in the present war'" (as quoted in Raitt 150). She donated over half of her wartime earnings to the war effort (Raitt 152) and very likely originated the idea of sending an ambulance unit to Belgium, choosing an eccentric Scottish doctor, Hector Munro, to lead it (Raitt 153). Evidently she was attracted to him and idealized him, claiming that he is "not only a psychologist & psychotherapist, but a 'psychic', & he has the 'psychic's' uncanny power over certain people (they are generally women)" (as quoted in Raitt 154). She was fifty-two and initially resisted going herself, but revealingly agreed only after *imagining* being challenged by him about being too fearful (*Journal* 15). Her compulsive overachievement, belying a need to belong, seems to have motivated her. Also characteristic of an avoidant attachment pattern, she apparently thrilled at losing awareness of self in the "ecstasy" of threatened danger (Sinclair "From" 171); yet before heading out to the front on 25 September, Sinclair recorded experiencing a great deal of anxiety, and "shameful and appalling horror," in nightmares: "Every night before I went to sleep I saw an interminable spectacle of horrors, trunks without heads, heads without trunks, limbs tangled in intestines, corpses by every roadside, murders, mutilations, my friends shot dead before my eyes" (Sinclair "From" 170). This suggests that the perceived threat of death triggered intense anxiety and preoccupation arising from her earlier experiences of loss. In *Mary Olivier* Sinclair describes how a visit to the cemetery in childhood provoked similarly repeated graphic nightmares:

> and the dreams went on just the same: the dream of the ghost in the passage, the dream of the black coffin coming around the turn of the staircase and squeezing you against the banister; the dream of the corpse that came to your bed. She could see the round back and the curled arms under the white sheet. (57)

While in Belgium she struggled to participate, but was on several occasions physically restrained by others from moving out with the ambulance (Raitt 157). Her lack of training and her age worked against her, and she spent most of her time being bored and observing others saving lives. When actually confronted by the horrors, she repeatedly states that, "I see nothing and feel nothing" (Sinclair "From" 170, 176, 177, 179), at least in her journal recollection, surely as clear a manifestation of the avoidant response as could be imagined. Another female recruit recalled that Sinclair "was a very intellectual, highly strung woman who managed to survive for only a few weeks before the horrors of war overcame her and she was sent home" (as quoted in Raitt 153). Not only was she ineffective in being unable to lift stretchers and bandage wounds, but she acted independently from her orders (Boll 107; Raitt 157). During the remainder of the war, two of Sinclair's three nephews who enlisted were killed in 1915, and the third incarcerated in a POW camp. According to biographer Suzanne Raitt, Sinclair "anxiously followed news of the war" and felt depressed at having lost her opportunity to participate directly (165).

After the war, Sinclair tended to play down its significance, despite having written obsessively on the subject (Raitt 181). She continued to react intensely to death, particularly to that of several of her cats (Illustration 5.2), on whom she was emotionally dependent, referring to the events as tragedies; Raitt claims that Sinclair coped in a typical manner by throwing herself into her work (Boll 118; Raitt 84–85). Sinclair developed the avoidant-resistant pattern of attachment, and typical of that pattern she elided the uncomfortable parts of her past, at least in interviews. Raitt summarizes that "Sinclair was not above falsifying or at least repressing the uncomfortable details of her own past" (22).

Much has been written about the disruptions to Woolf's attachments in early life, and so my aim is to bring into relief the most salient examples of loss and Woolf's avoidant-resistant response to it. Thomas Caramagno, for example, has detailed the evidence for the biological basis of Woolf's bipolarity or manic depression and the contributions of various losses and complications in mourning to that illness. Woolf was the fourth child born to Leslie Stephen and Julia, and the seventh including their children from previous marriages. Her parents came together in an atmosphere of mutual bereavement. Leslie Stephen had lost his first wife Minnie on his forty-third birthday after which he was shattered and desolate for an extended period (Bell 12). Julia had lost and "mourned her husband by the time she was 24" (*Moments* 32). In her autobiographical "Reminiscences," written when Virginia was twenty-five between 1907 and 1908, she claimed that her mother "found

Illustration 5.2 May Sinclair with her cat. Reprinted by permission of The Rare Book and Manuscript Library, The University of Pennsylvania Libraries

one who had equal reasons with herself to believe in the sorrow of life" (*Moments* 33). In her later memoir, "A Sketch of the Past," she praises her mother highly and claims that she lived "so completely in her mother's atmosphere that one never got far enough away from her to see her as a person" (*Moments* 84). Nevertheless, the overwhelming evidence suggests that her mother was aloof (Lee 81) and preoccupied with charitable work; her family of eight children, including mentally challenged Laura; an older husband, "difficult, exacting, dependent on her"; and living "at high pressure" (*Moments* 35, 83). Julia weaned Virginia very quickly, within three months, probably because of her health; the next child, Adrian, was conceived a year after Virginia's birth. According to one of Woolf's most perceptive biographers, Hermione Lee, Adrian quickly displaced her as the favored youngest child (Lee 99, 105). An early anxious resistant response, noted by Lee, was Virginia's "manipulativeness and desire to get her own way" (105). In a more candid comment, Woolf asks, "Can I remember ever being alone with [Julia] for more than a few

Illustration 5.3 Julia Stephen with Virginia as a child, 1884

minutes? Someone was always interrupting" (*Moments* 83). The photograph of Virginia at the age of two with her mother gives a hint of the nature of their relationship, with Julia looking down, contemplative, inward focused, not connecting with Virginia, who stares at the camera inquisitively from beneath a bang (Illustration 5.3). The photograph of her parents reading with Virginia Woolf in the background similarly captures something of their preoccupation (Illustration 5.4), and of Virginia's memory of "my father, sitting reading with one leg curled round the other, twisting his lock of hair; 'Go and take the crumb out of his beard' [Julia] whispers to me; and off I trot" (*Moments* 83). Virginia was there in the background, not always seen or heard. Perhaps being lost in the crowd and left to her own devices partially explains why Virginia did not speak properly until the age of three and could turn "purple with rage" in the nursery (Bell 22, 24). She summarized her early family life, claiming "we lived in a state of anxious growth" (*Moments* 30). For Woolf that anxiety would have been increased by the sexual abuse she suffered at the hands of her half-brothers, George and Gerald

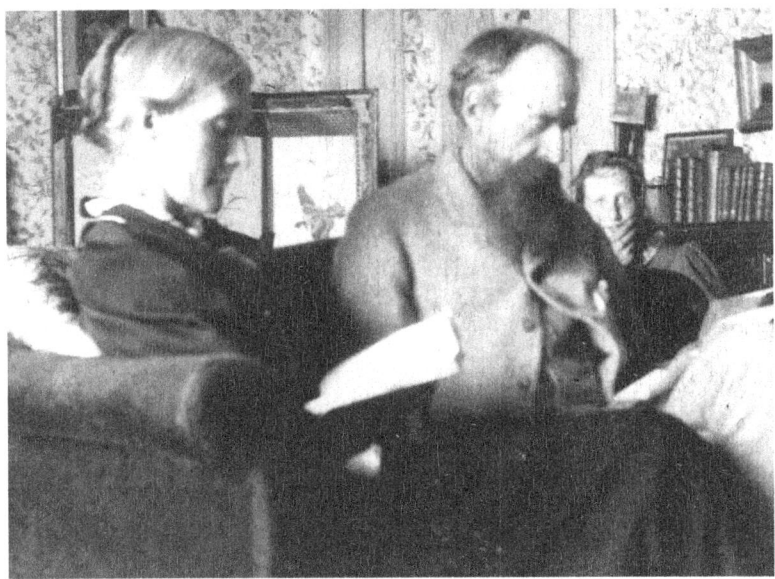

Illustration 5.4 Virginia peering out behind preoccupied parents Julia and Leslie Stephen

Duckworth. With incredible courage and insight, Woolf articulated in "A Sketch of the Past" that "I must have been ashamed or afraid of my own body," and then an explanation: "once when I was very small Gerald Duckworth lifted me onto this [slab for putting dishes on], and as I sat there he began to explore my body ... His hand explored my private parts too. I remember resenting, disliking it – what is the word for so dumb and mixed a feeling? It must have been strong, since I still recall it" (*Moments* 69). Louise DeSalvo has elaborated on this trauma, repeated when Woolf was in her early teens, which would only have exacerbated Woolf's intense avoidant attachment pattern.

Julia's death in 1895 at the age of forty-eight when Virginia was thirteen (Illustration 5.5) she described as "the greatest disaster that could happen" (*Moments* 40). Yet when she went to kiss her dead mother, she said to herself, "as I have often done at moments of crisis since, 'I feel nothing whatsoever'" (*Moments* 92; Lee 131), a clear indication of an avoidant pattern of response. In retrospect, Woolf was able to present a critical view of Julia, whom she described as quick-tempered when teaching her children, impetuous and a little impervious, "sharp," "ruthless," and most pertinently "quite indifferent, if she saw good, to any amount

Illustration 5.5 Virginia in mourning clothes after the death of her mother Julia. Private Collection

of personal suffering" (*Moments* 39, 42, 82). Julia's death began "a period of Oriental gloom, for surely there was something in the darkened rooms, the groans, the passionate lamentations that pass the normal limits of sorrow ..." (*Moments* 40). Leslie was the main cause of that excessive grieving, and his mourning was complicated and extended to depression. Virginia refused to participate in that melodramatic display of emotion, but on numerous occasions she saw an apparition of her mother: "beautiful, emphatic, with her familiar phrase and her laugh; closer than any of the living are" (*Moments* 40). She was not above using this vision to draw attention to herself (*Moments* 92). The family was left in a "chronic state of confusion" (*Moments* 45), especially after Virginia's step-sister Stella, who filled the role of mother, died two years later. Woolf recollected being in a "morbid state, haunted by great ghosts" (*Moments* 53).

At twenty-two Virginia lost her father; her ambivalence towards him was even more pronounced than towards her mother. His self-pity, rage, and "brutal" behavior towards Vanessa and Virginia, expressed in his anger about the household accounts, provoked in Virginia "such rage and frustration. For not a word of my feeling could be expressed" (*Moments* 125). After his death she became preoccupied with these scenes: "I would find my lips moving; I would be arguing with him; raging against him; saying to myself all that I never said to him" (*Moments* 1985 108). Yet his death provoked more positive feelings of attachment as well. Woolf reflected that without his early death "he would not have been so dumb, yet genuinely, bound to us. If there is any good (I doubt it) in this mutilation [of] natural feelings, it is that it sensitizes – if to be aware of the insecurity of life; [to] remember something gone; to feel, now and then, as I felt for father when he made no claim, an odd fumbling fellowship" (*Moments* 117).

Her brother Thoby succumbed to typhoid nearly three years later, in 1906. Hermione Lee describes Virginia's response as "intensely sad, but also calm" (231). In 1929 she imagined him as a ghost with whom she could speak: "That queer ghost. I think of death sometimes as the end of an excursion which I went on when he died. As if I should come in & say well, here you are" (*Diary* III 275). In "A Sketch" she imagines what he might have become had his life not been cut short (*Moments* 120), and she renegotiated her relationship with him in fiction, as we shall see.

She experienced serious nervous breakdowns after the deaths of her parents in 1895 and 1904, and also one in 1913. A thread running through these years is her avoidant response to emotional crises, whether it was the death of a loved one or finding herself in the company of a stranger (Bell 55, 76). At society events such as dances, she described that she and Vanessa "sit in corners & look like mutes who are longing for a funeral" (as quoted in Bell 77). Lee remarks on Woolf's passionate need for solitude and independence (Lee 113). Her avoidance of feeling most remarkably appeared in what Lee describes as Woolf's "alarming" need "to think of people as if they were books" (403).

At the outset of the First World War, Woolf, unlike the other subjects of this study, was a pacifist. She experienced numerous losses during the conflict: her childhood friend and fellow writer, Rupert Brooke, died in Greece, in 1915, two of her Fisher cousins died (Lee 351), one brother-in-law, Philip Woolf, was severely wounded, and another, Cecil Woolf, killed, both in 1917 (Levenback 48). After the war, in October 1922, Woolf's friend Kitty Maxse died suddenly in a fall from a flight of stairs. Woolf believed that Maxse had committed suicide, and Quentin Bell argues that Maxse can be identified with Clarissa Dalloway, since Woolf was in the early stages of transforming the first draft, entitled "The Hours," in which Clarissa commits suicide, into the novel *Mrs. Dalloway* (Friedman 211, 218–19).

Further evidence of Sinclair and Woolf's avoidant-resistant pattern of attachment can be discovered in their adaptations to loss. For both of them inner states were of supreme importance and they learned early on that an inner focus could transcend the pain and suffering in the external world. To a greater or lesser degree, both developed idealist, transcendent philosophies at the center of which was mystical experience. They also developed the facility of describing and analyzing these, eventually embracing fiction writing as a means of renegotiating relationships. Although Sinclair left no autobiographical account of when she first experienced psychic moments, she described them as being familiar by the age of eleven in *Mary Olivier*:

> By the gate of the field her sudden, secret happiness came to her. She could never tell when it was coming, nor what it would come from. It had something to do with the trees standing up in the golden white light. It had come before with a certain sharp white light flooding the fields, flooding the room. It had happened so often that she received it now with a shock of recognition; and when it was over she wanted it to happen again. She would go back and back to the places where it had come, looking for it, thinking that any minute it might happen again. But it never came twice to the same place in the same way. (*Mary* 93, 94)

These moments enable Mary to transcend family conflict and bring insight and happiness.

From an early age Sinclair was attracted to books, having access to her father's library. In *Mary Olivier* physical books serve as transitional objects, helping Mary overcome her insecure attachment to her mother: "When she looked at them [her brother Mark's books] she could still feel her old, childish lust for possession, her childish sense of insecurity, defeat" (*Mary* 301). Sinclair particularly sought out intellectual tracts, philosophy that emphasized consciousness as reality. Throughout her life she pursued the study of Idealism with extraordinary obsessive determination, publishing two major treatises defending and reviving philosophical Idealism, *A Defence of Idealism* (1917) and *The New Idealism* (1922). Her achievement was recognized to the extent that she was elected to the Aristotelian Society (Boll 112). While this writing might merely have reflected her avoidance expressed in a rigid and intellectualized form, she also discovered early on the pleasure of re-enacting mental and emotional states in fictional form, beginning with poetry. In *Mary Olivier*, she analyzes the writing process, including its sublimation of desire and vividly describes, "Happiness, the happiness that came from writing poems; happiness that other people couldn't have, that you couldn't give to them; happiness that was no good to Mamma, no good to anybody but you, secret and selfish; that was your happiness. It was deadly sin" (234). Notice the emphasis on creativity as a solitary secret pursuit, and as selfish and sinful, because of the self-negating way in which as a girl she has been raised. Later in the novel, the play that she drafts is significantly titled "Dream-Play" and it also makes her "intensely happy" (301). Sinclair wrote several novels focusing on the creative process, indicative of her preoccupation with its origins, and she considered the possibility that it was linked with madness, a prevalent medical view in her day. In *The Divine Fire* (1904), genius is described as a kind of possession, and in *The Creators* (1910) an enlightened doctor tells an insightful female novelist that genius is not simply a manifestation of neurosis but that her nervous system is perfectly adapted for her genius (*Creators* 420). This writer Jane Holland, whom Sinclair self-consciously modeled after herself, also experiences mystical moments, when the world became "luminous and insubstantial and divinely still" (111), or when she experiences a ghostlike presence, a "nascent ecstasy" accompanying the onset of creativity (*Creators* 459).

Sinclair probed mystic consciousness and the psychological root of mystical moments in a chapter entitled "The New Mysticism" of her philosophical treatise *A Defence of Idealism*, published just prior to *The Tree of Heaven* in 1917. She defines her experience and ideas against those of Evelyn Underhill, with whom she had become friends before 1907, and whose manuscript of *Mysticism* she had critiqued before publication in 1911 (Boll 79; *Mysticism* xi). Though she agrees with Underhill that the final goal of Christian mysticism is the unitive life, unlike Underhill Sinclair believes that this unitive life was also achieved in Eastern mysticism, the purest form according to Sinclair (*Defence* 273, 272). This reflects her more inclusive approach to mysticism. Sinclair also agrees with Underhill that the mystic life involves the instincts, and in fact a total remaking of the personality (*Mysticism* 448) and that sometimes the mystic's nervous system is not fully adapted to her consciousness, to the more organized spirit, a consequence of which is "mystical ill-health" (*Defence* 257). However, Sinclair, with her deep reading in dynamic psychology, probed this further. She concurred with Pierre Janet that, as with other neuroses and psychoses, the basis lay in dissociation, defined as "the break between one idea, or group of ideas, and its normal context and logical connections; the cutting off of one psychic state, or group of states, from the stream of consciousness itself" (*Defence* 290). Mystic detachment is dissociation, which can be a dangerous state (*Defence* 259), and yet mysticism can surmount the illusion of separation when at one with ultimate reality (*Defence* 315). Sinclair makes the connection between mysticism and war in claiming that the most intense certainty of this union with ultimate Reality occurs when facing death:

> there is an even higher state of certainty than these. Almost every hero knows it: the exquisite and incredible assurance, the positively ecstatic vision of Reality that comes to him when he faces death for the first time. There is no certainty that life can give that surpasses or even comes anywhere near it. And the world has been full of these mystics, these visionaries, since August 1914. (*Defence* 302)

To her credit, however, Sinclair acknowledges that "the secret of mystic passion and of mystic certainty remain alike insoluble" (*Defence* 322), and she concludes her analysis with a summary of mystical moments:

> No reasoning allows or accounts for these moments. But lovers and poets and painters and mystics and heroes know them: moments when eternal Beauty is seized travelling through time; moments when things that we have seen all our lives without truly seeing them, the flowers in the garden, the trees in the field, the hawthorn on the hillside, change to us in an instant of time, and show the secret and imperishable life they harbour; moments when the human creature we have known all our life without truly knowing it, reveals its incredible godhead; moments of danger that are moments of pure and perfect happiness, because then the adorable Reality gives itself to our very sight and touch. There is no arguing against certainties like these. (*Defence* 379)

Virginia Woolf termed these mystical states "moments of being," and for her, at least as a child, they had a more negative impact than for Sinclair. Woolf felt them as horrible shocks because they overwhelmed her and involved a severing; two of the examples she cites from her childhood, including the horror of a man's suicide, evoked pain and despair (*Moments* 71–72). Later she understood them as exceptional and valuable, "a token of some real thing behind appearances" (*Moments* 72). Her description evokes, in terms of Idealism, a glimpse of the Absolute, and she does actually call her ideas on this "a philosophy; at any rate it is a constant idea of mine; that behind the cotton wool is hidden a pattern; that we – I mean all human beings – are connected with this" (*Moments* 72). The real connection between human beings lies in the transcendental realm. Although these moments "were the invisible and silent part of my life as a child," she learned to write about them, and describes this with great insight as a reparative strategy (73). She reveals that "the shock-receiving capacity is what makes me a writer" (*Moments* 72): "it is only by putting [a shock] into words that I make it whole; this wholeness means that it has lost its power to hurt me; it gives me, perhaps because by doing so I take away the pain, a great delight to put the severed parts together" (*Moments* 72). Through writing she renegotiates reality and relationships: "making a scene come right; making a character come together" (*Moments* 72). She also articulates how loss sharpens the perceptions, claiming that her father told her and his other children to use "our sorrow to quicken the feeling that remained" (*Moments* 46). She elaborates: "for when you examine feelings with the intense microscope that sorrow lends, it is amazing how they stretch, like the finest goldbeater's skin, over immense tracts of substance" (*Moments* 59). This process of examining sorrow minutely and transforming it, making severed parts whole becomes the substance of her fiction. When she begins to write fiction she describes entering an inner, dreamlike world, as if in a trance. To Madge Vaughan, the niece of Idealist philosopher T. H. Green, she writes in 1906, "my present feeling is that this vague and dream like world, without love, or heart, or passion, or sex, is the world I really care about, and find interesting" (*Letters* I 227). When this "perfectly real" world took shape as her first novel, initially titled "Melymbrosia," she wrote to her brother-in-law Clive Bell, "for I wrote it originally in a dream-like state, which was at any rate, unbroken" (*Letters* I 383). Thus, Woolf's mysticism, even more so than Sinclair's took on a very individual form, and she was less influenced by the mystical tradition than Sinclair. However, for both, mystical states became a crucial means of absorbing shocks and through writing about them, of transforming them into something whole.

Sinclair found a focus for her mystical impulse, this sense of a realm beyond that knowable through the five senses, in the Society for Psychical Research, whose main aim was to prove by experimental means the survival of personality beyond death. To that end, the SPR examined various phenomena suggestive of a realm beyond the five senses, including telepathy, hypnosis, trances, automatic writing, and collective hallucination. Sinclair made allusions to psychical research from her first novel, *Audrey Craven* (1897 134), on, and was elected a member of the SPR on 14 May 1914 (Boll 105). Neither of Sinclair's biographers, Boll or Raitt, has recognized the full extent of Sinclair's interest in the Society,[4] or the impact of psychical research on her fiction (cf. Johnson "May Sinclair"). Sinclair wrote a review of a book on psychical research in 1917 ("The Spirits") and contributed letters to the *Journal* of the SPR in 1917 and 1918 that testify to the seriousness with which she took psychical research.[5] She also demonstrated an extensive knowledge of psychical research in *A Defence of Idealism*, concluding there that "telepathy is a fact" (351), and she continued to participate in psychical experiments in the 1920s with Catherine Dawson Scott. For five months she attended séances at which appeared the spirit of her favorite brother Frank, who had died in 1889. In a letter to Dawson Scott she revealed that:

> I was very anxious to get proof of [the spirits'] presence, something that cd.n't be explained away as yr. or my subconsciousness. So on Wednesday night I called Frank & asked if he cd. show a light in my room in a place where it cd.n't come from the outside. Nothing happened on Wednesday night but last night I'd no sooner called to Frank when a bright rod of light appeared, intensely pulsating, with a steady light below, in the very place I had asked for. It remained some time. (as quoted in Raitt 134)

We do not know the degree to which Sinclair was convinced, but in the introduction to Catherine Dawson Scott's account of some of these séances in *From Four Who Are Dead* in 1926 Sinclair wrote that Scott's script "is the only reasonable account of the life beyond death that I have yet seen" (5). She also explored a variety of psychical phenomena in her fiction, from telepathy to psychic invasion to persistence of strong feeling beyond death, as I have detailed in *Dynamic Psychology* (127–29).

Virginia Woolf was more ambivalent about psychical research than Sinclair. However, as I have argued elsewhere (Johnson "Spirit"), she was quite well informed about it, probably mainly through her friendships with Lytton and James Strachey, but also through reviewing a number of books treating the topic, including Dorothy Scarborough's *The Supernatural in Modern Fiction* (1917). Certainly by 1909 she demonstrated knowledge of psychical research in a letter, musing that:

> There should be threads floating in the air, which would merely have to be taken hold of, in order to talk. You would walk about the world like a spider in the middle of a web. In 100 years time, I daresay these psychical people will have made all this apparent now seen only by the eye of genius. (13 April 1909, *Letters* I 390)

She also held a view remarkably similar to that of Frederic Myers that strong emotions could persist beyond the time in which they occurred and that we could reconnect with them:

> I often wonder – that things we have felt with great intensity have an existence independent of our minds; are in fact still in existence? And if so, will it not be possible, in time, that some device will be invented by which we can tap them? I see it – the past – as an avenue lying behind; a long ribbon of scenes, emotions. There at the end of the avenue still, are the garden and the nursery. Instead of remembering here a scene and there a sound, I shall fit a plug into the wall; and listen in to the past. I shall turn up August 1890. I feel that strong emotion must leave its trace; and it is only a question of discovering how we can get ourselves again attached to it, so that we shall be able to live our lives through from the start. (*Moments* 67)

The electrical metaphor might be seen as flippant, but it was not uncommon in this period to draw parallels between the recent "invisible" technologies and telepathy. Despite this, the passage genuinely evinces a longing to reconnect to the past and the strong emotions associated with it.

That Sinclair's and Woolf's early disruptions to significant attachments and their various adaptations, including mystical transcendence, significantly shaped their response to war can be seen through their fiction. Sinclair's first novel to treat the war was *Tasker Jevons*, which accurately parallels details about her time at the front through the vulgar protagonist, who, like Sinclair, is middle-aged and tries to organize an ambulance unit, with the difference that his wife Viola accompanies him. Nevertheless, the novel mainly focuses on class distinctions and their effect on Jevons, a writer, and his socially superior wife. The war only figures in the last quarter of the novel and is primarily used as a device to gain Jevons' acceptance by his wife's family, thus solving marital tension. Hrisey Zegger accurately describes the novel as clever and superficial (85). Woolf's first attempt at capturing the impact of war on a character was much more subtle and indirect. The novel draws on her relationship with and loss of her brother Thoby, who died at twenty-five of typhoid in 1906. Anxiety about war loss revives anxiety about knowing and understanding this brother and her fading memory of him. In a sense it is her memorial to him, overlaid by her ambivalent testament to the unknown, universal soldier; hence the name she chose of Jacob Flanders, identifying him with the fields where the most intense losses occurred in the First World War. Woolf was extremely fond of Thoby and his loss was a terrible blow after the earlier losses of those dearest to her. For a month she denied his death to her friend Violet Dickinson in letters; then her "desire was to know more of him" (Bell 112), and she idealized him as "the best in us" (*Letters* I 374). Nevertheless, in "A Sketch" she associated him with one of those violent shocks, or moments of being, in fact the first one, and one associated with fighting:

> the first: I was fighting with Thoby on the lawn. We were pummelling each other with our fists. Just as I raised my fist to hit him, I felt: why hurt another person? I dropped my hand instantly, and stood there, and let him beat me. I remember the feeling. It was a feeling of hopeless sadness. It was as if I became aware of something terrible; and of my own powerlessness. I slunk off alone, feeling horribly depressed. (*Moments* 71)

Thoby "dominated" the children and possessed power in the family, as the favored child and as a male who received privileges, notably a Cambridge education, while Woolf did not (*Moments* 107–8). When Woolf came to write *Jacob's Room*, she expressed her ambivalence towards him, and portrayed him honestly with all his flaws, as perceived by others. His status is described succinctly as "Wealthy. Highly connected" (*Jacob's* 102). Yet he is "a little regal and pompous," "majestic, a little overbearing," and could get into the doldrums, when he was dull, grumpy, and morose (*Jacob's* 116, 119). More significantly, he can be callous, indifferent, and hurtful, particularly of women such as Fanny, with whom he has had a sexual relationship and whom he abandons without a second thought (*Jacob's* 137). He is constantly reading, mostly the classics, and remains detached from real life even when an argument breaks out in the street below his room (*Jacob's* 87). He is described as "dignified and aloof": for him "there is a stopper upon all emotions whatsoever" (*Jacob's* 93, 109). Woolf later wrote about Thoby that "He was amazingly reserved. Not a word of feeling was allowed to escape him" (*Moments* 109). Not only does Woolf honor his memory by being honest about his character, but we can see that he shared her avoidant pattern of attachment. Repeatedly, the narrator tells us that Jacob tells his mother nothing she wants to know (*Jacob's* 101, 104, 111). Woolf seems to have felt considerable anxiety about trying to capture this life in all its elusiveness and fluctuations. At one point she says it is no use trying to sum people up (*Jacob's* 22), at another that "Character-drawing is a frivolous fireside art" (*Jacob's* 124–25). Jacob always seems to be disappearing from the narrative, as he is lost to a minor character who meets him on a train, lost "as the crooked pin dropped by a child into the wishing well twirls in the water and disappears for ever" (*Jacob's* 22).

Jacob's Room is saturated by images of separations and loss and death from beginning to end. Mrs Flanders announces a leave-taking at the outset and we discover that she is a widow, since her husband Seabrook has been dead for two years. Most of the imagery of death is dissociated from Jacob and deflected, even into names of minor characters, such as Miss Wargraves (*Jacob's* 71). Other references are mysterious in their indirectness: "and now Jimmy feeds crows in Flanders and Helen visits hospitals" (*Jacob's* 76). There are few direct references to the war, as in "the battleships ray out over the North Sea, keeping their stations accurately apart" before firing simultaneously (*Jacob's* 125). The perspective on the war is distanced, remote, and unreal, as in the simile "Like blocks of tin soldiers the Army covers the cornfield, moves up the hillside, stops, reels slightly this way and that, and falls flat, save that, through the field glasses, it can be seen that one or two pieces still agitate up and down like fragments of broken matchstick" (*Jacob's* 125). War only becomes personal at the end when Mrs Flanders thinks she hears the guns, which evokes memories of earlier lost loved ones and of "her sons fighting for their country" (*Jacob's* 143). Thoby has been transformed into Jacob, the soldier, and yet Woolf never gives the details of his military service nor the circumstances of his death, since this sort of memorial would be false. Physical memorials are pushed to the margins. At the Wellington Monument, Clara reads "'this statue was erected by the women of England'" and she reacts with "a foolish little laugh," suggesting her incomprehension and also that the monument does not have its intended effect of evoking sorrow and memory (*Jacob's* 134). Jacob's father's tombstone epigraph, "Merchant of this city," is false, and Mrs Flanders's reaction to this memorial is to anxiously wonder "Had he, then, been nothing?" (*Jacob's* 9, 10). "At first, part of herself," he has now "merged in the grass" and the emblems of the cemetery in which he lies, now "one of a company," and anonymous (*Jacob's* 10). Woolf has prevented this from happening to Thoby through her renegotiated, more mature perspective on him in the novel, which involves mystical possibility. Woolf parodies the mystic in the minor character, Jinny Carslake, who "frequented Indian philosophers,'" and now reads

> ordinary pebbles picked off the road. But if you look at them steadily, she says, multiplicity becomes unity, which is somehow the secret of life, though it does not prevent her from following the macaroni as

it goes around the table, and sometimes, on spring nights, she makes the strangest confidences to shy young Englishmen. (*Jacob's* 105).

Nevertheless, at the novel's close, Jacob's is "an empty room," but we are told that "the wicker armchair creaks, though no one sits there" (*Jacob's* 143). Jacob's friend Bonamy stands at Jacob's window observing life going on, when "suddenly all the leaves seem to raise themselves," causing him to cry out "Jacob! Jacob!" as though his presence persists. Grief is muted and deflected into Mrs Flanders's exclamation, "Such confusion everywhere!" but this response echoes Woolf's earliest experience of the aftermath of death. When Mrs Flanders holds up "a pair of Jacob's old shoes" and asks "What am I to do with these?" Woolf subtly and powerfully conveys this mother's sense of being overwhelmed. Jacob's absence and her loss are magnified by the unasked question, who can fill these shoes now? Mrs Flanders is left without consolation, and there is just the most tentative intimation that Jacob might persist beyond death in some way.

Woolf and Sinclair probe a mystical response to loss more fully in *The Tree of Heaven* (1917) and *Mrs. Dalloway* (1925), as a comparative analysis will demonstrate. On the surface the novels do not seem to have much in common. A family chronicle, *The Tree of Heaven* traces the responses to social change of various members of the extended Harrison family during the period from 1895 to 1916. It focuses on the mixed emotions surrounding suffragism, an issue overtaken by the initial frenzied enthusiasm for the war. *Mrs. Dalloway* conveys the impressions and memories of various characters during one day in June 1923. The most dramatic action of the novel consists of war veteran Septimus Smith committing suicide, but the focus falls more consistently on Clarissa Dalloway and her preparations for her party, which closes the novel. In technique there are differences as well. Sinclair employs omniscient narration, though she carefully selects details and makes the reader privy to the thoughts of characters in succession, beginning with the mother, Frances Harrison. Woolf makes the reader more intimate with characters through a succession of indirect internal monologues that sound curiously alike, as Caramagno (210) and others have pointed out. Nevertheless, beneath the level of plot and technique, Sinclair's and Woolf's novels manifest remarkable similarities. I do not want to suggest a direct influence, although I think that a case could be made for anxiety of influence on Woolf's part, since Sinclair was the best-known female Edwardian novelist, and Woolf tended to deny knowledge of her work (*Letters* I 317; *Letters* II 503); Woolf is known to have drawn, for example, on Sinclair's essay "The Novels of Dorothy Richardson" in her article "Modern Fiction" (Silver 18–19, 155–56; Zegger 98). Rather, I would suggest that some of the similarities arise because of the resemblance in imaginative strategies engaged to cope with the human catastrophe of loss that the war represented.

Recall that a literary application of object relations and attachment theory makes the assumption that the text is a form of symbolic play, a projection of fantasy, the writer's means of managing or at least containing relational anxiety, including separation and loss, and possibly even of achieving some degree of reparation and wholeness, however fleeting. The narrator's psyche is typically split into constellations of self and other; displacements, dissociations, condensations, and sublimations ameliorate psychic conflict too painful to deal with directly. Sinclair herself was aware of some of these psychic processes, as has been shown in the case of dissociation, from her reading of Janet. In *A Defence of Idealism*, Sinclair also describes a dream for which she can vouch involving a complex dramatic incident implicating three people as well as the dreamer: "The dreamer, so far, was simply dreaming the outline of a very ordinary novel or a play. But no sooner did the outline and the parts to be played by the three persons become clear, than the dreamer *became* the three persons, and experienced, in one and the same moment, three sets of emotions, all distinct from each other, two of which were mutually exclusive, besides maintaining three distinct and appropriate attitudes to the total event" (376). Woolf, too, demonstrates tremendous insight into the psychic processes involved in writing, into its reparative and transformative capability: About *To The Lighthouse* she reflects, "I suppose that I did for myself what psycho-analysts do for their patients. I expressed some very long felt and deeply felt emotion. And in expressing it I explained it and then laid it to rest" (*Moments* 81). Nevertheless, she also recognizes that the process is not quite this tidy, going on to ask "what is the meaning of 'explained' it?" (*Moments* 81).

Viewed from an object relations stance, both novels deflect the harshest effects of war by splitting off and superficially containing it in a figure of the "other," labeled mad. In *The Tree of Heaven* the figure is Maurice, a troublesome uncle with a hereditary taint. The Harrisons view his being packed off to the Boer War as a solution to a problem. However, when he returns slightly wounded and with an even greater alcohol addiction, he relays the horrors of the war in graphic detail:

> You people here don't know what war is ... It's dirt and funk and stinks and more funk all the time ... You'll find a chap lying on his

> back all nice and comfy, and when you start to pick him up you can't lift him because his head's glued to the ground. You try a bit, gently, and the flesh gives way like rotten fruit, and the bone like a cup you've broken and stuck together without any seccotine, and you heave up a body with half a head on it. And all the brains are in the other half, the one that's glued down. That's war. (*Tree* 80)

None of the family can realize his experience, although the Harrison parents, Anthony and Frances, do vow temporarily not to let their sons have anything to do with war (*Tree* 83). Sinclair's later description of Maurice goes so far as to dehumanize him, further devaluing his experience: "Maurice a thing of battered, sodden flesh hanging loose on brittle bone, a rickety prop for the irreproachable summer suit bought with Anthony's money" (*Tree* 257–58). War has had a similarly profound impact on Woolf's Septimus Smith, including an intense, frequently mentioned anxiety that he can no longer feel, but he is more severely isolated than Maurice. No one understands his outbursts about Evans, his close friend and officer who was killed in the war, or about human cruelty (*Dalloway* 125), even though he has made the reparative effort to have his wife write them out (*Dalloway* 124). His wife and others fear him, and his doctors treat him with suspicion.[6]

The effects of war are otherwise dispersed, played down, and, in the case of Sinclair imaged positively, the negative impact even denied. In Woolf, the dispersal is particularly diffuse. However, from the outset both novels are intensely preoccupied with unfulfilled and unfulfilling attachments as well as separations, and show evidence of unresolved mourning. These preoccupations can be seen as a displacement of response to war losses. In Sinclair, the personal and the public become entangled and merged. In Woolf's case in particular, references to war keep erupting into the text, subverting the narrative flow.

In response to loss and mourning, both narratives evince an intense struggle for selfhood, a struggle impinged on by large societal forces, the most threatening of which is the war. *The Tree of Heaven* is dominated by anxiety about loss of self, and it provides a striking illustration of Sinclair's attitude to selfhood as expressed in *A Defence of Idealism*:

> though our selfhood would seem to remain inviolable, our individuality holds its own precariously, at times, and with difficulty against the forces that tend to draw us back to our racial consciousness again. The facts of multiple personality, telepathy and suggestion, the higher as well as the lower forms of dream–consciousness,

indicated that our psychic life is not a water-tight compartment, but has porous walls, and is continually threatened with leakage and the flooding in of many streams. (*Defence* 375)

In the novel Sinclair splits and projects herself primarily into the Harrison children, Michael, Nicky, and Dorothea, as well as a cousin, Veronica. The focus is on their responses, first to family experiences – especially their mother Frances's over-controlling behavior – and then to larger forces at work in society, the many streams that threaten psychic integrity. Their grandfather's death dominates the first section of the novel, and his wife, "Grannie," and unmarried daughters are absorbed by their bereavement (*Tree* 24). Frances feels "almost unbearable" sorrow for them, and guilt "for not being what she ought to be" (*Tree* 23). Since her relations are unsatisfactory with her husband Anthony, who is rather wooden emotionally and is, ironically, a timber merchant, she invests her emotion in her children. Their growth into adulthood is described as a death to her (*Tree* 44). She worries that her children will be swept away from her into "an unclean moral vortex" (*Tree* 158), as well as several other vortices, including feminism and revolutionary art, although she herself might be described as a maternal vortex, away from whose dominance her children must initially move.

All of the children adopt what W. R. D. Fairbairn terms a pseudo-independent stance in response to their Grandpapa's death. Disruptions in early attachments typically result in persistence to an exaggerated degree of infantile emotional dependence, claims Fairbairn. He adds that, "a deeply repressed attitude of infantile dependence may persist underneath, and be masked by, a more superficial attitude of exaggerated independence or pseudo-independence" ("War" 270). Michael responds most intensely, uncertain whether his Grandpapa is still a presence (*Tree* 6). He remains extremely sensitive to loss, a tree-felling upsetting him because he believes that "The trees died horrible deaths" (*Tree* 186). He also undergoes the most intense struggle to develop and maintain his individuality against the onslaught of collective behavior. His rebellion consists in rejecting his father's plans to enter the family business and in taking up revolutionary art as a poet, associating with figures considered morally unacceptable by his parents. His psychic withdrawal is described from the perspective of his over-controlling mother: "Frances was afraid for Michael now ... Because of his strange thoughts he was the one of all her children who had most hidden himself from her; who would perhaps hide himself from her to the very end" (*Heaven* 232). However, his independence is really a form of pseudo-independence, since his choice makes him dependent financially on his parents and he lives at home.

Nicky responds to the household grieving and to his mother's overcontrolling behavior in a slightly different way. He internalizes the powerful emotions or "bad objects," including his mother's frustration, and invents his own punishments (*Tree* 43), even taking on the guilt of others. His "bad objects" are projected onto his invention of a moving fortress, or tank, described as a "monomaniacal" obsession (*Tree* 161). Marrying a woman, Phyllis Desmond, whom he does not love, in order to conceal her pregnancy by another man constitutes his rebellion. That this is a pseudo-independent act is suggested when he returns to live with his parents after the child dies in infancy and the woman leaves him for another man.

Dorothea, the daughter rejected by her mother, takes up the suffragist cause in opposition both to her parents and to her boyfriend Frank, a gunner. Like Michael, she too remains in the family household, and after Frank is killed in the war, her grief is poisoned with remorse over her independent stance and the time wasted: she thinks "I could bear it if I hadn't wasted the time we might have had together. All those years – like a fool – over that silly suffrage" (*Tree* 317).

Sinclair imbues with battle imagery the children's various rebellions and their struggles with the vortices that threaten to sweep away their individuality. Dorothea, for instance, likens the high voices of the suffragists to "battle-cries" (*Tree* 124). In having her do so, Sinclair suggests the continuity between the psychological battles fought on the home front and those fought in the trenches. The most striking representation of the pseudo-independent response to disrupted object relations occurs in Nicky and Michael's letters home from the battlefront. To his second wife, Veronica, Nicky writes that "when you're up first out of the trench and stand alone on the parapet, it's absolute happiness. And the charge is – well, it's simply heaven. It's as if you'd never really lived till then" (*Tree* 368). In his discussion of the war neuroses, Fairbairn would find this sort of attitude psychopathic, and even brother Michael suggests it as a form of sex-madness, although Nicky denies that it is (*Tree* 368). Nevertheless, after Nicky is killed, Michael enlists; Sinclair makes it quite clear that this is the death of his selfhood and soul (*Tree* 384). He too exalts in acting independently (*Tree* 394) and denies the horror, claiming that in battle "You get the same ecstasy, the same shock of recognition, and the same utter satisfaction [as] when you see a beautiful thing" (*Tree* 397). He too is killed in battle. That the family has not resolved the losses is suggested in that the parents keep Nicky's workshop and Nicky's and Michael's bedrooms intact long after their deaths (*Tree* 401). Sinclair projects another strategy for coping with loss through the other unwanted daughter in the novel, Veronica, who as a child had "no peace or quietness or security" (*Tree* 101–2). She develops a psychic, telepathic power, both taking on the suffering of others – in object relational terms introjecting their bad objects – and telepathically healing others. When Nicky embarks on his false marriage to Phyllis Desmond, for example, Veronica undergoes a spiritual death (*Tree* 188). She later marries Nicky and, at the moment of his death, has a vision of him as happy (*Tree* 370). Through her power, Veronica transcends the pain of death. The fantasy would appear to be of omnipotence. After Michael's death, Veronica alone has the power to connect with the two sons, making the mother Frances both cling to Veronica and feel envious of her: "It was as if Veronica held the souls of Michael and Nicholas in her hands. She offered her [Frances] the souls of her dead sons. She was the mediator between her and their dead souls" (*Tree* 402). Even this strategy proves illusory, however, as Frances laments that "I want their bodies with me just as they used to be" (*Tree* 403); Veronica can only stand "ashamed and beaten before this irreparable, mortal grief" (*Tree* 403). Furthermore, the novel closes with another separation, as the last victim, the youngest son John, is driven off to battle "and was gone" (*Tree* 408). The presence at this moment of Uncle Maurice, who offers "a crapulous salute" to John, serves to remind us of the horror of war, and the last scene offers no consolation or resolution of the tragedy, perhaps understandable on one level since the war was ongoing when Sinclair finished the work (*Tree* 408).

Woolf's *Mrs. Dalloway* is similarly preoccupied with unfulfilling attachments as well as partings and lost relationships. Despite the psychic maneuver of attempting to contain the harshest effects of war within Septimus Smith, early in the novel war loss enters the consciousness of Clarissa Dalloway:

> For it was the middle of June. The War was over, except for someone like Mrs Foxcroft at the Embassy last night eating her heart out because that nice boy was killed and now the manor house must go to a cousin; or Lady Bexborough who opened a bazaar, they said, with the telegram in her hand, John, her favourite, killed; but it was over, thank Heaven – over. (*Dalloway* 6)

Since the novel takes place five years after the end of the war, clearly mourning remains unresolved. That it does so for Clarissa herself surfaces soon after this reflection, as she remembers in detail her separation from Peter. She rationalizes that "she had to break with him or they would have been destroyed, both of them ruined, she was convinced; though she had borne about her for years like an arrow sticking through her heart the grief, the anguish," and she also still feels anger (*Dalloway* 9). Also early on, Woolf conveys Clarissa's struggle for selfhood in the face of fear: "She had a perpetual sense, as she watched the taxicabs, of being out, out, far out to sea and alone; she always had the feeling that it was very, very dangerous to live even one day" (*Dalloway* 9). She feels insecure to the extent that it is a battle for her to go out to the shops (*Dalloway* 28), and she lacks a solid sense of self in spite of a definite, well-defined social self: "she had the oddest sense of being herself invisible; unseen; unknown …" (*Dalloway* 11). The personal roots of this anxiety lie deeply buried in the text and suggest schizoid detachment and an avoidant attachment as a response to loss. Well on in the novel, we discover that Clarissa has witnessed her sister killed by a falling tree, an event described briefly and without emotion (*Dalloway* 70). Even more briefly (and avoidantly), Clarissa responds at her party to Mrs Hilbery's memory of her mother: "And really Clarissa's eyes filled with tears. Her mother, walking in a garden, but alas she [Clarissa] must go" (*Dalloway* 156).

Despite the brevity of reference on the conscious level, on the level of fantasy the impact of these unresolved separations and losses can be seen to be extensive, though diffuse. As did Sinclair, Woolf splits herself into several characters, in this case primarily Clarissa Dalloway, Peter Walsh, and Septimus Smith, enabling a variety of responses to loss, including primary maternal loss, to be envisioned. It could be argued that Clarissa's response consists, on the one hand, of creating an idealized good object in the figure of Sally Seton. Clarissa remembers her love for Sally in their youth, and claims that "Sally's power was amazing, her gift, her personality" (*Dalloway* 31). Her anger, on the other hand, is projected into the denigrated bad object of Miss Kilman, a mothering figure in her role as the embittered governess of Clarissa's daughter, Elizabeth. Clarissa herself has the insights that her hatred of this woman involves fantasy and that Kilman is one of many specters:

> For it was not her one hated but the idea of her, which undoubtedly had gathered in to itself a great deal that was not Miss Kilman; had become one of those spectres with which one battles in the night; one of those spectres who stand astride us and suck up half our lifeblood, dominators and tyrants; for no doubt with another throw of

the dice, had the black been uppermost and not the white, she would have loved Miss Kilman! But not in this world. No. (*Dalloway* 13)

Other highly dissociated maternal images emerge during Peter's dream on a park bench, otherwise a rather puzzling sequence. First he envisions a figure, perhaps derived from the gray nurse sitting beside him, that "had risen from the troubled sea – as a shape might be sucked up out of the waves to shower down from her magnificent hands, compassion, comprehension, absolution" (*Dalloway* 52–53). This image is not clearly maternal, but another one follows, of "the figure of the mother whose sons have been killed in the battles of the world" (*Dalloway* 53), once again making the link between maternal loss and war loss.

Although all three main characters are described as solitary travelers, as Peter is in the dream state, a generalized yearning for connection is expressed through linking devices – again highly dissociated – of the motor car and plane. If thought of as transitional objects between self and other in the Winnicottian sense, these devices are certainly not comforting, being mechanical and mysterious, suggesting instead a projection of bad objects.[7]

These three characters also exhibit pseudo-independence, particularly Peter. He has lived an extraordinarily independent life, now aged fifty-two without wife and children, although in love with the wife of an officer in India, and he feels intense freedom as he walks through London (*Dalloway* 48). Nevertheless, this behavior masks a deep need for dependence, still focused on Clarissa after all the years of their separation. He fantasizes about being "sufficient to himself; and yet nobody of course was more dependent upon others ... it had been his undoing" (*Dalloway* 140). At Clarissa's party, Sally realizes that Peter "was longing for" Clarissa "all the time" (*Dalloway* 170). Septimus manifests the most extreme independent, even avoidant behavior, yelling out at one point that he must get "away from people" (*Dalloway* 24), imagining that his marriage is over and that he is free (*Dalloway* 61), and generally moving in and out of complete psychotic isolation. However, he too has been deeply dependent, in this case on his officer Evans; he commits suicide only after he can no longer hear Evans's and others' messages from the dead, and fears being "alone for ever" (*Dalloway* 129), one might say in permanent schizoid withdrawal. Clarissa lives a life of enormous independence, partly because of her social standing, but also because her marriage lacks intimacy. Her infantile dependency needs emerge through her preoccupation with the memory of Sally and other early attachments.[8]

Pseudo-independence as a strategy does not succeed, suggested by references to war-related loss that keep erupting into the text, most dramatically through the discussion of Septimus's suicide at Clarissa's party. Similarly to Sinclair, Woolf explores mystical transcendence as an alternative strategy for negotiating loss and accomplishing mourning. Woolf, like Sinclair, clearly believed that "our psychic life is not a watertight compartment, but has porous walls, and is continually threatened with leakage and the flooding in of many streams," and Woolf voices this belief through Clarissa's transcendental theory, first alluded to near the outset of the novel (*Dalloway* 10). Peter later recollects that:

> Odd affinities she [Clarissa] had with people she had never spoken to, some woman in the street, some man behind a counter – even trees, or barns. It ended in a transcendental theory which, with her horror of death, allowed her to believe, or say that she believed (for all her scepticism), that since our apparitions, the part of us which appears, are so momentary compared with the other, unseen part of us which spreads wide, the unseen might survive, be recovered somehow attached to this person or that, or even haunting certain places, after death. Perhaps – perhaps. (*Dalloway* 136)

Although Septimus's and Clarissa's streams of consciousness have overlapped during the novel, particularly through repetition of the consoling funeral song lines from Shakespeare's *Cymbeline*, "Fear no more the heat o' the sun" (IV, ii, 258), at the party Clarissa definitely experiences an "odd affinity" with the departed Septimus. She psychically envisions the details of the death and understands its defiant and yet dependent nature: "Death was an attempt to communicate, people feeling the impossibility of reaching the centre which, mystically, evaded them; closeness drew apart; rapture faded; one was alone. There was an embrace in death" (*Dalloway* 163). Similarly to Sinclair's Veronica, Clarissa takes on or introjects death, referring to Septimus's as "her disaster – her disgrace" (*Dalloway* 164). Clearly Clarissa identifies profoundly with him: "She felt somehow very like him – the young man who had killed himself" (*Dalloway* 165); yet there is the sense that he has acted out her unacceptable impulse, which clarifies her statement that "She felt glad that he had done it; thrown it away while they went on living" (*Dalloway* 165). Septimus's act is probably cathartic and possibly reparative for both Clarissa and Woolf. At the close of the novel, Clarissa is for the moment a life-affirming presence, but she may also be a projection of Peter's unresolved dependency, as he feels both a "terror" and an "ecstasy" at her appearance (*Dalloway* 172). Nothing would appear to be settled between the two old friends. Thus, neither novel confronts war experience directly, as it occurred in the trenches, but the psychic subtexts of both novels suggest "so prying and insidious were the fingers of the European War" (*Dalloway* 77), as Woolf has a character claim, that it has a profound emotional impact. War revives relational anxiety from early disruptions in attachments, and attachments become further destabilized during and in the aftermath of war, sometimes traumatically so, as in the case of Septimus Smith. Both novelists attempt to exert control over this anxiety, through omniscient narration in the case of Sinclair, and linked interior monologues in the case of Woolf, neither novelist plunging into stream of consciousness. Frank Swinnerton commented on Sinclair's method of "selection" in the novel, giving the impression "that it has been coolly and scientifically planned, and as strictly and rigorously performed" (137). Woolf did not allow herself a less edited stream of consciousness of the kind she had read in Joyce's *Ulysses*. Nevertheless, in both novels powerful emotion, notably grief, erupts through form and perhaps even subverts it. Potential romance plots, for example, succumb to preoccupation with unresolved mourning. In Sinclair, romance falsely flourishes under changed conditions and the stress of war, as in Dorothea and Frank's abrupt decision to marry (*Tree* 308), but losses and complicated responses to them predominate. Romance exists only in the memory of a time before the war in *Mrs. Dalloway*. Although *The Tree of Heaven* seems to suggest the need for sacrifice in the service of the patriotic effort, which might suggest why the novel was highly popular in 1918 (Boll 90), I would argue that the novel tapped into the collective psyche on a deeper level in the potential reparative strategy that it offers through Veronica's mystical connection with the dead soldiers. Woolf's novel fantasizes a similar strategy, though neither novel shows these strategies as fully comforting or as resolving relational anxiety.

Perhaps this helps explain why both novelists after finishing these war novels immediately plunged into writing their most autobiographical novels; having engaged with the more immediate trauma of war, they felt compelled to explore further the traumas of childhood aroused by the war. Sinclair delved into writing *Mary Olivier*, a scathing indictment of her family life, during which time she isolated herself: in early 1918, she wrote to Violet Hunt, "I want to be in Yorkshire, all alone, writing my novel. But I'm very, very tired, & don't know how I'm going to do it" (as quoted in Raitt 24). In the fall of 1918 she recorded that she was succumbing to despair in the writing (Raitt 240). She chronicled repeated emotional conflicts, particularly with her controlling mother, as well as multiple deaths of family members and others and departures of lovers. Although she employed a limited stream of consciousness, comparable to Woolf's, aiming to show the developing consciousness of her protagonist, she seems to have been too obsessive about details and not selective enough or creative enough in renegotiating the relationships. To Ezra Pound, a sympathetic innovator, she angrily defended her inclusive objectivity: "Mary's mind is 'objective' to me. You may hate Mary's mind, you may damn & blast Mary's mind, but that is irrelevant. I've got it, & I've got the objects reflected in it" (as quoted in Raitt 240). Perhaps too many of those objects were reflected too subjectively, rendering the novel neither therapeutic nor aesthetically satisfying.

Virginia Woolf similarly directly embarked on writing her most autobiographical novel, but with differing results from Sinclair. On the day she finished *Mrs. Dalloway*, she was making cryptic notes about her next novel, which would be called *To the Lighthouse*. Although she initially wrote fluently "after that battle Jacob's Room, that agony" (*Diary* III 59), she suffered a "nervous breakdown in miniature" during one month while writing it, and experienced depression as she completed the first draft (Lee 477–78). One of her anxieties was about how to avoid sentimentality by controlling emotions through form: to "split up emotions more completely" (as quoted in Lee 476). This she achieved by gaining perspective on her parents, fictionalized as Mr and Mrs Ramsay, through employing the perspective of the outsider, the painter, Lily Briscoe. This is signified by the symbol of "The Window," used as the title of the first section of this elegy. Mr and Mrs Ramsay are held up for scrutiny in all their complexity, with flaws as well as strengths, and by this Woolf honors the memory of her parents, as Lily attempts to "compose" Mrs Ramsay in her painting. In the second and briefest section, "Time Passes," Woolf contains losses during the war in parentheses, including Mrs Ramsay's death, daughter Prue's death through "illness connected with childbirth," and son Andrew's death in the war (*Lighthouse* 140, 144, 145), a typical avoidant strategy used here with powerful impact. Another avoidant strategy also used effectively is to displace the sense of loss onto the house by depicting its decaying and the inroads of nature on it: "The house was left; the house was deserted. It was left like a shell on a sandhill to fill with dry salt grains now that life had left it" (*Lighthouse* 149). Further, Woolf diffuses the creative impulse onto several characters, including Mrs Ramsay, Augustus Carmichael, and most significantly Lily Briscoe, who continues her creative quest in the final section, completing her painting just as Mr Ramsay reaches the lighthouse in a moment of mystical synchronicity. A numinous connection between Lily and Mrs Ramsay in the first section, in which Lily perceives Mrs Ramsay as "a triangular purple shape" and then Mrs Ramsay independently thinks of herself as "a wedge-shaped core of darkness" (*Lighthouse* 58, 69) is complemented by Lily's mystical vision in the third section, of Mrs Ramsay as "an odd-shaped triangular shadow over the step" (*Lighthouse* 218). Mrs Ramsay seems to be a not quite invisible presence that has persisted beyond death. Many possibilities have been suggested for the final vertical line that Lily draws in her painting, but if it represents Mr Ramsay, then perhaps Lily has "composed" him as well. Regardless of the aesthetic completeness of her painting, Lily remains alone, not having resolved relational issues, or perhaps in a more positive light, independent. After completing the novel, Woolf gained independence from her mother's ghost: "when [*To the Lighthouse*] was written, I ceased to be obsessed by my mother. I no longer hear her voice; I do not see her" (*Moments* 81). Woolf wrote those words as another war approached, and she again felt rising anxiety. Again she turned to re-visioning her past in "A Sketch of the Past," a more candid elaboration of her earliest years than the 1907–8 "Reminiscences" had been. She came to terms with writing this rather than "do[ing] something that will be useful if war comes," claiming "I feel that by writing I am doing what is far more necessary than anything else" (*Moments* 84).

Despite Woolf's and Sinclair's courageous, imaginative, and reparative response to trauma, involving a mystical dimension, which they explored with profound insight through writing "more necessary than anything else," ultimately both women succumbed to genetically conditioned illness. From the mid-1920s on Sinclair showed signs of the onset of Parkinson's disease, and after 1929 according to her niece "it was all silence as far as [Sinclair] was concerned" (Raitt 263). Woolf's decision to take her own life in 1941 at age sixty cannot be explained away, but she definitely believed "It is this madness," "this disease," the manic depression that she had struggled with in the past, which she feared was overtaking her again, as she wrote in her suicide note to her husband Leonard (Lee 760). Nevertheless, both of these writers had challenged the avoidant-resistant pattern of attachment and achieved intimacy, however compromised or fleeting. With Florence Bartrop, Sinclair's house-keeper and companion since 1919, and latterly her nurse, Sinclair, "was finally, even against her will, in the kind of intimate relationship that she had previously avoided or feared," according to biographer Suzanne Raitt (264). In her last letters to husband Leonard, Woolf repeatedly assured him that they couldn't have been happier together: "All I want to say is that until this disease came on we were perfectly happy. It was all due to you. No one could have been so good as you have been. From the very first day till now" (as quoted in Lee 760).

6
Purgatorial Passions: "The Ghost" (aka Wilfred Owen) in Owen's Poetry

> "They call me The Ghost, (which is a point in favour of their latent imaginations)."
> Wilfred Owen, Letter to his mother,
> 28 September 1918 (*Letters* 579)

A young man writhes on a humble cot, the darkness lying heavy, smothering him. In his mind's eye a horse-drawn cart rumbles along a broken road. A heavy object strikes one horse and both bolt. Two figures catapult from the cart, one falling beneath the rear wheel, blood smearing the face. The wheel spins, inducing nausea in the sleeper, and then it is a bicycle wheel, dangling and bent, and seen from muddy clay. A fresh-dug grave sinks into the mud and the young man stands at its edge, scorning and mocking, and stabbing at the putrid air, as the words of his creed hang in it. As he falls forward, gray Gorgon-faced despair clutches at him ... The sleeper cries out and sits bolt upright. His heart runs fast and irregularly, his dark eyes shrink back in his head. Shadowy phantasms swirl around him, bearing crosses, fingering his hair. He screams but nothing comes out and he chokes. His arm shoots up to ward off these ghosts, but he is thrown off balance, and falls to the floor, seeing nothing.

The young man is Wilfred Owen, the year 1913 – not during the war, but before it. Owen experienced the sort of "phantasies" or "horrors" here imagined, perhaps drawing on a bicycle accident he had and a local horse-cart tragedy (Hibberd 88, 91), after he broke with his evangelical faith, left his post at Dunsden as a minister's assistant, and, at the age of nineteen, returned home to his mother, where he succumbed to serious pulmonary illness. Biographer Dominic Hibberd claims that "leaving Dunsden in February 1913 was by far the most traumatic event in Wilfred's life until he saw the trenches in 1917" (99). What was the source of these "purgatorial shadows" that plagued him and about which he wrote to give him "ease," as he put it in his first consciously therapeutic poem, "On My Songs"? To answer this we need to probe his sexuality, as well as his early attachment pattern.

Owen is the only writer in *Mourning and Mysticism* who was a combatant on the front lines. However, he was not just a combatant, although he shared the fate of so many, nor was he simply a war poet. For many generations now, Wilfred Owen has been held up as *the* archetypal war poet, a compelling protester against the inhumanity of the Great War and civilian delusions about it, who at the age of twenty-five was tragically cut down a week before the Armistice was signed. In his famous "Preface" to his poems, Owen assigned himself the role of witness to "the pity of War," providing a warning of war's truth for the next generation (*Complete* 535); to a large extent he succeeded since our perception of the First World War, and perhaps of all war, has been indelibly impressed by his truth. Owing to his success, his poems have typically been read as personal only insofar as they convey experience directly related to the battlefront.

However, Owen was a poet of protest in quite another way as well, as a gay poet whose sexual preference was considered a crime by his society. Only latterly and gradually has the "Owen industry," concerned to protect the war hero poet's reputation, allowed him to emerge from the closet. In 1975, Paul Fussell broached the issue of Owen's sexuality but claimed that his was a "chaste," "temporary homosexuality" (272). Dominic Hibberd, in his early work circumspect about Owen's sexuality, has come not only to demonstrate the evidence of Owen's homosexuality, but to treat his sexual preference without prejudice. Nevertheless, in Hibberd's most recent biography of Owen, *Wilfred Owen: A New Biography*, he rather naïvely asserts that the "strong homoerotic impulse" in Owen's writing was "something that he seems to have recognized and accepted without much difficulty" (xix), and thus fails to probe the full implications for Owen's poetry. Owen's sexual orientation does matter because recognition that Owen needed to express his homosexual sensibility covertly reveals a whole "other" dimension to his poetry, as well as a more complex truth about his response to war and about the nature of relations between men in war in general. Owen's situation and his poetry remind us of the toll war exacts on "outsiders," those constructed as not fitting into a threatened society's narrowing norms, most pertinently gay soldiers whose sexual orientation increases their vulnerability in an institution like the military.

Given the evidence from Owen's biography and from the poems, I would argue that his "homoerotic impulse" caused him enormous anxiety, reflected in his poetry through obsessive "other-worldly" imagery of being haunted by ghosts and phantasms as well as in his development of pararhyme. This technique employs imperfect rhymes to create a jarring effect and, I would further argue, is indicative of anxiety-producing cognitive dissonance. Owen, nicknamed "The Ghost," engages the spectral as a means of managing anxiety in poems such as "Purgatorial Passions" and "Shadwell Stair." His poetic Fragments 88 and 117 represent first attempts at pararhyme which reveal cognitive dissonance. However, Owen did not fully utilize the technique until his war experience exacerbated earlier sexual anxiety. Oddly, Owen's most famous poem, "Strange Meeting," best illustrates how recognition of the role of both pararhyme and ghosts can open up new understanding of his response to war, since the ghostly other in the poem can be read as a projection of Owen's homosexual self that could not be acknowledged openly.

British object relations theory, in combination with attachment theory, can provide striking insight into how Owen negotiated relations with others, the roles poetry played for him, and his use of apparitions in that poetry. These theories apply well to Owen's situation for several reasons. Object relations theory differs from orthodox Freudian theory in shifting the focus from the father to the mother–infant dyad, particularly apropos in Owen's case since his mother played unusually significant roles in his life. Object relations theory supplies the most convincing psychoanalytic account of the origins and nature of creativity, which illuminates much about a creator like Owen. Attachment theory focuses on patterns of attachment and demonstrates that attachment to the original caretaker conditions, and to a certain extent, predicts later attachment patterns. Owen's pattern of attachment is quite distinct and consistent over time. Finally, both theories were developed specifically to understand and deal with men in Owen's situation, under duress in war and experiencing shell shock, as Owen himself did in 1917 (Hibberd 180, 340).

Owen's mother (Illustration 6.1) dominated Owen's development not only as a person but as a poet, since she served as both his Muse and as the original (and in some cases sole) audience for his poems, which he would include in letters to her. An understanding of his relations with her reveals much about the strategies he employs in his poetry because he certainly could not openly acknowledge to her his growing awareness of his sexual orientation. There can be no doubt that Owen

Illustration 6.1 Wilfred Owen (center) with his mother Susan, two of his siblings, and a nanny. Reprinted by permission of the Wilfred Owen Collection, English Faculty Library, Oxford

had an unusually close and yet conflicted relationship with his mother Susan; he was a self-proclaimed mother's boy (Hibberd 23), who several times in his extensive correspondence of over five hundred and fifty letters to his mother referred to his "psychological erraticness" [*sic*] or eccentricity, without specifying exactly what that was (*Letters*, 404, 150, 282). As Hibberd details, Susan had unusually high expectations for her eldest son, born on 18 March, the day after her birth date. Although of middle-class stock and married to a railway clerk, she referred to Wilfred at birth as "*Sir* Wilfred Edward Salter-Owen" (Hibberd 1), and she smothered him with affection (Hibberd 23); yet in his early years she also became preoccupied concurrently with several house moves and difficult pregnancies, as well as ill health stemming from these trials (Hibberd 23).

Wilfred for his part appears to have held several sharply incongruous attitudes towards her throughout his life. On the one hand, he idealized his mother, lavishing her with superlatives, such as "the gentlest of mothers" (*Letters* 376). He wrote passionately to her, treating her like a lover, as in a 1915 letter (at age twenty-one) when he claims to her that "[t]here is no other, with enough sympathy or understanding," or a few years later when he asserts, "not everybody of my years can boast, (or as many would say, confess) that their Mother is their absolute in their affections. But I believe it will always be so with me, always" (*Letters* 322, 569). On the other hand, he could be harshly critical and manipulative of her. On one occasion he summarized his attacks, writing "when I recall the past, I often feel pretty sick at all the abominable rudenesses, ingratitudes, huffs, grumps, snaps, and sulks levelled at you" (*Letters* 137). Owen detailed even his most minor ailments to Susan, seeking her solicitude, at times self-consciously: from Bordeaux he wrote, "[f]orgive me for pitying myself so loudly at you. It is simply to inveigle *tendernesses* from you and Home" (*Letters* 213). When he suffered more serious illness, he expected, and typically gained, his mother's undivided devotion. The most striking example occurred just after Owen, aged nineteen, returned home from Dunsden, as depicted at the outset of this chapter, but two points should be emphasized: First, that he had been fulfilling his evangelical mother's goal for him of embarking on a career in the church, and had lost his faith; second, that he suffered psychosomatic symptoms, including "phantasies" or "phantasms" (Hibberd 99), accompanying what was apparently pneumonia. This nervous collapse brought to a head bouts of despondency (Hibberd 99) he had experienced over several years, as well as dreams and fantasies of violence and illicit desire (Hibberd 67, 81), suggesting that by this time, as in a typical avoidant response to attachment, Wilfred had internalized conflict to a striking degree. The resistant component of his response is illustrated by his continued preoccupation for years afterwards with his mother's nursing him back to health on this occasion. A year later he wrote, "It must be getting near the date of my pneumonia-time. I have only to think of you as you were then to me, and I immediately get into a kind of sweet anguish, an ecstasy, (very difficult to describe, but something like the effect of a great music)" (*Letters* 322; cf. also 381). From an early age, Wilfred had also been preoccupied with the conduct of his younger siblings, and he continued to discuss their misdemeanors in letters to his mother; this attitude gained him another nickname, "The Judge" (*Letters* 178).

Even with his siblings, however, the avoidant pattern seemed to dominate. His brother Harold recollected that Wilfred was aloof and insensitive, and as Hibberd puts it, "at worst downright cruel, as when he shut the children up in dark cupboards or pretended to be a ghost to frighten them" (24). According to Hibberd, Harold was later puzzled that the famous poet of pity should have been so pitiless at home (24). Instances of Wilfred's aloofness pepper Hibberd's biography and Owen's letters. One of the great ironies of Owen's life is that the quintessential First World War poet actually avoided signing up for the war for over a year, even though he was living at the time in the war's battleground, France. In the midst of initial widespread patriotism about the war, his attitude seems particularly callous. On 28 August 1914 he wrote to Susan that, "I feel my own life all the more precious and more dear in the presence of this deflowering of Europe," and that "the guns will effect a little useful weeding" (*Letters* 282).

What is remarkable, however, is the degree of insight that Owen developed about his ambivalent, enmeshed relationship with his mother. In the last year of his life he admonished his mother not to cosset and deny his younger brother Colin, as he had been denied. Colin, now aged seventeen, was presumably smitten with love. Note how Wilfred's words are easily translatable into object-relational terms:

> A fever more scarlet is already inculcating in [Colin's] veins ... In the strangeness of his fever he will push you from him; and all your thought will not be able to quench his thirst. Deny him not the thing he craves, as I was denied, for I was denied, and the appeal which, if you watched, you must have seen in my eyes, you ignored. And because I knew you resisted, I stretched no hand to take the Doll that would have made my contentment.
> And my nights were terrible to be borne.
> For I was a child, and you laughed at my Toys, so that I loved them beyond measure; but never looked at them. (*Letters* 536)

Here, early loves are figured as "Dolls" or "Toys," as though they were transitional objects that would have become substitutes for the mother, except that she resisted their supplanting her; the child Wilfred consequently "never looked at them" (again an avoidant response) and yet "loved them beyond measure," a seeming contradiction unless Owen is implying that love for them was confined to his inner world.

Evidence from Owen's poetry suggests that he discovered poetic form itself could serve as a transitional object, an intermediate area of experience, where he could express those passions and other unacceptable feelings that could not be acted upon. He wrote the first of these therapeutic poems, "On My Songs," at the height of his crisis of faith in

1913, when he knew that leaving Dunsden "will mean a terrible bust-up" and when he recorded the "Pressure of Problems pushing me to seek relief in unstopping my mouth" (*Letters* 172). In the poem he describes the psychological process that led to his writing poetry. Poems by "unseen poets" initially serve as his "own soul's cry; easing the flow / Of my dumb tears with language sweet as sobs" (*Complete* 113, lines 4–5). However, at times these poetic containers hold nothing for Owen, perhaps because their emotion has been transformed into cognition, or in Owen's term "hoards of thought":

> Yet there are days when all these hoards of thought
> Hold nothing for me. Not one verse that throbs
> Throbs with my heart, or as my brain is fraught
>
> 'Tis then I voice mine own weird reveries:
> Low croonings of a motherless child, in gloom
> Singing his frightened self to sleep, are these.
> (*Complete* 113, lines 6–11)

His own "weird reveries" result from another kind of denial – abandonment – and an attempt to comfort his frightened self, or control anxiety.

The dynamics of his poetic expression are complicated because he oscillates between fear of abandonment by, and fusion with, his mother, who is symbolically figured as his Muse, and is literally his audience as well. In his first extant poem "To Poesy" (c.1909–10), for instance, Owen adopts the traditional supplicating attitude towards his Muse, and demands "help" and "pity" from her, but he also makes her his love, and in the conclusion reveals his desire that it be a secret love: "Loath would I be to show my exceeding bliss / Even to closest friends. But all unseen, / And far from men's gaze would I feel thy kiss; / No witness save the speechless star-lamps keen / When thou stoop'st over me" (*Complete* 5–6, lines 111–15). Her stooping over the poet suggests a maternal solicitude, and combined with the secrecy, infers a fantasy to possess the mother as Muse.

The mother's role as both Muse and audience requires not only that desires towards her be kept secret, but also that other intense, unacceptable feelings be coded; and in fact secrecy runs as a dominant motif throughout Owen's poetry. Object relations theorist Masud Khan has shown that secrets can act as potential spaces where "larval psychic experiences" can be sustained that cannot yet be actualized (261). In "The One Remains," for instance, Owen's speaker obsessively pores over "the secret traces / Left in my heart, of countenances seen, /And lost as soon as seen," his ultimate goal being to find "All beauty, once for ever, in one face" (*Complete* 103, lines 4–6, 14).

As in this poem, secrecy is most often invoked regarding homoerotic attraction, and Owen discovered that tropes of ghosts and spirits were the most effective and powerful means of cloaking his intense feelings and impulses arising from his sexuality.[1] Ghosts after all exist in a transitional or purgatorial space, neither here nor there, known or unknown. Since their former identities are uncertain, they possess a certain freedom to carry out acts that they couldn't or were prevented from carrying out during their lives. Paradoxically, however, they are also frequently chained by obsession, for instance over guilt and need for reparation. "The Peril of Love" reveals this dual role of spirits. The sonnet compares "men who call on spirits ... And woo successfully the coy Unseen" for amusement – later to become possessed by "dark spirits" that poison "love of life and kind" – with dalliance in love which finds too late "love's grave significance" (*Complete* 110, lines 1, 2, 4, 7, 10). This perilous love, described as "[a] fierce infatuation" that "[e]xhausts my faculties," implies a driven, perhaps destructive hypersexuality, an image reinforced by the final lines: "I am a prey / Of impulse, the marasmus of decay" (*Complete* 110, lines 13–14).

In "Shadwell Stair," drafted in early 1918, the speaker becomes the ghost, a ghost that is ambiguously both "shadow" and possessed of "flesh both firm and cool, / And eyes tumultuous" (*Complete* 183, lines 5–6). However, the realistically depicted East London dockland setting (that Owen had visited in 1915; Hibberd 301), where the ghost walks, watching "always," along with the closing line, "I with another ghost am lain," leave little doubt that this ghost has a sexual encounter, although the gender of the partners is left ambiguous (*Complete* 183, lines 10, 16). Editor Jon Stallworthy suggests that the ghost may be the female prostitute of Oscar Wilde's "Impression du Matin," since Owen is imitating that poem, but Hibberd points out that the French translation by Owen's homosexual friend (and possibly his lover) Charles Scott Moncrieff "identifies the first ghost as 'petit fantassin' (little infantryman), presumably 'little Owen' himself." (Owen was only five foot, five inches tall. Hibberd 314–15, 404, note 27.) A number of other poems, such as "Six O'Clock in Princes Street," similarly use ghosts to express various feelings about homoeroticism, including guilt, as in "Purgatorial Passions" and related Fragments (see Fragments 70–73). "Purgatorial Passions" depicts skeletal creatures whose "Wrong ... wrung their fingers / like a rack," whereas Fragment 73 begins "I know that I have paid for every drop of pleasure, / much / Paid ... in advance with ... anxiety / Paid ... afterward, with anguish; double measure" (*Complete* 455, 458).

Owen joined the military as an officer in the Artists' Rifles on 21 October 1915 (Illustration 6.2). While this move obviously brought him into much closer intimacy with men and, through his meeting at Craiglockhart in 1917 with homosexual poet Siegfried Sassoon and others, expanded his gay horizons,[2] it also intensified his conflicted feelings for his now mostly absent mother. Owen's war poetry is energized by his ambivalence towards her, as well as by his intense attraction to men and the restraints against acting on that attraction – particularly regarding those serving under him – which intensify his helplessness at witnessing their slaughter. Ghosts continue to serve as masks for expressing these feelings, as is well illustrated in "The Kind Ghosts." In the poem, "ghosts" becomes the collective term for "the boys on boys" whose

Illustration 6.2 Wilfred Owen in his officer's uniform. Reprinted by permission of the Wilfred Owen Collection, English Faculty Library, Oxford

sacrifice is ignored by Mother England (*Complete* 181, line 3). Owen's early dynamic with his mother, particularly his fear of abandonment, that had also been expressed in "On My Songs," provides the emotional charge behind his critique of Mother England, who is not "disturbed, or grieved at all" because the kind, considerate "shades keep down," not haunting her with their grievances (*Complete* 181, lines 7, 12). That his mother in effect haunts this poem about Mother England may not be as far-fetched as it might initially seem. In a pre-war letter to his mother, Owen asserted that in the household Susan "reigneth ... as a Queen" (*Letters* 206), and in the midst of battle wrote to his mother that the only "object for carrying on" that he could cling to was not his Motherland, but his mother (*Letters* 449).

Nevertheless, Owen transformed his self-pity, used to inveigle attention and pity from his mother, to pity for his "boys," in effect adopting the sort of mothering role that his mother had played for him. The transformation is suggested in Owen's description in a 1918 letter to his mother of nursing a dying soldier, "whose blood lies yet crimson on my shoulder where his head was – and where so lately yours was" (*Letters* 580). Yet pity is not quite the same thing as empathizing with someone, since it can imply an unequal stance, one of looking down on the object of pity, and can be tinged with sentimentality, which may well be what W. B. Yeats objected to when he excluded Owen's poems from *The Oxford Book of Modern Verse*, claiming that "passive suffering is not a theme for poetry" (xxxiv; cf. Pittock 205). Owen's stance is captured in his famous Preface where he asserted that "The poetry is in the Pity" (*Complete* 535). Also in the 1918 letter mentioned above, just prior to describing his nursing role Owen asserts that he shot a man, took the rest of the enemy "with a smile," and had entered the war to help his own boys "by watching their sufferings that I may speak of them" (*Letters* 580). These actions and attitudes suggest oscillation between a comforting, pitying, mothering role and a certain detachment, characteristic of the avoidant response to attachment.[3]

Just as Owen discovered prior to the war that ghosts could function as a trope of indeterminacy, in an intermediate space that enabled him to express homoerotic desire, he also discovered before the war a poetic technique, pararhyme, which creates a space or a gap between sounds that do not rhyme perfectly. Julian Wolfreys and others have argued that haunting causes a disruption, that the phantasm represents a gap (6). Pararhyme would thus seem to create an effect of haunting, arising from cognitive dissonance initially in his relation with his mother and subsequently through his homosexual orientation. In an essay on another technically innovative poet Gerard Manley Hopkins, Emilie Sobel reviews the object relations findings which suggest that children use sounds as transitional objects and that babbling represents the earliest aesthetic use of language because it is not goal-directed but actually attempts to reinstate experience (429). Creative types frequently possess considerable capacity to access and make use of this pre-symbolic phase of development. Sobel claims that, "When used by the mature poet, the medium of sound breaks through the symbolic function of language, yet still, within the modality of words, *reinstates* rather than *represents* an experience" (430). That Owen took pleasure in accessing this level of language is suggested in several letters to his mother in which he writes a kind of phonetic gibberish, in one instance supposedly replicating Hebrew: "My strethfaileth me cos miniquity'nbones acusume" (*Letters* 182; cf. also 184). More importantly, once he developed his new method of pararhyme, he defended it like "a child insisting, half humorously and half defiantly" that he was in the right, according to Frank Nicholson (as quoted in Hibberd 273), perhaps suggesting how deeply he felt its potential to capture or "re-model reality."

That defiance emanates from Owen's first sustained use of pararhyme, in poem 88, "Has your soul sipped," written in the summer of 1917. Shockingly, the poem expresses erotic desire for a murdered boy's bloody smile. Two rhetorical questions immediately engage readers: "Has your soul sipped / Of the sweetness of all sweets? / Has it well supped / But yet hungers and sweats?" (*Complete* 90, lines 1–4). Owen challenges us to remember a situation similar to the speaker's, when he thought he had experienced the essence of sweetness, but still hungered for more. The gaps created by the falling assonant sounds in sipped / supped and sweets / sweats reinstate this feeling of being haunted by desire. He then unfolds an incident which satisfied that desire: "I have been a witness / Of a strange sweetness, / All fancy surpassing / Past all supposing" (*Complete* 90, lines 5–8). The "strange sweetness" which he has "witnessed" – that word characteristic of Owen's avoidant detachment – is sweeter than all of life's experiences, including love; death "To one in dearth / Of life and its laughter"; the victor's "proud wound"; and even "the last end / Of all wars" (*Complete* 90, lines 25–26, 27, 29–30). Six stanzas of comparisons serve to build suspense about just what this superlative sweetness could be, until it is revealed as a smile at the beginning of the third to last stanza. Readers' expectations that it will be a smile of quintessential friendship or precious love are undermined at the end of this stanza when we read that the smile is "On a boy's murdered mouth" (*Complete* 91, line 38).

The final two stanzas deliberately shock with graphic details about the boy's condition, climaxing in the strange mixture of repulsion and attraction expressed in the final quatrain: "But with the bitter blood / And the death-smell / All his life's sweetness bled / Into a smile" (*Complete* 91, lines 43–46). Dissonance between detachment and desire, violence and love is captured on a visceral level by consistently falling assonant sounds in the pararhymes, for example, smell / smile. These suggest a falling away from perfect desire, from "the sweetness of all sweets," into a conventionally unacceptable and thus conflicted desire that haunts the speaker and the poem (*Complete* 90, line 2).

A strange sweetness is also expressed in Owen's most commented-on war poem "Strange Meeting," dating from early in 1918. Owen brings together ghosts and pararhyme to capture feelings around a fantasy of reunion with the other, the enemy and yet "my friend." The poem uses the device of prosopopeia, making an apostrophe to this unnamed soldier, yet this is done in an interiorized, transitional space, a dreamscape where Owen can safely renegotiate relations between spirit soldiers. Although identified as "Hell," there is nothing of its conventional depiction: "no blood" reaches this place and "no guns thumped" (*Complete* 148, lines 12–13). Instead, it more closely resembles a purgatory, a place where ghost soldiers can express intimate feelings about potential fates and where, at the denouement, after reparation and reconciliation occur, sleep is possible. There is neither animosity nor evil, but rather "piteous recognition"; strikingly, the speaker recognizes the other by his "dead smile" (*Complete*, 148, lines 7, 10); it is tempting to think of this fellow as resembling the murdered boy of "Has your soul sipped?"

In another sense, Owen may be projecting two aspects of himself: the avoidant, detached self, in the speaker, who claims "here is no cause to mourn" (*Complete* 148, line 14), and the more emotionally engaged homosexual self, whose impulse is towards identification and intimacy with the initial speaker. The second self is the one who says, "Whatever hope is yours / Was my life also," and in articulating the numerous losses of their unfulfilled lives may allude, albeit circumspectly, to loss of opportunity to tell the truth about his sexual orientation (*Complete* 148, lines 16–17). He states, "For by my glee might many men have laughed, / And of my weeping something had been left, / Which must die now. I mean the truth untold, / The pity of war, the pity war distilled" (*Complete* 148, lines 22–25). Most obviously, these lines evoke the loss of opportunity to tell of the piteous nature of war, but the secret might also be about his emotional impact on other men, about intimacy that wartime conditions brought about. Possibly this homosexual self could not be openly expressed, and so, in this mental landscape at least, was killed off. Nevertheless, after acknowledging the aggression inflicted on him, this second self invites his attacker to "sleep now," to reconcile, an offer that interestingly we do not know whether the initial speaker accepts. Once again, pararhyme supports on a visceral level a haunting effect, in this case arising from the feeling of one man, or one self, being in conflict with or haunted by another. A number of the assonant sounds fall in the pararhymes, and one or two, such as groined / groaned, and spoiled / spilled might even be sexually suggestive (*Complete* 148, lines 3, 4, 26, 27). While I would not want to reduce solely to the personal this powerfully poignant poem that confronts the consequences of killing in war, I would suggest that its emotional energy derives from the attraction and identification between the two men, and from the fantasy of their reconciliation.

"The key to many of my poems" Owen claimed he left to his cousin, Leslie Gunston (*Letters* 508); unfortunately, because of Gunston's reticence and probably Owen's brother Harold's censorship, we do not know exactly what that key was. I would suggest that Owen left just as significant a key when he revealed to his mother that his officers "call me The Ghost," and added in parentheses "(which is a point in favour of their latent imaginations)" (*Letters* 579). Hibberd omits the parenthetical remark, speculating that the nickname captured Owen's rising from the dead after a shell exploded very near him and he was blown into the air, rendered unconscious, and then observed pieces of his brother-officer Gaukroger "in various places round about" (Hibberd 240, 340). The nickname may refer to this shell shock trauma that caused him to be removed from the front, but as Hibberd admits, its source is obscure. In my mind, Owen is parenthetically and covertly suggesting that the men possessed some latent awareness of his sexual preference. As The Ghost, Owen haunted his own poems, refiguring purgatorial passions and relationships in secrecy and thus safety, but also possessed by guilt and the other oscillating emotions those encounters provoked. Given Owen's avoidant-resistant pattern of attachment, initiated through his interrelations with his mother, poetic form provided just the intermediate space between reality and fantasy that Owen needed. In poems he could enact internalized conflict, especially regarding homoerotic desire and the constraints on that desire, including his mother's moral stance and social propriety. In pararhyme, Owen intuited another means of opening a haunted space where conflicted feeling could be reinstated on a visceral level. The stress of war on the one hand exacerbated separation and sexual anxiety; when he succumbed to shell shock, his therapist

Dr Arthur Brock wrote of his having "faced the phantoms of the mind" (as quoted in Hibberd, 254–55); on the other hand, the pressure of emotion found a voice in the heightened intensity of his war poems like "Strange Meeting." If we recognize the strategies Owen developed in struggling to express the love that dares not speak its name, his poems gain a complexity and dynamism otherwise lost; he bears witness to truth not only of the war on the battlefront, but also of a war within.

Ironically, as a conflicted ghost, Owen continued to haunt the traumatized survivors of the war, notably Edmund Blunden. Although Blunden had never met Owen in the flesh, Owen entered his consciousness, inspiring Blunden to raise the alarm about the possibility of a second world war (Barlow). In "To Wilfred Owen (killed in action November 4th, 1918)," Blunden summoned Owen's spirit in poetic conversation, asking "Where does your spirit walk, kind soldier, now, / In this deep winter, bright with ready guns? / And have you found new poems in this war?" (as quoted in Barlow).

7
"Misty-schism": The Psychological Roots of Aldous Huxley's Mystical Modernism

A tall, lanky teenager sits in his room alone, hunched over in darkness, a darkness new to him, a darkness isolating him more than he has ever been isolated before. Slowly, he feels for the keys on a portable typewriter and presses one, then another.

So began Aldous Huxley's career as a writer, when at age sixteen he succumbed to an eye infection which totally blinded him for eighteen months. During that time he wrote an eighty thousand word novel (Bedford Vol. 1, 35). He would regain partial sight, but the consequences of this episode were far-reaching.[1] However, this trauma was not the first to darken his early years. When he was fourteen in 1908 his mother died suddenly of cancer. A third major trauma would follow in August of 1914, when Aldous's older brother Trevenon committed suicide. These events have long been seen as important by Huxley biographers, but their full significance in Huxley's life and writing has not been probed using the insights of theories particularly concerned with the impact of traumatic loss on attachment and creativity. Huxley himself said that, "I don't believe for a moment that creativity is a neurotic symptom. On the contrary, the neurotic who succeeds as an artist has had to overcome a tremendous handicap. He creates in spite of his neurosis, not because of it" (Fraser 5). This statement certainly applies to Huxley, since he overcame tremendous obstacles, scrutinizing them courageously in his fiction and transforming them into strengths, into opportunities for growth in self-awareness. Drawing on object relations and attachment theory, I will demonstrate that Huxley developed an avoidant-resistant pattern of attachment in childhood, which persisted into adulthood. This pattern shaped his creativity and helps explain his fascination with and ambivalence towards mysticism. In his earlier fiction he repeatedly portrays aloof, rebellious protagonists and satirizes mystical pursuits. Most famously, in *Brave New World* (1932) he constructs attachments, particularly to the mother, as vulgar and makes a mockery of spiritual communion in orgy-porgies. However, from 1933 to 1935 his avoidant-resistant patterning, manifested in a detached cynical outlook, began to work against him.

Huxley experienced a major physical, emotional, and spiritual crisis, brought on by a number of factors, including the death of his father in 1933 and his increasing depression and anxiety about the threat of war, which reactivated earlier responses to trauma, a dynamic that biographers have not analyzed. He worked through his depression and trauma by renegotiating early upheaval in *Eyeless in Gaza* (1936), a nonlinear autobiographical novel that he claimed "show[ed] the pressure of the past on the present" (Fraser 9). As did Huxley, his protagonist Anthony Beavis embraces mysticism and spiritually-engaged pacifism as a means of countering avoidance and achieving unity and peace. Ironically, Huxley employed modernist technique to compellingly expose and illuminate his emotional and spiritual growth. He articulated his new position in his best-selling non-fiction book *Ends and Means*, where he advocated pacifism and non-attachment. Even after the outbreak of the Second World War he continued to hold uncompromising spiritually-based pacifist views. During the conflict he again re-visioned his relationships through fiction in *Time Must Have a Stop* (1944). This novel broaches the possibility of positive change in attachment patterning by showing the protagonist, Sebastian Barnack, becoming an engaged spiritual seeker at an earlier age than John Beavis (father of Anthony mentioned above). Although technically more conservative than *Eyeless*, *Time Must Have a Stop* is more daring in its subject matter in that it explores the connections between spiritualism and mysticism, going so far as to portray a character in the afterlife attempting to communicate with those left behind. Huxley himself continued as an engaged spiritual seeker, who advocated non-attachment but also embraced the importance of human connectedness, as in his novel *Island*. Although Huxley was still searching for insight and access to childhood memories, as evidenced in a novel he was writing when he died, through reparative work in fiction he achieved a rare degree of self-awareness and integration.

Aldous Huxley, the third child of three sons and a daughter, was born in 1894 into a distinguished family on both sides, and this heritage had both advantages and disadvantages. His grandfather was Thomas Henry Huxley, the social Darwinist, and his mother, Julia, was the granddaughter of Dr Thomas Arnold of Rugby, niece of the poet and essayist Matthew Arnold and sister of novelist Mrs Humphrey Ward.

This pedigree provided many opportunities, one, for instance in due course giving him entrée to the intelligentsia, but Huxley also inherited the burden of expectation (exacerbated because his father, Leonard, had not lived up to Huxley standards), and of depression. Thomas Henry, considered "a god in the family" (Dunaway 9), was prone to depression, and Aldous's brother Julian suffered multiple nervous breakdowns (Dunaway 9) and was called "a manic-depressive by temperament" by his son Francis (Dunaway 11). Aldous's depressions were less severe, but he suffered from a more chronic melancholy (Dunaway 10). Various relatives observed that from an early age he was moody and had a temper (Bedford Vol. 1, 6). Perhaps revealingly, his nickname was Ogie, a diminutive of ogre (Bedford Vol. 1, 2). He also recalled with "horrible vividness" being mocked and humiliated by his family at age six, presumably for being a complainer: "I was presented with one of those yellow mugs to drink my evening milk out of, with the following inscription on it: 'Oh isn't the world extremely flat / With nothing whatever to grumble at.' It hurt my feelings most horribly at the time and so did the mockery of the family" (Smith 169).

His relationship with his mother seems to have been ambivalent. She was described as "the pivot" of the family (Dunaway 6), whom Aldous "loved passionately" according to his brother Julian (Bedford Vol. 1, 6). She read to him and formally taught him at the Prior's Field School for girls that she founded in 1902 (Bedford Vol. 1, 5). However, he rarely spoke of her (Bedford Vol. 1, 7)[2] and left no direct reminiscence of her (Murray 15) though he did fictionalize her repeatedly, as we shall see. From the scant evidence, it seems as though she may not have been as available to him as he would have liked. Aldous formed a significant attachment to the governess, Ella Salkowski, suggested by the fact that when he became a father he employed her to look after his son, Matthew (Bedford Vol. 1, 2). A certain neediness might be suggested in that Aldous also carried around with him a rag doll until he was eight (Bedford Vol. 1, 3). At nine years old he was sent away to boarding school, where "a lot of bad bullying went on" according to his favorite cousin Gervas, who also attended (Bedford Vol. 1, 12). What does emerge clearly from almost everyone who knew Aldous is that from an early age he was detached and would sit in silence (Bedford Vol. 1, 3, 10). Later, he would frequently absent himself from conversation (Dunaway 11). Childhood friend Enid Bagnold remembered him at the age of eight as "silent, inscrutable, antagonistic" (Bedford Vol. 1, 10) (Illustration 7.1). When his mother died, fourteen-year-old Aldous "stood in stony misery" (Dunaway 6). By this time it seems he had

Illustration 7.1 Aldous Huxley at age 8. Reprinted by permission of Georges Borchardt, Inc., for the Aldous and Laura Huxley Literary Trust, Mark Trevenen Huxley, and Teresa Huxley

developed an avoidant-resistant response to frustration in attachments and to significant loss that would persist into adulthood. His sister-in-law Juliette recalled that, "Aldous's silences were always dominant" (Dunaway 28).

Huxley's relationship with his father Leonard (Illustration 7.2) was much more fraught. Gervas remembered that Aldous was fond of Leonard, but "thought he was silly. He *was* silly. He wasn't the kind of father one looked up to or went to when one was in trouble" (Bedford Vol. 1, 14). Aldous's resentment deepened when from his perspective, his father failed to take his eye infection seriously, and as a consequence he did not get to a doctor until the damage was done (Dunaway 8). Aldous's loss of sight was compounded by his being "cut off" from his schoolmates at Eton when he was forced to leave early in 1911

Illustration 7.2 Aldous Huxley with his father Leonard

(Bedford Vol. 1, 34), and by the fact that, since his father could not accommodate Aldous in his bachelor flat, he was passed around to relatives and friends (Murray 34).[3] To make matters worse, during this eighteen-month period of anxiety and instability for Aldous, Leonard abruptly decided to remarry, in February 1912, to a woman thirty years younger than him, just slightly older than Aldous and younger than his two older brothers (Murray 35). Aldous's fictionalized portraits of his step-mother Rosalind, and of Leonard for that matter, were unflattering, to the point that they caused a rift between him and his father (Bedford Vol. 1, 142).

Regarding the third family trauma, the suicide of Trevenon, apparently Aldous and his remaining brother, Julian, blamed their father for it (Dunaway 9). Trevenon had become depressed at not having met the family expectations by obtaining a first-class degree at university, and he had fallen in love with a girl beneath the Huxleys in social standing. In August 1914 the family had decided to go on a vacation in Scotland, even though Trevenon had been confined to a nursing home for a rest cure. On 15 August he disappeared from there, and hanged himself sometime before 23 August 1914, when his body was found. Aldous's sister Margaret, who described 'Trev' as the hub in the family after Julia's death, captured the impact on the family: "When Trev died, it was as if a bomb had exploded in the family. It got separated" (Dunaway 5).

This metaphor is apropos since the war had begun, and Aldous was to suffer another trauma when he returned to Oxford for his second year only to find his friends had gone to war (Bedford Vol. 1, 48). He felt abandoned, as he had felt when forced to leave Eton, and was described by Aldous's tutor and friend Sir George Clark as "impaired" (Bedford Vol. 1, 49). Typical of the avoidant response, Huxley plunged himself into his studies, and began writing poetry. One poem, "Soles Occidere Et Redire Possunt," strongly suggests, however, that Huxley had discovered the reparative potential of writing. In 1918 when an Oxford acquaintance-turned-soldier asked Huxley, tongue-in-cheek, to immortalize him in verse, Huxley did so after the young man died, writing an elegy of nearly five hundred lines, a testament far in excess of the extent of his friendship (Bedford Vol. 1, 111).[4]

Huxley emerged from the war period writing rebellious, detached, and cynical poetry and prose. Fortunately for him, his writing in this vein captured precisely the mood of his society, suffering from collective war trauma. In his novels of the 1920s, the characters are frequently isolated solipsists, such as poet Denis Stone in *Crome Yellow* (1921) who asks, "Did one ever establish contact with anyone? We are all parallel straight lines" (16). Huxley wrote prolifically in order to make a living as a writer, but overwork and the intrusion of past trauma into his present began to take its toll (Bedford Vol. 1, 153). A striking example occurs in *Those Barren Leaves* (1925), a novel populated by cynical, jaded egotists, although two writer characters, Mary Thriplow and Mr Calamy reveal a desire to move beyond this negative stance. Mary lacks a solid identity and writes smart, "cynical and elegantly brutal" novels (much like Huxley's), but she is frustrated because her audience does not see "the tragedy and tenderness underneath" (*Those* 49–50). At the end of the first section of *Those Barren Leaves*, that tenderness is revealed in a moving passage when thoughts of her dead brother Jim obtrude on her consciousness and conscience. She wonders whether he has communicated with her and enacts an apostrophe to him, asking "poor darling, darling Jim" for his forgiveness for forgetting him, and remembering "that the only visible reason why we exist in the world is to love, and be loved" (*Those* 71). Not only does this brother evoke Trevenon, but Mary's expression of love echoes Aldous's mother's deathbed letter to him to "love much" (Dunaway vii). Mary reveals that she has tried to meditate without success, and her cynical self finds her genuine grief suspect, but at the close of this chapter, she has the impulse to use writing as therapy:

> She picked up her pen again and wrote, very quickly, as though she were writing an exorcizing spell and the sooner it had been put on paper the sooner the evil thoughts would vanish.
> 'Do you remember, Jim, that time we went out in the canoe together and nearly got drowned?' (*Those* 73)

The successful writer and amorist Mr Calamy similarly resists deeper thoughts and questions, but "They loomed up enormously behind the distracting bustle of life" (*Those* 169) and "forced themselves on him" (*Those* 170). Unsatisfied by his love affair with Mary, he gropes towards embracing a mystical approach to life, but the question of whether he will be able to commit to this remains open. Huxley wrote about *Those Barren Leaves* that "the main theme is the undercutting of everything by a sort of despairing skepticism and then the undercutting of that by mysticism" (as quoted in Bedford Vol. 1, 152). That Huxley himself could not yet find solace in mysticism is suggested by his suffering from depression and writer's block in 1927 while he was writing his next, most complex, novel *Point Counter Point* (Bedford Vol. 1, 182).

Then in 1930 he experienced the death of D. H. Lawrence, whom Huxley described as "the most extraordinary and impressive human being I have ever known," and for whom he expressed love (Smith 332). Huxley and his wife Maria had moved near to Vence, France to be with Lawrence and were with him when he died, which Aldous described as "a very painful thing" (Murray 232). Maria was devastated, but Huxley's response was typically avoidant. He made plans to edit an edition of Lawrence's letters, interspersed with friends' recollections, and he embarked on writing a play, *The World of Light*, which he repeatedly referred to in his letters as "amusing" (Smith 334, 338).

The "comedy" deals with the apparent loss of a son, Hugo, in a plane crash, and continues a vein in Huxley's writing of satirizing spiritualism, the belief in the ability to communicate with the dead, which Huxley typically associates with the older generation. In this case Mr Wenham, Hugo's father, has written a book on a medium's, Hubert

Capes, spiritualist communication with Hugo, which is invalidated when Hugo returns alive. Ironically, Mr Wenham does lose his son in the end, since Hugo decides to take off surreptitiously for another adventure. Nevertheless, the play does not simply satirize spiritualism, but reveals Huxley grappling with issues of emotional attachment and loss and belief in psychic communication. Mr Wenham clearly resembles Huxley's father Leonard in circumstance, since Mr Wenham like Leonard has married a much younger wife, and most importantly has failed to understand the younger generation and particularly his son, Hugo. There is a touch of D. H. Lawrence in Hugo's friend, Bill Hamblin, with his aquiline face, "very bright blue eyes," quick movements, and worship of life adventures (*World* 14). He provokes Hugo to escape from his "ghastly academic prison" and the unpleasant prospect of becoming engaged to Enid Deckle, and to accompany him on an adventure to the jungle, en route to which their plane crashes. The loss prompts Enid to realize that Hugo did not love her and that "You can be deeply attached and at the same time have a kind of hatred of the person you're attached to" (*World* 39). She is saved from suicidal thoughts and genuinely consoled by spiritualist messages conveyed through Hubert, claiming to him that "You made me realize that he [Hugo] was not really dead but still near, still interested and wanting me to go on living" (*World* 47). When Hugo ironically does reappear fifteen months later, Enid has the strength to broach the emotional truth about her relations with both Hugo and Hubert, including being able to admit that she "bullied" Hugo (*World* 92–93). Bill, blinded in the accident, similarly wants the truth, not to be patronized because of his disability (*World* 96). Finally, the spiritualist incident enables Hugo to express the truth to his father, that Wenham's spiritualist "theory was always much more real than I was. So far as you're concerned father, I've never really been there at all. I was a kind of ghost while I was alive ... more of a ghost really than when I was dead. There was always a gulf fixed between us" (*World* 100). Hugo's realization, expressed to his father that "you'd rather have your theory than me" (*World* 99) leads him towards his decision to free himself by leaving (with a thousand pounds from Wenham's publisher). Nevertheless, before departing Hugo has confirmed that Capes has been bringing messages telepathically from him in this world, and claims that "clairvoyance and telepathy and so on – those are the facts" (*World* 82).

Huxley had long demonstrated ambivalence towards not just spiritualism, but the broader conception of mysticism, or "Misty-schism," as Huxley referred to it in an essay written at about this time. He drew on Cardinal Newman's quip that mysticism begins in mist and ends in schism (as quoted in Deery 132). For Huxley, mysticism is misty because it is a literature about the inexpressible, but the metaphor he employs to describe it, of light and darkness, is revealing of the schism in him: the best mystical writers reveal "A strange alternation of light and darkness: light to the limits of the possibly illuminable and after that the darkness of paradox and incomprehensibility, or the yet deeper, the absolute night of silence" ("Music" 317–18). Huxley continuously struggled not only with physical darkness because of eye strain and fatigue, but also moral and emotional darkness, the darkness of isolation from fellow beings. In one letter he wrote, "for me the most vital problem is not the mental so much as the ethical and emotional. The fundamental problem is love and humility ... – a difficulty greater now, I feel, than ever, because men are more solitary now than they were ..." (Smith 245).

Huxley was not quite ready to embrace mysticism but instead expressed a horrific vision of moral and emotional darkness in *Brave New World*, which can in part be seen as another avoidant response to attachment and Lawrence's death in particular. When Huxley had first met Lawrence in 1915, Lawrence had persuaded Huxley to join him in his plan to establish a utopian community in Florida, a plan which came to nothing (Bedford Vol. 1, 61). *Brave New World* can be seen as the dark dystopian response to that dream. Bernard Marx, the loner protagonist, seeks out attachment in a world where attachments, particularly to the mother, are considered pornographic, where spiritual communion has been reduced to soma-induced orgy-porgies, and where death conditioning has eliminated grief. Bernard seeks out the primitive world and finds John the savage, a Lawrentian figure who overshadows Bernard but whose emotional attachments and moral integrity cause him such anguish that he hangs himself, a recurring pattern for Huxley characters who cannot cope with overwhelming emotions.

On finishing *Brave New World*, published in 1932 to critical and popular success, Huxley embarked on what would be called *Eyeless in Gaza*, which Charles Holmes, among other biographers and critics, has recognized as "the fullest, frankest confessional [Huxley] ever wrote" (98). After he began "meditating" on it (Holmes 97), his father Leonard died in May 1933 while Aldous was in New York (Murray 271). Sybille Bedford, who met with the Huxleys a few weeks after Leonard's death, claims she did not know what Aldous's reaction was, since "Silence was expected" (Vol. 1, 285). We do know that, typical of the avoidant-resistant strategy, Huxley worked "feverishly" on his novel through the summer of that year, according to Maria (Smith 371), but the strategy began to break down and Huxley started to experience depression and chronic insomnia, bringing his work to a standstill by 1935 (Holmes 97). Huxley had begun to seek out help, however. F. Matthias Alexander, a guru of mind-body therapy, introduced him to "kinesthetic re-education" and meditation (Woodcock 194). Huxley wrote to Robert Nichols that he "found [he] could do something to help the drugs by means of breathing exercise of the Yoga sort with accompanying mental concentration and finally attempted elimination of irrelevant thoughts and feelings – the latter a very difficult process which I don't pretend ever to have succeeded in mastering" (Smith 389). *Eyeless in Gaza* stands as a testament to that struggle. Sybille Bedford wrote that "Aldous projected himself into Anthony Beavis," the protagonist, but she does not probe the interconnections, concluding that "Perhaps it had best be left by saying that Anthony Beavis was a much distorted portrait of Aldous by Aldous" (307). Through the lens of attachment theory and object relations much more can be revealed, and the relational patterning shown to be consistent with Aldous's earlier life and works.

The first thing to note is that the non-chronological structure strongly reinforces Beavis's emotional struggle. The novel covers three periods of his life, at prep school, his early twenties, and early middle age (May 118), but six series of events from these periods are intertwined. Thus, the past frequently intrudes on the present narrative, reflecting one important moral lesson Beavis must learn, that one's past actions condition one's present behavior. Huxley wrote that the novel followed a person who became first materially and then mentally and emotionally free (Smith 376), and by the last he meant overcoming "a dread and avoidance of emotion" that Huxley admitted about himself in his letters of this period (Smith 390). Significantly, the novel begins on Anthony's birthday, 30 August 1933, his forty-second, which turns out to be his birth into a new way of engaging with the world. Initially, however, he is preoccupied with the past, with examining old photos, referred to as his "old corpses" (*Eyeless* 5). One is of his mother shortly before she died, and the other of a former lover, Mary Amberley, whom we later discover he first met as a boy at his mother's funeral when Mary was pregnant, and who is ten years older than him. He evinces desire for both as he compares them, reflecting on his mother's "swan-like loins! That long slanting cascade of bosom – without any apparent relation to the naked body beneath!" (*Eyeless* 1). Yet his avoidant stance rapidly becomes clear, as we are told "he had no time, no energy for emotions and responsibilities. His work came first" (*Eyeless* 4). This is driven home when his current lover Helen, the daughter of Mary, enters, and expresses her dissatisfaction at his emotional unavailability: "he had shut the door against her" (*Eyeless* 6).

In the first chapters the past continues to intrude, including the suicide of Anthony's school friend, Brian Foxe, but the death of Anthony's mother Maisie dominates. At her funeral in 1902, Anthony at age eleven does express grief by weeping "uncontrollably," but neither his father nor Mary nor anyone else responds to him; among the mourners in black "he walked as though at the bottom of a well" (*Eyeless* 35). He clearly learns an avoidant response. His attitude towards his mother emerges as ambivalent as well, since he repeatedly remembers her instilling fear in him about germs (*Eyeless* 36, 65, 111), and on one occasion when she insists on him skating and he cries in fear, "he almost hated her" (*Eyeless* 39).

Not only does Huxley split the mother figure into Mary, who ends as a drug addict after Anthony has thrown her over as a lover, but he brings in another in the form of Mrs Foxe, the mother of his friend Brian. She mainly represents the good mother, in that she brings him into her home and comforts him after the death of his own mother. She recognizes him as a spiritual cripple because he doesn't know how to feel properly (*Eyeless* 99), reads to him dramatically, as Aldous's mother had done, and shows Beavis the way to healing by remembering Maisie. She advises:

> Sadness is necessary sometimes – like an operation; you can't be well without it. If you think about her, Anthony, it'll hurt you. But if you don't think about her, you condemn her to a second death. The spirit of the dead lives on in God. But it also lives on in the minds of the living – helping them, making them better and stronger. The dead can only have this kind of immortality if the living are prepared to give it them. (*Eyeless* 108)

Significantly, Mrs Foxe's son Brian helps Anthony find a transitional object for his mother, a boat which he and Brian take out at night while at school. Anthony transforms it in his imagination into a beautiful sailing ship, and Brian's sympathy enables Anthony to move from anger to genuine grief: "this first hardening of resistance melted away, and now, without feeling ashamed of what he was doing, he began to cry" (*Eyeless* 74). Mrs Foxe turns out, however, to be a possessive, overcontrolling mother, overinvested in her son because lacking love from her husband (*Eyeless* 114, 248). She has instilled an impossibly high moral standard in Brian and a fear of physical intimacy, which compromises his relations with his girlfriend Joan, and indirectly leads to his suicide when he discovers that Joan has kissed his friend Anthony.

In a letter to his stepmother, Huxley defended using a direct portrait of his brother Trev, who committed suicide, in his portrait of Brian, claiming that he "preserved the stammer and insisted on the ascetic obsession" (Smith 409) for artistic reasons. There is no evidence to suggest that Huxley interfered with his brother's lover, as Anthony does; rather it seems as though Huxley magnified his guilt at being on holiday in Scotland and not with Trev when he was suffering his mental breakdown (Bedford Vol. 1, 46). Interestingly, in *Eyeless*, after Brian's death Anthony parts ways with both the forbidden mother, Mary, who has put Anthony up to the scheme of seducing Joan, and with Mrs Foxe, whom he avoids afterwards (*Eyeless* 588). In fictionalizing and renegotiating his relationship with Trevenon, Huxley seems to have expunged his guilt.

Illustration 7.3 Aldous Huxley with fellow pacifist Gerald Heard in 1937

Eyeless in Gaza contains several father figures as well, including John Beavis, Anthony's actual father, treated with ambivalence; the idealized father figures, Purchas, based on the pacifist preacher Dick Sheppard; and James Miller, a condensation of Sheppard, Gerald Heard (Illustration 7.3), F. M. Alexander, and others (Woodcock 202). Essentially, John Beavis comes across as self-absorbed and responds sentimentally to his wife's death, spewing platitudes and memorializing her through rituals of marking anniversaries and handling her dresses, a sensuous experience (*Eyeless* 194), that is, until he becomes infatuated with an adoring plump twenty-seven-year-old, whom he marries (*Eyeless* 197). Through Anthony's response to John we can observe the resistant dimension of his attachment patterning, since Anthony becomes preoccupied with resisting his father's conventional approach to mourning (*Eyeless* 95). Even John is aware that Anthony "seems strangely indifferent" and "seemed to resist and reject suffering" (*Eyeless* 101). Nevertheless, as an adult Anthony, by way of resisting his father's indifference to the possibility of war, broaches the central question of the novel in an early chapter: "How to be simultaneously dispassionate and not indifferent, serene like an old man and active like a young one?" (*Eyeless* 86). James Miller mentors Anthony into understanding the difference between detachment and non-attachment and into accepting love as central, expressed through his adoption of a spiritually energized pacifism. Anthony meets Miller after he experiences the trauma of having a man pull a gun on him while he is in Mexico (*Eyeless* 498–99). This revives anxiety from two earlier traumas, being accidentally hit by a bomb in war training (*Eyeless* 89), and being splattered by the blood of a dog dropped from an airplane while sunbathing with his then lover Helen (*Eyeless* 153). Anthony demonstrates an avoidant response to both of the earlier experiences, but after the third incident, when the gunshot misses him, he feels "abjectly humiliated" (*Eyeless* 499) and in a state open to change. Miller advocates increasing his self-awareness through journal writing – a prime example of writing as therapy – and a significant number of the fifty-four dated entries consist of Anthony's meditations. They become less based on reason and more incantatory, as he moves from isolation towards unity, from spiritual darkness to illumination. The last passage is left open-ended, suggesting that this mystical movement will continue: "For now there is only the darkness expanding and deepening, deepening into light; there is only this final peace, this consciousness of being no more separate, this illumination …" (*Eyeless* 619). His meditation is interrupted by the realization that the time has come to go to a pacifist meeting where he knows he will face hostile forces, but he accepts this "dispassionately, and with a serene lucidity" (*Eyeless* 619). He is engaged and yet aware of the inevitability of conflict, and this stance parallels Huxley's since he advocated in speeches and print an absolute, constructive pacifism, despite intense opposition (Murray 293).

Huxley achieved considerable insight into the psychological dimension of mysticism, for instance suggesting that the absolute appealed to the introvert as compensation for external hostile objects (*Proper* 49) and that mysticism embodied resistance. He claimed that, "Mystical religion is the ideal religion for doubters – those ultimate schismatics who have separated themselves from all belief. For the mystic is dispensed from intellectually believing in God; he feels God" ("Music" 318–19). Mysticism appealed partly because it was an iconoclastic pursuit in the modernist age, similar to his uncompromising stance on pacifism. Nevertheless, through mysticism and pacifism, physical therapy and meditation, and perhaps most significantly writing about the process of engaging with these beliefs and therapies, Huxley overcame his physical, mental, and spiritual blocks. In *Eyeless in Gaza* Huxley wrote an unflattering, candid, even ruthless account of painful growth out of a stunted, bitter darkness, but in doing so he renegotiated relationships and trauma, and achieved self-awareness and enlightenment.

Huxley explored his new stance in *Ends and Means*, which Maria saw as "in essence a practical continuation of Eyeless" and the best thing he had done "spiritually" (as quoted in Murray 307). By this time he had traveled to the USA to spread his pacifist message, which was contained in *Ends*, but it is a much broader analysis of human motivation and ideals and the ends by which they might be realized. In the book Huxley advocates non-attachment to worldly desires and instead attachment to ultimate reality. Non-attachment is not detachment, of course, and non-attachment enables the practice of all the virtues, including charity, courage, and compassion. Huxley affirms "the existence of a spiritual reality underlying the phenomenal world" (*Ends* 4), and argues that metaphysical beliefs act as a determining factor in all our actions (as quoted in Murray 308). As evidence for the power of mind he points to studies of psychosomatic illness and of parapsychology. The latter field "leaves no doubt as to the existence of telepathy and clairvoyance and very little doubt as to the existence of pre-vision" (*Ends* 259), and these extensions of consciousness suggest the power of the mind to heal. Huxley admits that the development of self-awareness may as easily produce undesirable as desirable results. The development of personality may be regarded as an end in itself or, alternatively, as a means towards an ulterior end – the transcendence of personality through immediate cognition of ultimate reality and through moral action towards fellow individuals, action that is inspired and directed by this immediate cognition. Where personality is developed for its own sake, and not in order that it may be transcended, there tends to be a raising of the barriers of separateness and an increase of egotism. (*Ends* 326–27)

Huxley probes these differing consequences of developing self-awareness and the nature of the spiritual world underlying the phenomenal world in his novel *Time Must Have a Stop* (1944), which he claimed was "the most successful" and "the one that I like best" (as quoted in Fraser 8). As with *Eyeless*, this novel is highly autobiographical, a coming-of-age story about a son, Sebastian Barnack, whose behavior is conditioned by the early loss of his mother and his angry, bullying father. Sebastian has traces of Denis Stone, in that he transforms his fraught experiences into poetry, and also of John Beavis, who becomes a seeker, but this novel demonstrates more hope about surmounting trauma and suggests that Huxley's reparative renegotiations in fiction were succeeding in the sense that Huxley's fictionalized persona, Sebastian, grows much more quickly from a traumatized, self-absorbed, manipulative, avoidant-resistant character to a wise seeker after mystical truth, who has learned to love. On his path he is influenced by two father figures. At the age of thirty-two he is on the brink of an understanding with his biological father, yet another re-working of Huxley's fraught relations with his father. Huxley also renegotiates his relations with and loss of Lawrence through one of these father figures to Sebastian, the mystic Bruno Rontini. In addition Huxley, daringly depicts afterlife communication, and opens readers to its possibility, perhaps even convincing some, by his deft employment of satire.

As in *Eyeless*, the protagonist's trauma and his characteristic response to it emerge early on in the novel. Sebastian encounters a middle-aged woman, Mrs Ockham, at the library, and she projects her feelings for her son who died in the war onto Sebastian. His first impulse is to judge and condemn her, but instead he manipulates her into giving him an entire box of chocolates. Immediately after she departs, he associates her with his dead mother who would have been about the same age as Mrs Ockham. This touches off musing about large-scale trauma and suffering, with "millions dying at this very moment," and makes Sebastian feel "a vast impersonal sadness" (*Time* 3). Once again the link between personal trauma and collective trauma is made, and Sebastian responds by associating with Keats's line "The giant agony of the world!," egotistically critiquing a passage from "The Fall of Hyperion," and then composing lines himself. His anger intrudes when a phrase pops out, "the women in cages," and he decides he will write "a poem in which he would take vengeance on the whole female sex" (*Time* 5). Later on, and only after she has died, we discover that his mother has abandoned him and his father to take up a lover. At this point he has the therapeutic impulse to write poetry, but unresolved negative emotion obtrudes, and in the typical avoidant strategy he escapes into a technical discussion about the diction and subject matter of his lines. An encounter with his cousin Susan, only one day apart in age, reveals that Sebastian has been transforming experience into fiction from as early as age five; the earliest story she can remember involved transforming a wart on a rubber ball into a "tummy-button" and his imaginative and horrifying account of how tummy-buttons are opened and cleaned. This symbolically connects storytelling with his mother, since the tummy-button is the manifestation of separation from her. Sebastian has been raised by his Aunt Alice because his father also has often been absent (*Time* 14), but her daughter Susan has clearly become Sebastian's maternal substitute – in fact, he "invited her [Susan] to love him in yet another way – protectively and maternally" (*Time* 17). He continues to tell her stories to shock her, and "sometimes his words hurt her" (*Time* 17). Despite this, Susan harbors passion for him and is distraught when he taunts her with his story of his older lover, Mrs Esdaile (*Time* 17). This too is a fiction since in actuality Sebastian has had a sordid encounter with a prostitute and has had to lie to and manipulate their servant Ellen in order to obtain one pound to pay off the prostitute (*Time* 24–27).

Not only has Sebastian essentially been abandoned by his parents and transferred his anger and ambivalence toward them onto his cousin Susan, but there are signs of trauma and avoidant-resistant patterning in his extended family. Significantly, we encounter them on the anniversary of their revered patriarch's death, a fact to which the depressive Uncle Fred Poulshot draws their attention in order to shame his son (*Time* 50–51). Sebastian's grandfather was a successful and self-denying industrialist, ascetic and parsimonious, whose wife died early (*Time* 39–40). Aunt Alice and Uncle Fred worship him, but his accomplishments bring into relief their flaws and failures. Fred inflicts his black moods on all (*Time* 46), and Aunt Alice has over-regulated

Sebastian's "native moodiness" as a consequence (*Time* 49). However, Sebastian's own father, John, has had the greatest impact of the men on conditioning Sebastian's behavior, and in fact Sebastian's conflict with his father sets the entire plot in motion. In the early chapters of the novel Sebastian is preoccupied with developing a strategy to ask his father for a set of evening clothes. John has been consistently stingy with Sebastian, and his opposition is "the last humiliation" for Sebastian (*Time* 23). The clothes represent his growth into manhood, but John sees them as a class symbol clashing with his reformist politics (*Time* 30). Sebastian adopts the avoidant strategy of not showing too much emotion, so as to avoid rejection (Howe 96):

> The great thing, Sebastian had learned from long and bitter experience, was never to seem too anxious or insistent. He must ask for the dinner jacket – but in such a way that his father wouldn't think that he really longed for it. (*Time* 30)

To Sebastian, John appears emotionless and difficult to read:

> To Sebastian that was one of the most disquieting things about his father: you never knew from his expression what he was feeling or thinking. He would look at you unwaveringly, his gray eyes brightly blank, as though you were a perfect stranger. The first intimation of his state of mind always came verbally, in that loud, authoritative, barrister's voice of his ... (*Time* 33–34)

John's pronouncements typically bully Sebastian, as when John sarcastically refuses the evening clothes. With characteristic insight, Huxley shows that John clearly projects onto his son his memories and ambivalence towards his unfaithful wife. Sebastian mentions that he wants the suit to attend a party, and John "recalled the ecstatic note in which Rosie used to pronounce that hated word [party]" (*Time* 57). When Sebastian entreats his father, his voice "unsteady with emotion" and looking childish, John "sees the image of the childish wife who had betrayed him, and was now dead" (*Time* 59). Their antagonism towards one another does not abate until the Epilogue.

Nevertheless, two other father figures supplant John: Uncle Eustace Barnack and cousin Bruno Rontini, both key to the plot, the narrative and thematic strategies, and Sebastian's character development. Eustace presents a complete contrast to his brother John's hard, emotionless asceticism, in being a decadent, debauched sensualist. Unlike John, who mirrors their father's obsessive asceticism, Eustace has responded to the trauma of his upbringing by adopting an avoidant-resistant attachment pattern. He has become a good reader of others' emotional states (though not of his own) (Howe 102), as attested by his perceptions of his sister Alice's marriage and his brother John's psychology (*Time* 45–47). His resistance has taken the form of rebellion against the Barnack "low-living, high-minded" values and radical political principles (*Time* 44), and he has married a rich widow (now dead), enabling him to live as a civilized aesthete in Florence. Though he has provoked "outrage" and "insult" in his siblings, and is called "the Prodigal" by his sister (*Time* 44), he has not entirely rejected his family's values, as he retains their antagonism towards religion and God, "The Gaseous Vertebrate," as he jokes (*Time* 43). This attitude has led him to avoid thinking about death or the afterlife (*Time* 128), a stance Huxley exploits for comic effect. In fact, Huxley conveys much of his comedy and satire through Eustace, who defends against pain through his irreverence and by laughing at himself as well as others; he has a "front-row seat at the human comedy" (*Time* 48). For instance, Huxley satirizes Freudianism through his description of Eustace's desire for his cigar, implying he is arrested at the oral stage of development:

> Damply, lovingly [Eustace's] lips closed over the butt; the match was ignited; he pulled at the flame. And suddenly Sebastian was reminded of his cousin Marjorie's baby, nuzzling with blind concupiscence for the nipple, seizing it at last between the soft prehensile flaps of its little mouth and working away, working away in a noiseless frenzy of enjoyment. True, Uncle Eustace had rather better manners; and in this case the nipple was coffee-coloured and six inches long. (*Time* 52)

Sebastian the budding poet immediately begins to transform this scene into mock-heroic verse, describing his uncle as "Old but an infant ..." (*Time* 52). Huxley cleverly undercuts this veneer of psychological comedy with his serious insights into attachments and the impact of loss in particular, and he employs a similar tactic in dealing with the afterlife, as we shall see.

Eustace is initially attracted to Sebastian because his mother was "the loveliest of irresponsible gypsies" and because he relishes the opportunity of educating him in opposition to his brother's wishes (*Time* 42), but he also is moved by Sebastian's beauty and his "essential purity" (*Time* 112). As a young man, Eustace possessed similar ideals and aspirations, for example to write verse, but he became degraded, suggested by the fact that he only writes lewd limericks (*Time* 113). We see Sebastian's incipient flaws of manipulation and lying magnified in Eustace, such as when he lies on the telephone to his dying former lover, Laurina, while in the company of his mistress Mimi (*Time* 94). Despite opportunities to improve himself morally and spiritually, such as through his contact with his mystic cousin Bruno, Eustace has chosen to indulge himself in a variety of fleshly and aesthetic pleasures, including fifty years of indiscriminate reading (*Time* 130). He is the cultivated man of leisure who has developed his personality for its own sake, a use of self-awareness that Huxley warned about in *Ends and Means*. Eustace quickly takes "possession" of Sebastian from Bruno (*Time* 110) and corrupts and seduces him, advising pleasure-seeking and "flight" as "your only strategy" when amusement with a woman becomes incompatible with his talent (*Time* 125). Sebastian responds to Eustace's Degas painting by penning a lewd verse, which delights Eustace so much that he offers the painting in exchange for it (*Time* 127). Following this gift of a painting, an offer of evening clothes from Eustace (*Time* 111), and feeling that he is being listened to and taken seriously (*Time* 126), Sebastian forms an attachment to his uncle. It is ironic, then, that when Eustace calls out for help from the lavatory, where he is in pain from overindulgence, Sebastian has likewise overindulged in his uncle's wine to the extent that he has passed out and does not hear.

It is also ironic that Uncle Eustace has the greatest impact on Sebastian after he dies. First, Sebastian enters into a moral quagmire by selling the promised but not bequeathed Degas to buy his evening clothes, and the Degas is discovered missing. This leads him to Bruno Rontini who will save him from his sin. Second, and more immediately, Eustace exerts an impact through his communication from the afterlife. Within Eustace's household lives his mother-in-law, Mrs Gamble, another of Huxley's blind seers (although she is mocked). An ardent believer in spirit communication, she is having Oliver Lodge's *Raymond* read to her when first encountered (*Time* 65). Following Eustace's death, she immediately calls for a medium (who ironically cannot be contacted right away). Meanwhile, several chapters are devoted to Eustace's experience of the afterlife. These are dominated by his awareness of light and darkness, the latter figured as a hideous absence (*Time* 139). The phrase "backwards and downwards" is among the most important fragments which come back to him from his life, since this phrase captures his movement away from the light, light which is identified with Bruno (*Time* 173). Although the séance Mrs Gamble arranges is treated comically, partly because her companion, Mrs Thrale, flirts with Sebastian during it, but more importantly because Eustace is shown to be frustrated by how his words and jokes are garbled through the medium's control, Huxley makes it clear that Eustace genuinely communicates and that he possesses clairvoyance in predicting Mrs Thrale's marriage (*Time* 180). He later predicts the death of Jim Poulshot (*Time* 233) and the fate of others. Also, Sebastian, a skeptic, realizes that Eustace's voice is buried in the medium's "idiotic squeak," and that his Degas verse has even been recited though misquoted (*Time* 183). This technique of undermining the satire with genuine belief succeeds even for a skeptic such as Edmund Wilson, who wrote in an early review of *Time Must Have a Stop*:

> Now, one may not be prepared to accept Huxley's views about spiritualistic phenomena and the Platonic rebirth of souls, but the whole thing has been given plausibility – though queer it is never creepy – by treating the disembodied vicissitudes of Eustace Barnack's soul in the same dry droll way as the adventures of his consciousness while still in the flesh. (348)

As derision begins to dominate Eustace's spirit and he moves towards pain and away from the light, which becomes his enemy (*Time* 232), Sebastian moves towards the light, associated with the good father, Bruno.

Bruno, the son of Eustace's cousin Mary, has been raised as a Quaker (*Time* 43) and has become a mystic, his words framed "in a setting of silence" (*Time* 237). On meeting Sebastian he immediately intuits that Sebastian, like his namesake, will be prey to the arrows of various lusts and temptations (*Time* 109). Thus he is not surprised when Sebastian comes to him for help in retrieving the Degas. As a second-hand book dealer, he knows the unscrupulous art dealer Weyl, who has re-purchased the painting from Sebastian at a large profit. Bruno does not condemn Sebastian's selfish act, but instead shows compassion and mentors him. He suggests that Eustace's séance communication may have come from a "temporary pseudo-Eustace," who is not necessarily "happy and jolly" (*Time* 239). He also helps Sebastian to understand that his offence has a genealogy, with antecedents and consequences (*Time* 243), the truth of which is played out. A young servant girl is falsely accused of the crime, and in retaliation her father kills Mrs Gamble's dog (*Time* 272). More significantly, Bruno's contact with Weyl has caused him to be taken by the fascists, and Sebastian is accused of being responsible for this by an angry young man who strikes him (*Time* 271).

Sebastian's contact with Bruno has set him on the path of moral questioning, and this trauma of losing Bruno has evidently brought about transformation in Sebastian, as we learn in an Epilogue, set on New Year's Day, 1944, when Sebastian takes stock by reading over his notes to himself from the previous few months. These testaments to Sebastian's spiritual growth have been criticized because of their expository nature, but it could be argued that Huxley aimed for this jarring effect, since he has Sebastian observe that this is the age not of the novelist but of the "Document" (*Time* 301). Sebastian's "documents" may make readers uncomfortable but their striking appearance in a novel forces readers to attend to them. We discover that Sebastian has not only reconnected with Bruno but that he has rented a house in Vence and attends the man dying of throat cancer. During these fifteen weeks Sebastian receives Bruno's wisdom and his blessing, and this he claims, was the "most memorable period of his life" (*Time* 286). This scenario is clearly a re-working of Huxley's loss of Lawrence, with more acceptance and wisdom from Lawrence and less guilt on the part of Huxley. Sebastian has also suffered the loss of a wife through miscarriage and he has had an affair with Mrs Gamble's companion Veronica Thrale, after her marriage. As Bruno says, he is not Joan of Arc, but needs to make the only redemptive sacrifice "of self-will to make room for the knowledge of God" (*Time* 288). Sebastian subsequently has adopted the mystic stance and lays out the principles of mysticism, including that to achieve "unitive knowledge, to realize the supreme identity, is the final end and purpose of human existence" (*Time* 294). This is the ground for Sebastian's wide-ranging views, including his advanced insights into environmental degradation: "where natural resources are concerned, we sacrifice a pretty accurately predictable future to present greed. We know, for example, that if we abuse the soil, it will lose its fertility ..." (*Time* 298). He also holds Huxley's continuing, uncompromising stance on pacifism: "a shared theology is one of the indispensable conditions of peace" (*Time* 299).

Sebastian has suffered war trauma, having lost his hand in battle (*Time* 276), and his ensuing insights into suffering, that most return from battle unchanged, many are worse and "a few – men with an adequate philosophy and a desire to act upon it – are better" (*Time* 301), are interrupted by the arrival of his father, source of his original trauma. This final encounter shows that Sebastian has become wiser and more mature than his father, both through his contact with Bruno and the experience of suffering that clearly has made him one of the few better men. Sebastian's attitude towards his father displays that characteristic

Huxleyan harshness; for example Sebastian sees John as a Peter Pan, arrested in his development and typical of his generation, and as a "spiritual abortion" (*Time* 304, 308), but he demonstrates more patience in explaining his views of peace, and more understanding of his father's avoidant stance towards other people (*Time* 309). This prompts John to attempt to show affection and, when he mysteriously evokes the spirit of Bruno, to pay Sebastian a compliment for "the first time" (309). At the close of the novel John shows a new willingness to listen to Sebastian, who himself responds with affection. Huxley seems to have renegotiated his relations with his father yet again, but in a more positive light than previously.

Domineering mother figures reappear in this novel as well, such as Mrs Ockham, whose multiple personal losses provoke "maternal lust" for Sebastian (*Time* 217), but he comes to an understanding of the psychology of her "passionate pity" and expresses sympathy for her (*Time* 301). Mrs Thrale doubles as mother and seductress, but she also mentors Sebastian, chastising him frankly about his childish manipulations and advising him to use an "outrage or *non sequitur* in action" to deal with bullies like Mrs Gamble, a strategy which in attachment terms resembles resistance (*Time* 162–63).

Thus *Time Must Have a Stop* advances Huxley's therapeutic renegotiations of his past trauma, but it also demonstrates more insight into and compassion for his characters, "as living patterns in space, how incredibly subtle, rich and complex!" as Sebastian exclaims (*Time* 146). Through adept use of comedy and satire, particularly through the figure of Uncle Eustace, Huxley courageously explores more of his growing conviction about the spiritual nature of the universe and of the interconnectedness of the corporeal world and afterlife, subject matter new to fiction and "a brilliant performance," as early reviewer Edmund Wilson recognized (348).

Huxley demonstrated his commitment to mysticism and to sharing its greatest insights in *The Perennial Philosophy*, published the next year. He felt that many would want to do something with the war ending, and that an introduction to what he called the perennial philosophy, the common features among various mystical and religious traditions, would provide a good ground for seeking oneness with the Divine Ground (Murray 353). He defined "the divine ground of all existence [as] a spiritual absolute, ineffable in terms of discursive thought, but (in certain circumstances) susceptible of being directly experienced and realized by the human being" (*Perennial* 21). Through the 1950s until his death he tried various means of experiencing this absolute, from hypnosis and automatic writing to taking LSD and mescaline under controlled circumstances, as Laura Huxley, his second wife, recounts in her memoir, *This Timeless Moment* (10, 30, 131ff.). By 1956 he could sum up in *Heaven and Hell* that:

> My own guess is that modern spiritualism and ancient traditions are both correct. There *is* a posthumous state of the kind described in Sir Oliver Lodge's book, *Raymond*; but there is also a heaven of blissful visionary experience; there is also a hell of the same kind of appalling visionary experience as is suffered here by schizophrenics and some of those who take mescaline; and there is also an experience, beyond time, of union with the Divine Ground. (*Doors* 112)

Huxley characteristically extracted what he saw as the element of truth from various traditions and his own experience, as "a minimum working hypothesis" as Sebastian puts it in *Time Must Have a Stop* (294).

Huxley also used these means to access his childhood, a point Laura Huxley repeatedly mentions: "Aldous wanted to recover the memory of a two-year period around the age of eleven, of which he remembers very little. He needs to recapture this period for his writing" (*Timeless* 10, cf. also 138, 145). This time period would have been when his mother was alive, before her illness, and perhaps represented a happier time before this first tragedy, but it does suggest that Huxley continued to be preoccupied with past relations. Under the influence of LSD Huxley recorded that, "You realize that, well, after all, all your psychotherapy is in a sense a preparation for death in as much as you die to these memories which are allowed to haunt you as though they were in the present" (*Timeless* 182).[5] For her book on recipes for living and loving, *You are Not the Target*, Laura Huxley claims that Aldous suggested the phrase "Lay the ghost," which deals with the problem of haunting emotional memories that interfere with our present (*Timeless* 182). She also includes the first chapter of a first-person retrospective novel Huxley was working on when he died. After discussing "the complex realities of the autobiographical process," the protagonist remembers his eleventh birthday (in 1900), and a dream in which he calls out for his mother, runs to her and kisses her repeatedly:

> "that's enough," she said but I went on kissing her. "That's enough," she repeated and dipped her pen and ink. "Run along and play. I'm writing." "But, mother ..." I heard myself protesting as I woke up. (*Timeless* 213)

The protagonist realizes that he is not with his parents in India but at his Aunt Frances's house in Surrey. He recounts that, "the mood of sadness in which I had woken from my dream gave place to a gloating exultation," but only because the boy realizes it is his birthday (*Timeless* 214). This telling scene about a boy's attempt to reach out to his preoccupied mother, who is then lost to him, is followed by a reminiscence of his mother's disapproval at immature behavior and his embarrassment (*Timeless* 214). Enraged at receiving "a book for babies!" for his birthday, the narrator is about to throw the "insulting gift across the room" when he becomes intrigued by a question posed in the book: "tell me, what am I?" The narrator asks:

> What was I really? The brilliant boy, two years ahead of his contemporaries in book learning? Or the crybaby, two years behind them in self-control and the art of behaving like an English gentleman? The model child who won all the prizes was also the feeble outsider, bullied, made fun of, at the best contemptuously tolerated by the louts he envied and despised. Which was the genuine me? (*Timeless* 217)

Here the narrator retreats from bullying and criticism into a book, which prompts introspection. The protagonist also recalls that his German governess "was the grown up with whom I had the closest and most continuous feelings" (*Timeless* 220). A memory of his tenth birthday with his parents confirms the reason why. After spending a brief time with her boy, his mother claims "time to go to work" and he responds, "my happiness collapsed like a pricked balloon" (*Timeless* 221). Despite his pleading and crying and his father's anger towards his wife: "Scribble, scribble, scribble. It's an addiction – like chewing Bethel," his mother, "stony with repressed anger," leaves him "to my misery and resentment" (*Timeless* 221). His father stays to play soldiers with him, "but my mind was with my mother in the study. Even on my birthday, I was thinking, her work meant more to her than I did" (*Timeless* 221–22). He hates her "bloody novels" but is also proud of them, demonstrating an intense ambivalence (*Timeless* 222). More conflict follows, with the boy "full of hatred" yet unable to express it (*Timeless* 223). He exclaims at one point: "How vividly, even after more than sixty years, I remember these things!" (*Timeless* 233). Although this is fiction, it is tempting to suggest that Huxley captured something of his family's dynamic, with a preoccupied mother, a precocious, bullied, resentful son, and an ineffective father, in this self-proclaimed autobiographical first draft, where the emotions may have been expressed in a more raw form than they would have been in a more polished draft.

Huxley continued to embrace spiritualism, mysticism, and psychical research up to his death on 22 November 1963 and beyond, according to Laura Huxley. Not only did Oliver Lodge's *Raymond* remain a touchstone, but Huxley repeatedly championed F. W. H. Myers's work in a variety of venues, from lectures, letters, and popular articles in *Esquire* magazine to the Foreword he contributed to a new edition of Myers's *Human Personality and its Survival of Bodily Death* in 1961 (Bedford Vol. 2, 261; Smith 647, 656; "Oddest" 326). Huxley noted that William James "attributed the beginning of the new psychology, with its stress upon the dynamic unconscious, to the publication of a paper in 1886 by F. W. H. Myers" on the subliminal self (as quoted in Bedford Vol. 2, 261). Freud's account of the psyche eclipsed Myers's, but Freud's is distorted because, as a doctor, he focused on illness, whereas Myers's was more comprehensive and balanced:

> in this great book Myers brought together an immense store of information about the always strange and often wonderful goings on in the upper stories of a man's soul house. And this information he presents within a theoretical frame of reference that takes account not only of the rats and beetles in the cellarage, but also of those treasures, birds and angels so largely ignored by Freud and his followers.
>
> For some tastes, Myers's theoretical framework may seem excessively "spiritual." But at least it has the merit of "saving the appearances," of covering all the facts. His account of the unconscious is superior to Freud's in at least one respect; it is more comprehensive and true to the data of experience. ("Foreword" *Human* 7)

Huxley not only shared Myers's synthetic approach to "that impersonal spiritual world which transcends and interpenetrates our bodies, our conscious minds and our personal unconscious" ("Foreword" 7–8), but he also, like Myers, communicated with others after his death, at least according to Laura Huxley (*Timeless* 311ff.). During several sittings with a medium, K. M. R., Laura Huxley received messages "that Aldous was very keen on giving proof of survival," and she was directed to several books and pages in Aldous's library which turned out to contain passages about him (*Timeless* 324). One of these was a book on parapsychology (*Timeless* 327). Laura Huxley scrupulously eliminates rational explanations for this occurrence, before wisely concluding with one of Aldous's favorite passages from his grandfather T. H. Huxley on the most fruitful approach to science: "sit down before fact like a little child, and be prepared to give up every preconceived notion, follow humbly wherever and to whatever abysses nature leads or you shall learn nothing" (*Timeless* 330).

Like his grandfather, Aldous Huxley realized that preconceived notions blocked understanding. Attempts to explain mysticism "in a variety of different languages" were always limited (*Timeless* 195). However, he asks "within what larger frame of reference can these divergently sense-making explanations be combined so as to make a deeper, more comprehensive sense? Into what totally expressive lingua franca can the various dialects of chemistry, psychiatry, theology, and transcendental operationalism be translated?" (*Timeless* 196). Huxley's quest was not only to find that larger frame of reference but also to experience mysticism, the union with the Divine Ground. The origins of the quest were in childhood trauma, which Huxley surmounted through creative expression of emotion within the imaginative forms of poems, short stories, novels, and plays. By renegotiating damaged and even severed relationships in these forms, Huxley was able to overcome his dread and avoidance of emotion, an avoidant-resistant relationship pattern, and to move toward secure, human connectedness through non-attachment.

Ironically, he began as the great cultural hero of the "lost" or war generation, expressing its cynicism and disillusionment, but he became the hero of the new-age movement and the 1960s counterculture, anticipating and facilitating their quest for spiritual, mystical experience outside of organized religion.

8
After-life/After-word: The Culture of Mourning and Mysticism

"I was in a staid London hotel at eleven o'clock in the morning, most prim of all the hours of the day, when a lady, well-dressed and conventional, came through the turning doors, waltzed slowly round the hall with a flag in either hand, and departed without saying a word. It was the first sign that things were happening" (*Memories* 386). So wrote Arthur Conan Doyle about the cessation of war on 11 November 1918. He then rushed out to Buckingham Palace and witnessed singing, cheering, and a man downing a bottle of whisky raw, which angered him, when he felt "It was the moment for prayer" (*Memories* 386). Doyle's eldest son Kingsley had died two weeks earlier, just shy of his twenty-sixth birthday.

Throughout Britain, sporadic reveling broke out, or what Huxley referred to as "the Jollifications of the first days of peace" (Smith 169), but the overwhelming mood was exhaustion with death, combined with survivors' guilt. Rudyard Kipling captured the shock in a rather graphic image: he wrote, "here we are in England – dazed and stupefied with the guts of Central Europe trailing round our legs – the whole shoot collapsed like the last scene of some Wagnerian opera" (*Letters* 520). He then expressed his anger that the "Hun" was not pursued further, back into Germany. Finally his personal grief surfaced, in this letter to a fellow bereaved father: "we feel the loss of our young 'uns more bitterly now in peace, even than we did in the heat of the war of the early years." He closed the letter by revealing that he had escaped the peace celebrations and "bolted home from town and had my dark hour alone" (*Letters* 520). His mixed, yet intense reactions expressed in the confines of a letter and his impulse to grieve alone typify the avoidant-resistant response to loss. In Paris on the 11th, J. M. Barrie found most memorable "the happy faces," but they revealed to him, "it is finished" rather than "we have won" (*Letters* 125). On Armistice Day, Virginia Woolf wrote to her sister, the painter Vanessa Bell, that "I, on the whole though rather emotional ... feel also immensely melancholy" (*Letters* Vol. 2, 290). She added, "I think the rejoicing, so far as I've seen it, has been very sordid and depressing" (*Letters* Vol. 2, 292). She lamented the "very sentimental or completely stolid reaction of the London poor," and then added, "but I suppose the poor wretches haven't much notion how to express their feelings" (*Letters* Vol. 2, 293). This reaction seems unfeeling and perhaps reflects the threat of perceived chaos to her own jumble of emotions. She implies, however, that she, and others like her, writers and artists, had the advantage of being able to articulate their feelings of grief and to renegotiate severed relationships in formally ordered texts; that is what this study has attempted to demonstrate.

That is not to say that the general public did not find ways to express their grief. In *Loss*, Bowlby wrote that the bereaved typically continue to search for the lost loved one (27–28). With 499,000 soldiers listed as missing in action, 173,000 found but not identified, and well over 700,000 men confirmed dead, the losses were overwhelming, the searchers manifold. Thousands visited graves at the battlefronts of Europe, and they also held onto transitional objects of their lost loved ones, requesting photographs of gravesites, creating memorial books and domestic shrines (replete with medals, the Dead Man's Penny, and items of clothing or kit), and documenting the last days of their fallen men. Hundreds of thousands paid tribute at national memorials and thousands contributed to their local war memorials. Those who were educated enough and so inclined also read histories of the war, and there were plenty to choose from, along with photographic journalism and stories, poems, or plays about the conflict. *Punch* magazine in August 1918 made fun of this, stating that "War has not only stimulated the composition, but the perusal of poetry, especially among women" and published a verse depicting women "prescribing" themselves the works of various authors, depending on their condition:

> When the man-slump makes her fretty
> Susie takes to D. Rossetti,
> Though her sister Arabella
> Rather fancies Wilcox (Ella) ...
> And when Auntie heard by chance
> That the Curate was in France,
> Browning's enigmatic lyrics
> Helped to save her from hysterics (*Mr. Punch's* 247–48)

Interestingly, all of the writers called upon were safely Victorian, although Ella Wheeler Wilcox was still living and wrote spiritualist-influenced lines, such as her mantra: "The dead live: And they speak through us and to us" (359). Parody such as *Punch*'s reveals that the idea of literature as therapeutic, or what we now refer to as bibliotherapy, was definitely in the air, and of course harks back to the Romantic poets and beyond, but which during this period was being studied and applied more systematically by mental scientists. Students of the Orthopsychics Society, the educational branch of the Medico-Psychological Clinic of London, in which May Sinclair was heavily involved, read her novel *The Tree of Heaven* (1917) both as literature and as therapy (Boll 234). Wilfred Owen's doctor, Dr Arthur Brock, encouraged his shellshocked patient to write poems and later observed that, "In the powerful war-poems of Wilfred Owen we read the heroic testimony of one who having in the most literal sense 'faced the phantoms of the mind' had *all* but laid them ere the last call came; they still appear in his poetry but he fears them no longer" (as quoted in Hibberd 254–55). Nevertheless, formalized therapy such as this was only for the select few; there was no state system for dealing with the psychological dimension of mental distress, with psychological scars. Yet this was a culture most horrifically scarred and wounded. The physical evidence could not be avoided; according to Hanson:

> In almost every street there were blind men turning their sightless faces to the light, the maimed and disabled, standing with the arm of a jacket or a trouser leg flapping empty or hobbling on crutches down the street, and scarred or disfigured ex-servicemen – the French called them 'men with broken faces' and sculptors made metal masks to cover the ravaged features. (407)

He notes that there were 250,000 British amputees, and even by 1928 2.5 million war veterans still collected pensions for "wounds, disability or shell shock" (407). Psychological trauma was less easy to discern or quantify but it was pervasive.

Thus, many turned to the wounded healers, the writers, among them those studied here, to provide solace and in some cases insights into the afterlife. Their own conflicted feelings and attempts to renegotiate loss caught the collective mood. Sinclair's *Tree of Heaven*, for instance, was a bestseller, reaching its fourth print run by February 1918, and with further reprinting in the 1920s. Barrie's play *Dear Brutus* was a success both at home and in Europe and the US (Chaney 331; Mackail 534).

Huxley's early novels with their avoidant satire and mockery and Woolf's elegies *Jacob's Room* and *To the Lighthouse* galvanized the younger, post-war generation. The writers in this study continued to mediate the anxieties, sorrows, and anger related to the war, as well as attempts at transcendence right through to the 1930s with Huxley's bestselling *Eyeless in Gaza*. Ghosts lived among this culture, and people were keen to understand more about spirit phenomena, as we have seen. The survivors, the widows, were particularly prone to visions. Van Emden mentions a post-war study, which found that 14 percent of widows saw the ghosts of their dead husbands (227). The enormous popularity of Oliver Lodge's *Raymond*, fueled by the controversy around its claims of spirit communication, attests to this, as do all the numerous spirit soldier testimonies which followed in its wake. Psychical research and spiritualist texts proliferated. A cheaper, one-volume edition of Frederic Myers's *Human Personality and its Survival of Bodily Death*, edited by Myers's son Leo, was reprinted every year from 1917 until the 1920s. Another classic of psychical research, Edmund Gurney's *Phantasms of the Living* was similarly reprinted in a one-volume edition in November 1918, and ran into several impressions. Popular books, such as Lodge's *Ether and Reality* and *Phantom Walls* and Doyle's *The Vital Message*, continued to meet the demand for and give shape to notions about immortality. Although membership in the Church of England declined after the war, the Spiritualist movement burgeoned, with a quarter of a million joining the Spiritualists' National Union and a quarter of a million more practicing some form of spiritualism, with the aid of professional mediums or relying on their own talents. Ridicule of the claims of psychical research and especially spiritualism betrayed anxiety about the existence and nature of an afterlife and kept these issues in the forefront of consciousness through the popular press.

Nevertheless, the dominant mode of coping with war loss was avoidance (Jalland xiii, 9, 10, 56). In Britain, almost 250,000 widows and, depending on estimates, between 360,000 and 381,000 children lost fathers (van Emden 3; Newcombe 8). Reactions varied widely, as one would expect, some widows absorbing and grieving the loss, moving on, and remarrying, others responding in hysterical outbursts, anger, and breakdown, and for still more retreating into silence. Sociologist Tony Walter described "a pattern in families in which stress by women as well as by men, is coped with by not talking about it ... Children in the interwar period typically had parents who chose to remain silent about wartime experience and who bore the depression of the 1930s with quiet stoicism" (as quoted in Jalland 9). This response was not effective and could be harmful, with the unspoken emotions eating away at a person. In the same survey mentioned above, it was found that 12 percent of widows died within one year of losing their spouse (van Emden 227). In *Loss*, John Bowlby writes that parents who suppress feelings after a loss make it "almost impossible" for children to express their feelings, since they take their cue from parents: "Children are quick to read the signs. When a parent is afraid of feelings the children will hide their own. When a parent prefers silence the children, sooner or later, will cease their enquiries" (272). Van Emden provides anecdotal evidence from numerous children who experienced this in their homes after their father was killed. One such child, Letitia, recalled that her father "was never mentioned again as far as Mother was concerned," but she was fully aware of her mother's inner turmoil, writing that "because Mum bottled her emotions up it made the pain much worse" (as quoted in van Emden 116). In 1980, Bowlby wrote that there was no way of knowing what proportion of parents withhold expressing and sharing their emotion with children, but that various studies show that "it is common in both Britain and America" (272). We have even less means of discovering the proportion from the post-First World War period, since the first study focusing on children's reactions to war loss, psychoanalysts Anna Freud and Dorothy Burlingham's *War and Children*, was not published until 1943 and dealt with children who lost fathers during the Second World War. A collective study of those children who lost fathers or brothers in the First World War and then who became writers, such as Cynthia Asquith, Vera Brittain, Christopher Isherwood, Mollie Panter-Downes, and H.D., would give valuable insight into how the post-war generation coped.

Regarding the writers in this study, we have seen that their losses and trauma occurred in various forms, but that all of them discovered early on a means of addressing these challenges through writing. All of them developed an avoidant-resistant pattern of attachment, in some cases complicated by other issues, including alcoholism, poverty, bullying, and the imperative of concealing their sexual identity. This pattern of responding to loss gave them several advantages as writers. With a need to observe closely and to develop a rich inner life, they harbored strong emotional conflicts that could be drawn on, and which indeed generated impassioned energy in their writing. Frederic Myers first expressed strong feelings about the death of his father in his poetry, but subsequent losses, particularly of his love Annie Marshall, drove him to spend the rest of his life gathering evidence to support the possibility of survival beyond death. His writing, along with that of other prominent psychical researchers, helped shape a new conception of the afterlife, as well as expansion of human capabilities in areas such as automatic writing, telepathy, and spirit communication. Oliver Lodge built upon this foundation with his conception of the ether as well as many popular writings on immortality. Arthur Conan Doyle similarly proselytized about spirit communication after the war.

For those in this study who lived through the war, the losses experienced revived earlier trauma and they either developed or extended some form of mysticism as a means of renegotiating those losses. How successful was their mystical quest? In some cases, their written testaments to lost loved ones comprised an ethical form of communication allowing exploration of the person's identity, relationship with the mourner, and renegotiation of that relationship. Lodge's *Raymond*, Barrie's "A Well-Remembered Voice," Kipling's "Mary Postgate," and Virginia Woolf's *Jacob's Room* stand out in this regard, though re-visioning of severed relationships occurred in many of the works examined here. These testaments, whether in non-fiction or fictional form, in some cases enabled the writer in subsequent works to probe and expunge their childhood traumas, although the long-term therapeutic effectiveness of this effort varied. Barrie and Kipling were arguably the most crippled by their losses, and yet they still managed to create some of their most compelling, dense, and compressed writing after the war. Of course, owing to Owen's death we do not know whether his strategy proved successful, although the indications from poems like "Strange Meeting" suggest that he was on his way to reconciling the trauma of his war experience. Virginia Woolf's death by suicide brings up the specter of failure, and yet she managed her manic-depression for sixty years and lived more intensely and with a greater appreciation of the manifold joys of life than many of us.

In seeking consolation for their losses and understanding of the significance of them, and in questioning their permanence, the writers in this study turned to mysticism in its diverse forms, with varying degrees of commitment and with mixed consequences. Frederic Myers tried to maintain a scientific stance in describing supernormal phenomena in his magnum opus *Human Personality and its Survival of Bodily Death*, and yet on reaching the shadowy margins of his subject turned mystic. Oliver Lodge and Arthur Conan Doyle embraced the form of mysticism known as spiritualism and gained strength and clarity from it, to the extent that it absorbed their lives and channeled their writing into exposition of its truths. For the others, mysticism and spiritualism answered deep-seated needs and also became part of their aesthetic, enabling them to make tentative forays into the unseen, to ask questions, to play with the possibilities, and providing them with another layer to their work. The most enduring works of literature often have a dimension to them that resists analysis and closure, leaving intriguing questions unanswered, and this often involved mystical speculation. Aldous Huxley probably embraced mysticism most fully, as a discipline and experience, and yet even at the end of his life had doubts about it and felt compelled to rework childhood trauma. May Sinclair developed her experience of mysticism into her philosophical stance, in support of Idealism, but in her novels this does not obtrude. Sensuous mystical moments offering the possibility of transcendence arise naturally and play a defining role in her fiction, as has been more broadly recognized in Woolf's work. Owen had his own particular goal in giving shape to ghosts and the unseen as a mask for his sexual proclivities. Barrie and Kipling were the most ambivalent about the findings of psychical research and the practice of spiritualism, and yet gave form to unseen voices and visions throughout their work. As Evelyn Underhill wrote, mysticism paradoxically involves "withdrawal of attention from the bewildering multiplicity of things" and a retreat into unity of spirit, but also an openness or receptivity to "messages from another plane" (*Practical* 42–43) and a renewal and reengagement with life on a more vital plane. My hope is that this study has illuminated the benefits of employing psychobiography, drawing on the insights of object relations and attachment theory, to show how writers experienced this process and how it enhanced their creativity. Myers, Lodge, Doyle, Barrie, Kipling, Sinclair, Woolf, Owen, and Huxley collectively gave weight and respectability to the culture of mourning, defining its nature and shaping its outlets both during and after the First World War, and in most cases enhancing the appeal of imaginative writing on this subject. Perhaps the ideas of Myers, the ghost man, hover over the other writers. In *Irreducible Mind: Toward a Psychology for the 21st Century*, the Kellys and several other psychologists argue for a central position for Myers's work and for recognition of the role of mysticism in psychology, suggesting that his views of survival will continue to have an impact, as will the expression of loss and the grappling with ghosts in the works of all of these writers.

Notes

Introduction: Attachment, Mourning, and Mysticism

1. Telepathy was one of the most significant and accepted phenomena studied by the Society for Psychical Research. However, in the conclusion to his study of Myers's invention of telepathy, Roger Luckhurst feels compelled to dissociate himself from his subject matter, claiming "But no, in case you're asking, I don't believe in telepathy" (*Invention* 278).
2. Eisenstadt reports that in the 1921 Census from England and Wales, parental loss between the ages of 0–14 was 16.6 percent for the death of one parent, 11.9 percent for death of the father, 5.75 percent for death of the mother, and 1.2 percent for death of both parents (*Parental* 17).
3. Jalland mentions Bowlby's work in passing, but she does not apply the findings of attachment theory to her analysis of First World War loss (202, 244).
4. According to a contemporary phrase etymology website, "the stiff upper lip has gone out of favour in the UK and British heroes have been able to show more emotion. Footballers now cry when they lose and soldiers cry at comrades' funerals, both of which would have been unthinkable before WW II." http://www.phrases.org.uk/meanings/keep-a-stiff-upper-lip.html
5. This is the downfall of some psychoanalytically-informed so-called pathobiographies, of which Freud wrote one of the earliest, "Leonardo Da Vinci," in 1910, and of what Joyce Carol Oates has referred to as "pathographies," which focus to such a degree on psychological disorders that they denigrate the subject of the biography. See Joyce Carol Oates, "Adventures in Abandonment." http://www.nytimes.com/1988/08/28/books/adventures-in-abandonment.html (accessed 25 November 2014).

1 F. W. H. Myers: Loss and the Obsessive Study of Survival

1. As a child, Leopold Hamilton Myers was fearful of his father, and he later referred to him as a bore, according to his biographer G. H. Bantock (137). Interestingly, Bantock also remarks that Leopold's most striking characteristic was his "aloofness and detachment" (153). He committed suicide in 1944 at the age of sixty-two, after having had a career as an acclaimed writer of novels probing spiritual despair.
2. Myers published his observations about these characteristics of dreams as early as 1885 in *The Contemporary Review*, as quoted in Myers ("Subliminal" I 314).
3. Myers claimed that, "I here use the word 'self' as a brief descriptive term for any chain of memory sufficiently continuous, and embracing sufficient particulars, to acquire what is popularly called a character of its own. There will thus be one distinct supraliminal self at a time: but more than one subliminal self may exist, or may be called into existence" ("Subliminal" I 305–6).

4. Alan Gauld agreed, claiming that, "There was however without a doubt a mystical streak in both Myers's thinking and his personality." Myers had experienced mystic states at intervals from his youth. To Wilfred Ward he wrote that "It has been my lot during many years of my life, to feel in the most vivid manner almost the whole range (if I can judge from the well-known records of experience such as those of St Augustine, St Teresa, etc.) of spiritual conflict and ecstasy" (Ward, as quoted in Gauld 327).
5. Prominent social scientists who belonged to the SPR included Hippolyte Bernheim, William James, Pierre Janet, Charles Richet, Cesare Lombroso, Albert von Schrenk-Notzing, Sigmund Freud, and Carl Jung. Cf. *Dynamic Psychology* for a more extensive list of renowned SPR members (56, 61).
6. Oliver Lodge later wrote a book, *Christopher*, about her son's spiritualist communications after he was killed in the war in 1918, as will be discussed in Chapter 2.
7. H. A. Dallas, *Mors Janua Vitae?* (London: Rider, 1910); Geraldine Cummins, *The Road to Immortality* (London: Psychic Press, 1932); *Beyond Human Personality* (London: Psychic Press, 1935), and *Swan on a Black Lake* (London: Routledge, 1965).

2 Spirit Soldiers: Oliver Lodge's *Raymond* and *Christopher*

1. Richard van Emden, in *The Quick and the Dead*, for example claims that "Sir Oliver had come to spiritualism after the death of his son Raymond in 1915" (197).
2. *Raymond* sold for eleven shillings (Byrne 76). Besterman lists the editions (110, 114, 128).
3. The memorial epitaph on Raymond's tombstone is also included (*Raymond* 7).
4. London: Methuen & Co., 1918. Spirit-soldier communications include Elsa Barker, *War Letters from the Living Dead Man* (London: William Rider & Son, 1915); Wellesley Tudor Pole (W.T.P.), *Private Dowding* (London: John M. Watkins, 1917); Thomas Tiplady, *The Soul of the Soldier* (Grand Rapids: Fleming H. Revell Company, 1918); Rev. Walter Wynn, *Rupert Lives!* (London: Kingsley Press, 1918); J. S. M. Ward, *A Subaltern in Spirit Land*, 1920, later collected in *Gone West: Three Narratives of After-Death Experiences* (London: Psychic Book Club, 1944); Olive C. B. Pixley, *Olive Pixley's Spiritual Journey: Comprising "Listening In", "The Trail", "Human Document"* (Shere: Armour of Light Trust Council, 1999) (the three works were originally published separately in 1928, 1934, and 1947 respectively).
5. Edward Clodd, *The Question: A Brief History and Examination of Modern Spiritualism* (London: Grant Richards, 1917), pp. 265–301; Walter Cook, *Reflections on "Raymond"* [the book by Sir Oliver J. Lodge]: *An Appreciation and Analysis* (London: Grant Richards, 1917); Rev. Francis Little Hayes, "The War and the Doctrine of Immortality," *The Biblical World* 53(2) (March 1919): 115–26; Paul Hookham, *"Raymond": A Rejoinder Questioning the Validity of Certain Evidence and of Sir Oliver Lodge's Conclusions Regarding It* (Oxford: B. H. Blackwell, 1917); Charles Arthur Mercier, *Spiritualism and Sir Oliver Lodge* (London: Mental Culture Enterprise, 1917); Charles Lindley Wood, Viscount Halifax, *"Raymond": Some Criticisms [on the Work of that Name by Sir Oliver J. Lodge]. A Lecture Given ... February 14, 1917, with the Addition of a Preface* (London: A. R. Mowbray & Co., 1917).

6. Lodge again defended such attacks in a chapter of *Raymond Revised* in 1922.
7. Glen T. Hamilton, *Intention and Survival* (Toronto: Macmillan, 1942); Margaret Lillian Hamilton, *Is Survival a Fact?* (London: Psychic Press, 1969).

3 From Parodist to Proselytizer: Arthur Conan Doyle's "Vital Message"

1. Andrew S. Malec claims that "Conan Doyle's wholehearted devotion to spiritualism and allied paranormal pursuits has baffled most of his biographers, who could not reconcile Sherlock Holmes as creator with a man of, they felt, almost limitless credulity" (67).
2. In his survey of Doyle biographies, Lellenberg claims that "many who look to Sherlock Holmes as a supreme literary spokesman for rationalism feel dismay and bewilderment about his Creator having become a leading champion of a doctrine that seems at odds with his education and literary ideas" (11). Daniel Stashower calls Sherlock Holmes "the embodiment of cold logic" and observes that "then as now, his detractors have considered it unseemly, and perhaps a trifle witless, that such a man should suddenly profess an interest in spirits" (Stashower 161). See also Booth 314.
3. These characteristics are somewhat controversial, as Kenneth J. Sher notes in "Psychological Characteristics of Children of Alcoholics," *Alcohol Health and Research World* 21(3) (1997): 247–54.
4. David Gow, the Editor of *Light*, was only one of many who recognized Doyle's "Many-sided personality" (Lellenberg *Letters* 660).

4 "Well-Remembered Voices": Mourning and Spirit Communication in Barrie's and Kipling's First World War Narratives

1. Others include Andrew Lycett's *Rudyard Kipling* (1999), Phillip Mallett's *Rudyard Kipling: A Literary Life* (2003), William Dillingham's *Rudyard Kipling: Hell and Heroism* (2005), and Jad Adams's *Rudyard Kipling* (2006).
2. It is a sad irony that Margaret was not able to see the impact of the loss on J. M. since she had experienced a similarly profound loss, of her mother, when she was about Barrie's age (Barrie *Margaret* 27).
3. Barrie had responded in an unusually intense way to the death of another sister's fiancé in 1892 (Chaney 109).
4. Although Barrie claims that it was a "Scotch custom" for a woman to retain the maiden name among friends, he "loved to name her" this himself, perhaps suggesting an Oedipal fantasy of eliminating the father, who is rarely mentioned in the memoir (Barrie *Margaret* 7).
5. Chairs become a motif, including a description of Hyde Park benches, which are the focus of Margaret's anxiety about Barrie's well-being in London (Barrie *Margaret* 56).
6. Leonée Ormond claims that "from at least 1901, Barrie was fascinated by the idea of the ghost mother who comes back to earth to look for her children" (125).
7. Kemp (1988), however, reductively suggests that Kipling's psychological probing resembles Freud's and was contemporaneous with Freud's *Studies*

in *Hysteria*, which she erroneously claims (56) was published in England in 1895 (actually first in English in the USA in 1909), and his *Psychopathology of Everyday Life*, which she states was published in English in 1901 (when actually the English translation was published in England in 1914). It is much more likely that Kipling assimilated the psychological findings of the Society for Psychical Research in his early writing, which would help account for his integration of the psychic and psychological.
8. Leonée Ormond claims about the parting of father and daughter that "this is Barrie at his most haunted, and one of the few places in his plays where his own dread of vacancy emerges" (215).
9. Barrie's preoccupation with the past transformed him into a "most individual and bewildering ghost," as Cynthia Asquith put it (224), a cruel irony given that Barrie had in his early years so desperately wanted to replace that ghost boy David.

5 Mourning, the War, and the "New Mysticism" in May Sinclair and Virginia Woolf

1. Woolf lived under the illusion of civilian immunity for at least the first half of the war (Levenback 45).
2. Her last brother died in 1905, four years after her mother (Boll 27).
3. Letters to Katherine Tynan, 1 January 1902; Letters from Gwendolyn "Zack" Keats, 12 July 1899; Boll 8, 27, 59; Zegger 80.
4. Raitt (115) defers to Boll, who erroneously claims that "she [Sinclair] never contributed to either the *Journal* or the *Proceedings*. She had an artist's interest in the occult story as a creative exercise, and in the mysteriously happening psychic phenomena in life, but had no patience with the assumption that psychic phenomena were matters for scientific exploration according to a scientific methodology" (Boll 105). He may not have wanted to associate his subject with an organization no longer considered within the realm of science, and may have been unaware of its impressive status in English society in 1914.
5. These concern the question of cross-correspondences. According to Alan Gauld, cross-correspondences are "the series of parallel or interlinked communications obtained through different mediums and automatists, and allegedly devised by the spirits of deceased members of the Sidgwick group [of SPR researchers] for the benefit of their colleagues still in the flesh" (274). Though "particularly impressed by the latest Willett scripts," Sinclair argues for the necessity of checking an alternative psychological hypothesis that such cross-correspondences may occur because of telepathy between the living experimenters, who have a common desire that survival will be proved, rather than as signals from the beyond (Letter, *Journal of SPR*, 26 April 1917, 67).
6. Dr Holmes labels his condition as "nerve symptoms and nothing more" (*Dalloway* 82), while Sir William Bradshaw, who doesn't like to speak of madness, claims Septimus lacks proportion.
7. They are also not comforting since they are unknowable. Neither the motor car's occupants nor the aeroplane's message can be determined.
8. For Clarissa, "the most exquisite moment of her whole life" was when Sally kissed her in the garden at Bourton (*Dalloway* 33).

6 Purgatorial Passions: "The Ghost" (aka Wilfred Owen) in Owen's Poetry

1. Evidence that he did not employ ghosts in the traditional way is suggested by his only known "table-turning" experience in 1915, when he apparently was not convinced that spirits from the dead could communicate in séances. Following the incident, he exposed his friend "Raoul's trickery and made him confess it on the way home" (*Letters* 346).
2. Sassoon introduced Owen to his gay friends in London, among them Robert Ross and Charles Scott Moncrieff (Hibberd 102, 314–15).
3. Fellow poet and soldier David Jones was astonished at how Owen was able to write in the trenches with "a unique and marvellous detachment" (as quoted in Nicholas Murray, *The Red Sweet Wine of Youth: The Brave and Brief Lives of the War Poets* (New York: Little, Brown, 2010), 147).

7 *"Misty-schism"*: The Psychological Roots of Aldous Huxley's Mystical Modernism

1. In 1933 Huxley wrote to his childhood friend and fellow writer, Naomi Mitchison, "of course I am also to a considerable extent a function of defective eyesight. Keratitis punctata shaped and shapes me; and I in my turn made and make use of it" (Smith 373).
2. He did write in a letter to Jelly d'Aranyi, "she was a very wonderful woman. Trev was most like her. I have just been reading again what she wrote me before she died ..." (Bedford 58).
3. Aldous later wrote that "I was much alone and thrown on my own resources" (as quoted in Murray 35).
4. Huxley wrote in 1920 to Edward Marsh that he found much of what he had written "strange and undesirable – the result of ... following a spiral inwards, instead of outwards" (as quoted in Holmes 17).
5. Huxley continues: "we have to be dying to these obsessive memories. I mean, again the paradox is to be able to remember with extreme clarity, but not to be haunted." Laura adds, with impressive clarity, "Aldous is speaking here of the difference between the two memories, the informational memory and the emotional memory. The informational memory is essential to us, to carry on our daily life. Emotional memory has a more subtle, powerful, and, at times, all pervading quality; especially when unconscious, it can haunt us with ghosts of our emotional past, robbing us of the energy and attention we need here and now" (*Timeless* 182–83).

Works Cited

Adult Children of Alcoholics World Service Organization, Inc. The Laundry List. http://www.adultchildren.org/lit/Laundry_List.php (accessed 10 July 2014).
Aller, Susan Bivin, *J. M. Barrie: The Magic Behind Peter Pan* (Minneapolis: Lerner, 1994).
Anisfeld, Leon and Arnold D. Richards, "The Replacement Child: Variations on a Theme in History and Psychoanalysis." *The Psychoanalytic Study of the Child* 55 (January 2000): 301–18.
Asquith, Cynthia, *Portrait of Barrie* (London: James Barrie, 1954).
Austin, James Bliss, "The Family's Counterattack." In Jon L. Lellenberg (ed.), *The Quest for Arthur Conan Doyle: Thirteen Biographers in Search of a Life* (Carbondale: Southern Illinois University Press, 1987), pp. 105–10.
Bantock, G. H., *L. H. Myers: A Critical Study* (London: Jonathan Cape, 1956).
Barlow, Adrian, "Commissioned Article: Mistaking Magdalen for the Menin Gate: Edmund Blunden, November 1 1931." 25 April 2010. http://www.edmundblunden.org/newsevent.php?newseventid=1141 (accessed 28 September 2014).
Barrie, J. M., *Better Dead* (1891 Author's Edition) (New York: Charles Scribner's Sons, 1896). Project Gutenberg. http://www.gutenberg.org/files/20807/20807-h/20807-h.htm (accessed 16 January 2008).
—— *Dear Brutus* (New York: Charles Scribner's Sons, 1922).
—— *The Greenwood Hat, being A Memoir of James Anon 1885–1887* (London: Peter Davies, 1937).
—— *Letters of J. M. Barrie*. Ed. Viola Meynell (London: Peter Davies, 1942).
—— *The Little White Bird* (London: Hodder & Stoughton, 1902).
—— *Margaret Ogilvy* (London: Hodder & Stoughton, 1896).
—— "The New Word." *Echoes of the War* (New York: Charles Scribner's Sons, 1918).
—— "A Well-Remembered Voice." *Echoes of the War* (New York: Charles Scribner's Sons, 1918).
Barrow, Logie, *Independent Spirits: Spiritualism and English Plebians 1850–1910* (New York: Routledge, 1986).
Bazin, Nancy Topping and Jane Hamovit Lauter, "Virginia Woolf's Keen Sensitivity to War: Its Roots and Its Impact on Her Novels." In Mark Hussey (ed. and "Introduction"), *Virginia Woolf and War: Fiction, Reality and Myth* (New York: Syracuse University Press, 1991), pp. 14–39.
Beckson, Karl, *London in the 1890s: A Cultural History* (New York: Norton, 1992).
Bedford, Sybille, *Aldous Huxley: A Biography* (2 vols.) (London: Chatto & Windus, 1973–74).
Beer, John, "Myers's Secret Message." In *Providence and Love: Studies in Wordsworth, Channing, Myers, George Elliott, and Ruskin* (Oxford: Oxford University Press, 1998).
Bell, Quentin, *Virginia Woolf: A Biography*. Vol. I: *Virginia Stephen 1882–1912* (London: Hogarth Press, 1972).

Benson, A. C., "Frederic Myers." In *The Leaves of the Tree: Studies in Biography* (London: Smith, Elder & Co., 1911).
Beresford, J. D., "The Crux of Psychical Research," Part I, *Westminster Gazette* (6 March 1920): 8; Part II, *Westminster Gazette* (13 March 1920): 8.
——— "More New Facts in Psychical Research," *Harper's* 144 (March 1922): 475–78.
Besterman, Theodore, *A Bibliography of Sir Oliver Lodge F. R. S.* Compiled by Theodore Besterman; Foreword by Sir Oliver Lodge (London: Humphrey Milford, Oxford University Press, 1935).
Birkenhead, Lord, *Rudyard Kipling* (New York: Random House, 1978).
Birkin, Andrew, *J. M. Barrie and the Lost Boys* (London: Constable, 1979).
Boll, Theophilus E. M., *Miss May Sinclair: Novelist. A Biographical and Critical Introduction* (Rutherford, NJ: Fairleigh Dickinson University Press, 1973).
Booth, Martin, *The Doctor, the Detective and Arthur Conan Doyle* (London: Hodder & Stoughton, 1997).
Bowlby, John, *Attachment and Loss*. Vol. III: *Loss: Sadness and Depression* (Harmondsworth: Penguin, 1985).
——— *The Making and Breaking of Affectional Bonds* (London: Tavistock, 1979).
——— *A Secure Base: Clinical Applications of Attachment Theory* (London: Routledge, 1988).
Brandon, Ruth, *The Spiritualists: The Passion for the Occult in the Nineteenth and Twentieth Centuries* (New York: Prometheus, 1985).
Briggs, Julia, *Night Visitors: The Rise and Fall of the English Ghost Story* (London: Faber and Faber, 1977).
Brink, Andrew, *Bertrand Russell: The Psychobiography of a Moralist* (Atlantic Highlands, NJ: Humanities Press International, 1989).
——— *Creativity as Repair* (Hamilton, Ont.: Cromlech Press, 1982).
——— *Desire and Avoidance in Art* (New York: Peter Lang, 2007).
——— *Loss and Symbolic Repair* (Hamilton, Ont.: Cromlech Press, 1977).
——— *Obsession and Culture: A Study of Sexual Obsession in Modern Fiction* (Madison, NJ: Fairleigh Dickinson University Press, 1996).
Browning, Don S., *Pluralism and Personality: William James and Some Contemporary Cultures of Psychology* (Lewisburg: Bucknell University Press, 1980).
Bullett, Gerald, *The English Mystics* (London: Michael Joseph, 1950).
Buse, Peter and Andrew Stott (eds.), *Ghosts: Deconstruction, Psychoanalysis, History* (Basingstoke: Palgrave Macmillan, 1999).
Byrne, Georgina, *Modern Spiritualism and the Church of England, 1850–1939* (Woodbridge: Boydell Press, 2010).
Cannadine, D., "War and Death, Grief and Mourning in Modern Britain." In J. Whaley (ed.), *Mirrors of Mortality: Studies in the Social History of Death* (New York: St Martin's Press, 1981).
Caramagno, Thomas C., *The Flight of the Mind: Virginia Woolf's Art and Manic-Depressive Illness* (Berkeley: University of California Press, 1992).
Carr, John Dickson, *The Life of Sir Arthur Conan Doyle* (New York: Carroll and Graf, 1987).
Carrington, Hereward, *Psychical Phenomena and the War* (New York: Dodd Mead, 1918).
Cassidy, Jude and Phillip R. Shaver (eds.), *Handbook of Attachment: Theory, Research, and Clinical Applications* (New York: Guilford Press, 2008).

Cavaliero, Glen, *The Supernatural and English Fiction* (Oxford: Oxford University Press, 1995).
Cerullo, John J., *The Secularization of the Soul: Psychical Research in Modern Britain* (Philadelphia: Institute for the Study of Human Issues, 1982).
Chaney, Lisa, *Hide-and-Seek with Angels: A Life of J. M. Barrie* (London: Hutchinson, 2005).
Cooke, Ivan (ed.), *The Return of Arthur Conan Doyle* (Liss, Hampshire: The White Eagle Publishing Trust, 1963). Rpt. of *Thy Kingdom Come* (London: Wright and Brown, 1933).
Cox, Don Richard, *Arthur Conan Doyle* (New York: Ungar, 1985).
Crabtree, Adam, "Automatism and Secondary Centers of Consciousness." In Edward F. Kelly, Emily Williams Kelly, Adam Crabtree, Alan Gauld, Michael Grosso, and Bruce Greyson (eds.), *Irreducible Mind: Toward a Psychology for the Twenty-First Century* (New York: Rowman & Littlefield, 2010), pp. 301–65.
Crittenden, Patricia McKinsey, "Teoria dell'attaccamento, psicopatologia e psicoterapia: L'approccio dinamico maturativo" [Attachment Theory, Psychopathology, and Psychotherapy: The Dynamic Maturational Approach]. *Psicoterapia* 30 (2005): 171–82.
Crittenden, Patricia McKinsey and Angelika Hartl Claussen, *The Organization of Attachment Relationships: Maturation, Culture, and Context* (Cambridge: Cambridge University Press, 2000).
Crittenden, Patricia McKinsey and Andrea Landini, *Assessing Adult Attachment: A Dynamic-Maturational Approach to Discourse Analysis* (New York: Norton, 2011).
Cummins, Geraldine, *Beyond Human Personality: Being a Detailed Description of the Future Life Purporting to be Communicated by the Late F. W. H. Myers. Containing an Account of the Gradual Development of Human Personality into Cosmic Personality* (London: Nicholson and Watson, 1935).
—— *The Road to Immortality* (London: Psychic Press, 1935).
—— *Swan on a Black Lake* (London: Routledge, 1965).
Dallas, Helen Alex, *Mors Janua Vitae? A Discussion of Certain Communications Purporting to Come from F. W. H. Myers* (London: Rider, 1910).
Dawson-Scott, Catherine, *From Four Who Are Dead* (London: Arrowsmith, 1926).
Deery, June, *Aldous Huxley and the Mysticism of Science* (New York: St Martin's Press, 1996).
DeSalvo, Louise, *Virginia Woolf: The Impact of Childhood Sexual Abuse on Her Life and Work* (Boston: Beacon, 1989).
Doyle, Arthur Conan, *The Complete Sherlock Holmes*. "Preface" Christopher Morley (2 vols.) (New York: Doubleday, 1953).
—— "Early Psychic Experiences." *Pearsons's Magazine* (March 1924): 208–9.
—— *The Edge of the Unknown* (New York: Putnam's, 1930).
—— *The Land of Mist* (New York: Doran, 1926).
—— *Memories and Adventures* (Boston: Little, Brown, 1924).
—— *The Mystery of Cloomber* (New York: Mershon [n.d.]).
—— *The New Revelation* (New York: Doran, 1918).
—— "The Parasite." 6 May 2004. http://tsat.transform.to/stories/parasite.html (accessed 10 August 2014).
—— *Pheneas Speaks: Direct Spirit Communications in the Family Circle* (London: Psychic Press, 1927).

Doyle, Arthur Conan, "The Poison Belt." In Jeffrey Meyers and Valerie Meyers (eds.), *The Sir Arthur Conan Doyle Reader: From Sherlock Holmes to Spiritualism* (New York: Copper Square Press, 2002), pp. 361–433.
—— *The Stark Munro Letters* (London: Longmans, Green, 1895).
—— *The Unknown Conan Doyle: Uncollected Stories*. Compiled and "Introduction" by John Michael Gibson and Richard Lancelyn Green (London: Secker & Warburg, 1982).
—— *The Vital Message* (London: Hodder & Stoughton, 1919).
—— *The Wanderings of a Spiritualist* (London: Hodder & Stoughton, 1921).
Doyle, Georgina, *Out of the Shadows: The Untold Story of Arthur Conan Doyle's First Family* (Ashcroft, BC: Calabash Press, 2004).
Dudgeon, Piers, *Captivated: J. M. Barrie, the du Mauriers and the Dark Side of Neverland* (London: Chatto & Windus, 2008).
Dunaway, David King, *Aldous Huxley Recollected: An Oral History* (New York: Carroll and Graf, 1995).
Dunbar, Janet, *J. M. Barrie: The Man Behind the Image* (London: Collins, 1970).
Dunlap, Knight, *Mysticism, Freudianism and Scientific Psychology* (1920) (Freeport, NY: Books for Libraries Press, 1971).
Eigen, Michael, *The Psychoanalytic Mystic* (Binghamton, NY: ESF Publishers, 1998).
Eisenstadt, Marvin, Andre Haynal, Pierre Rentchnick, and Pierre de Senarclens, *Parental Loss and Achievement* (Madison, CT: International Universities Press, 1989).
—— "Understanding Genius and Loss: The Psychology of Creative, Scientific, and Political Achievement." Unpublished typescript.
Erickson, Kai, "Notes on Trauma and Community." *American Imago* 48(4) (1991): 455–72.
Fairbairn, W. R. D., "Schizoid Factors in the Personality." In *Psychoanalytic Studies of the Personality* (London: Routledge, 1994a), pp. 3–27.
—— "A Synopsis of the Development of the Author's Views Regarding the Structure of the Personality." In *Psychoanalytic Studies of the Personality* (London: Routledge, 1994b) pp. 162–79.
—— "The War Neuroses – Their Nature and Significance." In *Psychoanalytic Studies of the Personality* (London: Routledge, 1994c), pp. 256–88.
Fleming, Alice, "My Brother, Rudyard Kipling." *The Kipling Journal* 84 (December 1947): 3–4.
Forster, Laurel, "Women and War Zones: May Sinclair's Personal Negotiation with the First World War." In T. Gomez-Reus and A. Usandizaga (eds.), *Inside Out: Women Negotiating, Subverting, Appropriating Public and Private Space* (Amsterdam: Rodopi, 2008), pp. 229–48.
Fraser, Raymond and George Wickes, Interview with Aldous Huxley. "The Art of Fiction No. 24." *The Paris Review* (Spring 1960). http://www.theparisreview.org/interviews/4698/the-art-of-fiction-no-24-aldous-huxley (accessed 16 March 2011).
Freedman, Ariela, *Death, Men and Modernism: Trauma and Narrative in British Fiction from Hardy to Woolf* (New York: Routledge, 2003).
Freud, Sigmund, "A Note on the Unconscious in Psychoanalysis." *Proceedings of the Society for Psychical Research* 26(66) (1912): 312–18.

——— "The Uncanny." In *Art and Literature* (The Pelican Freud Library) Vol. 14. Trans. James Strachey (Harmondsworth: Penguin, 1987).

Friedman, Alan Warren, *Fictional Death and the Modernist Enterprise* (Cambridge: Cambridge University Press, 1995).

Frosh, Stephen, *Hauntings: Psychoanalysis and Ghostly Transmissions* (Basingstoke: Palgrave Macmillan, 2013).

Fussell, Paul, *The Great War and Modern Memory* (Oxford: Oxford University Press, 1977).

Garrett, Eileen, *Many Voices: The Autobiography of a Medium* (New York: Putnam's, 1968).

Gauld, Alan, *The Founders of Psychical Research* (New York: Schocken Books, 1968).

Gaythorpe, Elizabeth (ed.), *Unpublished F. W. H. Myers Scripts Selected from the Richmond Material* (C.P.S. Paper No. 4) (London: College of Psychic Studies, 1950).

Gilbert, Elliot L., "Haunted Houses: Place and Dispossession in Rudyard Kipling's World." In Norman Page and Peter Preston (eds.), *The Literature of Place* (Basingstoke: Macmillan, 1993), pp. 87–106.

Goldman, Dorothy, Jane Gledhill, and Judith Hattaway, *Women Writers and the Great War* (New York: Twayne, 1995).

Gray, Donald, "Rudyard Kipling." In William F. Naufftus (ed. and intro.), *British Short-Fiction Writers, 1880–1914: The Romantic Tradition. Dictionary of Literary Biography*, Vol. 156 (Detroit, MI: Gale, 1995), pp. 181–99.

Green, Richard Lancelyn, "His Final Tale of Chivalry." In Jon L. Lellenberg (ed.), *The Quest for Arthur Conan Doyle: Thirteen Biographers in Search of a Life* (Carbondale: Southern Illinois University Press, 1987), pp. 38–63.

Grout, Leslie A. and Bronna D. Romanoff, "Replacement Children." In *Encyclopedia of Death and Dying*. http://www.deathreference.com/Py-Se/Replacement-Children.html (accessed 20 June 2014).

Hall, Trevor, *The Strange Case of Edmund Gurney* (London: Duckworth, 1980).

Hamilton, Trevor, *Immortal Longings: F. W. H. Myers and the Victorian Search for Life After Death* (Exeter: Imprint Academic, 2009).

Hanson, Neil, *The Unknown Soldier: The Story of the Missing of the Great War* (London: Corgi, 2007).

Haynes, Renée, *The Society For Psychical Research, 1882–1982: A History* (London: Macdonald & Co., 1982).

Hayward, Rhodri, *Resisting History: Popular Religion and the Origins of the Unconscious* (Manchester: Manchester University Press, 2007).

Hazelgrove, Jenny, *Spiritualism and British Society Between the Wars* (Manchester: Manchester University Press, 2000).

Hess, David J., *Science in the New Age* (Madison: University of Wisconsin Press, 1993).

Hibberd, Dominic, *Wilfred Owen: A New Biography* (London: Weidenfeld & Nicolson, 2002).

Higham, Charles, *The Adventures of Conan Doyle: The Life of the Creator of Sherlock Holmes* (New York: Norton, 1976).

Hill, J. Arthur, *Letters from Sir Oliver Lodge*. Compiled by J. Arthur Hill (London: Cassell, 1932).

Hipp, Daniel, *The Poetry of Shell Shock: Wartime Trauma and Healing in Wilfred Owen, Ivor Gurney and Siegfried Sassoon* (Jefferson, NC: McFarland & Co., 2005).

Hoffman, Frederick J., *The Mortal No: Death and the Modern Imagination* (Princeton: Princeton University Press, 1964).
Holberton, Philip, "Epitaphs of the War." Notes. 26 June 2012. http://www.kiplingsociety.co.uk/poems_epitaphs.htm (accessed 25 September 2014).
Holberton, Philip and Alastair Wilson, "London Stone." Notes. http://www.kiplingsociety.co.uk/rg_londonstone1.htm (accessed 25 September 2014).
Hollingdale, Peter (ed. and "Introduction"), *J. M. Barrie: Peter Pan and Other Plays: The Admirable Crichton; Peter Pan; When Wendy Grew Up; What Every Woman Knows; Mary Rose* (Oxford: Oxford University Press, 1995).
Holmes, Charles M., *Aldous Huxley and the Way to Reality* (Bloomington: Indiana University Press, 1970).
Howe, David, *Attachment Across the Life Course: A Brief Introduction* (Basingstoke: Palgrave Macmillan, 2011).
Huxley, Aldous, *Brave New World* (1932) (London: Flamingo, 1998).
——— *Collected Poetry of Aldous Huxley*. Ed. Donald Watt (London: Chatto & Windus, 1971).
——— *Crome Yellow* (1921) (Mineola, NY: Dover, 2004).
——— *The Doors of Perception and Heaven and Hell* (Harmondsworth: Penguin, 1960).
——— *Ends and Means* (London: Chatto & Windus, 1937).
——— *Eyeless in Gaza* (1936) (London: Chatto & Windus, 1955).
——— "Foreword." In *Human Personality and its Survival of Bodily Death* by F. W. H. Myers. Ed. Susy Smith (New York: University Books, 1961).
——— *Music at Night and Other Essays* (1931) (London: Chatto & Windus, 1949).
——— "The Oddest Science." In *Collected Essays* (New York: Harper & Row, 1958).
——— *The Perennial Philosophy* (London: Chatto & Windus, 1946).
——— *Proper Studies* (London: Chatto & Windus, 1927).
——— *Those Barren Leaves* (1925) (Harmondsworth: Penguin, 1972).
——— *Time Must Have a Stop* (London: Chatto & Windus, 1944).
——— *The World of Light: A Comedy in Three Acts* (London: Chatto & Windus, 1931).
Huxley, Laura, *This Timeless Moment* (New York: Farrar, Straus & Giroux, 1968).
Hynes, Samuel, *The Edwardian Turn of Mind* (1968) (Princeton: Princeton University Press, 1975).
Inglis, Brian, *Science and Parascience: A History of the Paranormal, 1914–1939* (London: Hodder & Stoughton, 1984).
Izzo, David Garrett, *A Change of Heart: A Novel* (Arlington, VA: Gival, 2003).
——— *The Influence of Mysticism on 20th Century British and American Literature* (Jefferson, NC: McFarland and Co., 2009).
Jalland, Patricia, *Death in War and Peace: A History of Loss and Grief in England, 1914–1970* (Oxford: Oxford University Press, 2010).
James, William, "Frederic Myers's Service to Psychology." *Proceedings of the Society for Psychical Research*. Vol. XVII, Part XLII, May 1901. Reprinted in Gardner Murphy and Robert O. Ballou (eds.), *William James on Psychical Research* (1960) (Clifton: Augustus M. Kelley, 1973).
——— Review of "*Human Personality and its Survival of Bodily Death*." *Proceedings of the Society for Psychical Research*. Vol. XVIII, Part XLVI, June 1903. Reprinted in Gardner Murphy and Robert O. Ballou (eds.), *William James on Psychical Research* (1960) (Clifton: Augustus M. Kelley, 1973).

―― *The Varieties of Religious Experience: A Study in Human Nature* (New York: Longmans, Green and Co., 1902).
Jarret, Derek, *The Sleep of Reason: Fantasy and Reality from the Victorian Age to the First World War* (London: Weidenfeld & Nicolson, 1988).
Jervis, John and Jo Collins, *Uncanny Modernity: Cultural Theories, Modern Anxieties* (Basingstoke: Palgrave Macmillan, 2008).
Johnson, George M., "Apparition of a Genre: The Psychical Case Study in the Pre-Modernist British Short Story." *Studies in the Fantastic* No. 1 (Summer 2008): 3–17.
―― *Dynamic Psychology in Modernist British Fiction* (Basingstoke: Palgrave Macmillan, 2006).
―― "A Haunted House: Ghostly Presences in Virginia Woolf's Essays and Early Fiction." In Jeanne Dubino and Beth C. Rosenberg (eds.), *Virginia Woolf and the Essay* (New York: St Martin's Press, 1997).
―― "May Sinclair: The Evolution of a Psychological Novelist." In Frederico Pereira (ed.), *Literature and Psychoanalysis* (Lisbon: Instituto Superior de Psicologia Aplicada, 1998), pp. 149–57.
―― "'The Spirit of the Age': Virginia Woolf's Response to Second Wave Psychology." *Twentieth Century Literature* 40(2) (Fall 1994): 139–64.
Jolly, W. P., *Sir Oliver Lodge* (Rutherford: Fairleigh Dickinson University Press, 1975).
Kahn, M. Masud R., "Secret as Potential Space." In Simon A. Grolnick and Leonard Barkin (eds.), *Between Reality and Fantasy: Transitional Objects and Phenomena* (New York: Aronson, 1978), pp. 259–70.
Kavaler-Adler, Susan, *The Compulsion to Create: A Psychoanalytic Study of Women Artists* (New York: Routledge, 1993).
Keating, Peter, *The Haunted Study: A Social History of the English Novel, 1875–1914* (London: Secker & Warburg, 1989).
Keeley, James P., "Subliminal Promptings: Psychoanalytical Theory and the Society for Psychical Research." *American Imago: Studies in Psychoanalysis and Culture* 58(4): 767–91.
Kelly, Edward F., Emily Williams Kelly, Adam Crabtree, Alan Gauld, Michael Grosso, and Bruce Greyson, *Irreducible Mind: Toward a Psychology of the 21st Century* (Lanham, MD: Rowman & Littlefield, 2010).
Kemp, Sandra, *Kipling's Hidden Narratives* (Oxford: Basil Blackwell, 1988).
Kerr, Douglas, *Conan Doyle: Writing, Profession, and Practice* (Oxford: Oxford University Press, 2013).
Kipling, Rudyard, "An Only Son." In *Epitaphs of the War*. http://www.kiplingsociety.co.uk/poems_epitaphs.htm (accessed 25 September 2014).
―― "Baa Baa, Black Sheep." In Thomas Pinney (ed.), *Something of Myself and Other Autobiographical Writings* (Cambridge: Cambridge University Press, 1990).
―― "The Brushwood Boy." In *The Day's Work* (London: Macmillan, 1898).
―― "Common Form." In *Epitaphs of the War*. http://www.kiplingsociety.co.uk/poems_epitaphs.htm (accessed 10 September 2014).
―― "En-dor." http://www.kiplingsociety.co.uk/rg_endor1.htm (accessed 15 September 2014).
―― "The Gardener." In *Debits and Credits* (London: Macmillan, 1926).
―― *The Letters of Rudyard Kipling*. Ed. Thomas Pinney. Volume 4: *1911–19* (Iowa City: University of Iowa Press, 1999).

Kipling, Rudyard, "London Stone." http://www.kiplingsociety.co.uk/poems_londonstone.htm (accessed 15 September 2014).
—— "A Madonna of the Trenches." In *Debits and Credits* (London: Macmillan, 1926).
—— "Mary Postgate." In *A Diversity of Creatures* (London: Macmillan, 1917).
—— "My Boy Jack." http://www.kiplingsociety.co.uk/poems_jack.htm (accessed 15 September 2014).
—— "My Own True Ghost Story." In John Beecroft (ed.), *Kipling: A Selection of His Stories and Poems* (New York: Doubleday, 1956).
—— "The Sending of Dana Da." In *In Black and White* (New York: Charles Scribner's Sons, 1907).
—— "Shock." In *Epitaphs of the War*. http://www.kiplingsociety.co.uk/poems_epitaphs.htm (accessed 10 September 2014).
—— *Something of Myself and Other Autobiographical Writings*. Ed. Thomas Pinney (Cambridge: Cambridge University Press, 1990).
—— "They." In *Traffics and Discoveries* (London: Macmillan, 1904).
—— "Wireless." In *Traffics and Discoveries* (London: Macmillan, 1904).
Kollar, Rene, *Searching for Raymond: Anglicanism, Spiritualism, and Bereavement Between the Two World Wars* (Lanham, MD: Lexington Books, 2000).
Lee, Hermione, *Virginia Woolf* (London: Vintage, 1997).
Leichtman, Robert R., *From Heaven to Earth: Sir Oliver Lodge Returns* (Columbus, OH: Ariel Press, 1979).
Lellenberg, Jon L. (ed.), *The Quest for Arthur Conan Doyle: Thirteen Biographers in Search of a Life* (Carbondale: Southern Illinois University Press, 1987).
Lellenberg, Jon L., Daniel Stashower, and Charles Foley (eds.), *Arthur Conan Doyle: A Life in Letters* (London: HarperCollins, 2007).
Lerner, Jeffrey C., "Changes in Attitudes Toward Death: The Widow in Great Britain in the Early Twentieth Century." In Bernard Schoenberg et al. (eds.), *Bereavement: Its Psychosocial Aspects* (New York: Columbia University Press, 1975).
Levenback, Karen L., "Virginia Woolf's 'War in the Village' and 'The War From the Street': An Illusion of Immunity." In Mark Hussey (ed. and "Introduction"), *Virginia Woolf and War: Fiction, Reality and Myth* (New York: Syracuse University Press, 1991), pp. 40–57.
Levy, Paul, "The Wounded Healer, Part 1." http://www.awakeninthedream.com/wordpress/the-wounded-healer-part-1/ (accessed 13 June 2014).
Lodge, Sir Oliver, "Christianity and Spiritualism." In J. Marchant (ed.), *Life after Death according to Christianity and Spiritualism* (London: Cassell, 1925).
—— *Christopher: A Study in Human Personality* (London: Cassell, 1918).
—— "Continuity," *Nature* 92 (11 September 1913): 33–48.
—— *Conviction of Survival: Two Discourses in Memory of F. W. H. Myers* (London: Methuen, 1930).
—— *Ether and Reality* (London: Hodder & Stoughton, 1925).
—— *The Ether of Space* (London: Harper, 1909).
—— *My Philosophy* (London: Ernest Benn, 1933).
—— *Past Years: An Autobiography* (1931) (New York: Charles Scribner's Sons, 1932).
—— *Raymond, or Life and Death* (New York: Doran, 1916).
—— *School Teaching and School Reform* (London: Williams and Norgate, 1905).

―――― *The Survival of Man* (New York: Moffat, Yard, 1909).
―――― *The War and After* (London: Methuen, 1915).
―――― *Why I Believe in Personal Immortality* (London: Cassell, 1928).
Luckhurst, Roger, *The Invention of Telepathy* (Oxford: Oxford University Press, 2002).
Lycett, Andrew, *Conan Doyle: The Man Who Created Sherlock Holmes* (London: Weidenfeld & Nicolson, 2007).
Mackail, Denis, *The Story of J.M.B: A Biography* (London: Peter Davies, 1941).
McCorristine, Shane, *Spectres of the Self: Thinking about Ghosts and Ghost-Seeing in England, 1750–1920* (Cambridge: Cambridge University Press, 2010).
―――― (ed.), *Spiritualism, Mesmerism and the Occult, 1800–1920* (London: Pickering & Chatto, 2012).
Malec, Andrew S., "Commitment to Great Causes." In Jon L. Lellenberg (ed.), *The Quest for Arthur Conan Doyle: Thirteen Biographers in Search of a Life* (Carbondale: Southern Illinois University Press, 1987, pp. 64–76.
May, Keith M., *Aldous Huxley* (London: Elek, 1972).
Melton, J. Gordon, "Frederic William Henry Myers." In *Encyclopedia of Occultism and Parapsychology* (5th edn.) (Farmington Hills: Gale Group, 2001).
Mercier, Charles A., *Spiritualism and Sir Oliver Lodge* (London: Watts, 1917).
Meyers, Jeffrey and Valerie Meyers (eds.), *The Sir Arthur Conan Doyle Reader: From Sherlock Holmes to Spiritualism* (New York: Copper Square Press, 2002).
Mitchell, T. W., *Beneath the Threshold* (London: Methuen, 1931).
Moore, E. Garth, *Try the Spirits: Christianity and Psychical Research* (New York: Oxford University Press, 1977).
Mr. Punch's History of the Great War (London: Cassell, 1919).
Mumford, Laura Stempel, "May Sinclair's *Tree of Heaven*: The Vortex of Feminism, the Community of War." In Helen Cooper, Adrienne Auslander Munich, and Susan Merrill Squier (eds.), *Arms and the Woman: War, Gender, and Literary Representation* (Chapel Hill: University of North Carolina Press, 1989), pp.168–83.
Murray, Nicholas, *Aldous Huxley* (New York: Thomas Dunne Books, 2002).
Myers, Frederic W. H., *Collected Poems*. Ed. Eveleen Myers (London: Macmillan, 1921).
―――― *Fragments of Inner Life*. 1893 (London: The Society for Psychical Research, 1961).
―――― "Fragments of Inner Life." In Eveleen Myers (ed.), *Fragments of Prose and Poetry* (London: Longmans, Green, 1904).
―――― *Human Personality and its Survival of Bodily Death* (2 vols.) (New York: Longmans, Green, 1903).
―――― "Hysteria and Genius." *Journal of the Society for Psychical Research* 8(138) (April 1897): 51–59.
―――― "The Mechanism of Hysteria." *Proceedings of the Society for Psychical Research* Vol. IX (June 1893): 3–25.
―――― "Multiplex Personality." *Nineteenth Century* 20 (20 November 1886): 648–66.
―――― "The Principles of Psychology." Review of William James's *The Principles of Psychology*. In *Proceedings of the Society for Psychical Research* Vol. VII (1891): 111–33.
―――― "The Subliminal Consciousness. Chapter I. General Characteristics of Subliminal Messages." *Proceedings of the Society for Psychical Research* Vol. VII (1892): 298–327.

Myers, Frederic W. H., "The Subliminal Consciousness. Chapter II. The Mechanism of Suggestion." *Proceedings of the Society for Psychical Research* Vol. VII (1892): 327–55.
—— "The Subliminal Consciousness. Chapter III. The Mechanism of Genius." *Proceedings of the Society for Psychical Research* Vol. VIII (1892): 333–61.
—— "The Subliminal Consciousness. Chapter IV. Hypermnesic Dreams." *Proceedings of the Society for Psychical Research* Vol. VIII (1892): 361–404.
—— "The Subliminal Consciousness. Chapter V. Sensory Automatism and Induced Hallucinations." *Proceedings of the Society for Psychical Research* Vol. VIII (1892): 436–535.
—— "The Subliminal Consciousness. Chapter VI. The Mechanism of Hysteria." *Proceedings of the Society for Psychical Research* Vol. IX (1893–94): 3–25.
—— "The Subliminal Consciousness. Chapter VII. Motor Automatism." *Proceedings of the Society for Psychical Research* Vol. IX (1893–94): 26–128.
—— "The Subliminal Consciousness. Chapter VIII. The Relation of Supernormal Phenomena to Time; – Retrocognition." *Proceedings of the Society for Psychical Research* Vol. XI (1895): 334–593.
Myers, W. L., *The Later Realism: A Study of Characterisation in the British Novel* (Chicago: University of Chicago Press, 1927).
Nelson, G. K., *Spiritualism and Society* (London: Routledge & Kegan Paul, 1969).
Newcombe, Nora and Jeffrey C. Lerner, "Britain Between the Wars: The Historical Context of Bowlby's Theory of Attachment." *Psychiatry* 45(1) (February 1982): 1–12.
Nordon, Pierre, *Conan Doyle* (London: John Murray, 1966).
Oppenheim, Janet, *The Other World: Spiritualism and Psychical Research in England, 1850–1914* (Cambridge: Cambridge University Press, 1985).
Ormond, Leonée, *J. M. Barrie* (Edinburgh: Scottish Academic Press, 1987).
Ouditt, Sharon, *Fighting Forces, Writing Women: Identity and Ideology in the First World War* (London: Routledge, 1994).
Owen, Alex, *The Place of Enchantment: British Occultism and the Culture of the Modern* (Chicago: University of Chicago Press, 2004).
Owen, Wilfred, *Collected Letters*. Ed. Harold Owen and John Bell (London: Oxford University Press, 1967).
—— *The Complete Poems and Fragments* (2 vols.). Ed. Jon Stallworthy (London: Chatto & Windus, 1983).
Palmer, Alan and Veronica Palmer, *Who's Who in Bloomsbury* (New York: St Martin's Press, 1987).
Penzoldt, Peter, *The Supernatural in Fiction* (New York: Humanities Press, 1965).
Pinney, Thomas, "Introduction." In Rudyard Kipling, *Something of Myself and Other Autobiographical Writings* (Cambridge: Cambridge University Press, 1990), pp. vii–xxxv.
Pittock, Malcolm, "The War Poetry of Wilfred Owen: A Dissenting Reappraisal." In Patrick Quinn and Steven Trout (eds.), *The Literature of the Great War Reconsidered: Beyond Modern Memory* (Basingstoke: Palgrave Macmillan, 2001).
Radcliffe, John and John McGivering, "En-dor." Notes. 12 July 2011. http://www.kiplingsociety.co.uk/rg_endor1.htm (accessed 15 September 2014).
Radke-Yarrow, Marion (ed.), *Children of Depressed Mothers: From Early Childhood to Maturity* (Cambridge: Cambridge University Press, 1998).
Rae, Patricia (ed.), *Modernism and Mourning* (Lewisburg: Bucknell University Press, 2007).

Raia, Courtenay Grean, "From Ether Theory to Ether Theology: Oliver Lodge and the Physics of Immortality." *Journal of the History of the Behavioral Sciences* 43(1) (Winter 2007): 18–43.
Raitt, Suzanne, *May Sinclair: A Modern Victorian* (Oxford: Oxford University Press, 2000).
Ricketts, Harry, *Strange Meetings* (London: Chatto & Windus, 2010).
——— *The Unforgiving Minute: A Life of Rudyard Kipling* (London: Chatto & Windus, 1999).
Roberts, R. Ellis, "Miss Sinclair Among the Ghosts." *The Bookman* (London) (October 1923): 32–33.
Rose, Gilbert J., "The Creativity of Everyday Life." In Simon A. Grolnick and Leonard Barkin (eds.), *Between Reality and Fantasy: Transitional Objects and Phenomena* (New York: Aronson, 1978).
Rose, Jonathan, *The Edwardian Temperament, 1895–1919* (Athens, OH: Ohio University Press, 1986).
Rosof, Barbara D., *The Worst Loss: How Families Heal from the Death of a Child* (New York: Holt, 1995).
Rowlands, Peter, "Lodge, Sir Oliver Joseph (1851–1940)." *Oxford Dictionary of National Biography* (online edition, accessed 26 March 2011).
Royle, Nicholas, *Telepathy and Literature: Essays on the Reading Mind* (Oxford: Basil Blackwell, 1990).
Sabbadini, Andrea, "The Replacement Child." *Contemporary Psychoanalysis* 24(4) (October 1988): 528–47.
Sassoon, Siegfried, "On Passing the New Menin Gate." http://www.ppu.org.uk/learn/poetry/poetry_ww1_4.html (accessed 24 June 2014).
Scarborough, Dorothy, *The Supernatural in Modern English Fiction* (1917) (New York: Octagon, 1967).
Scott-James, Rolfe A., *Modernism and Romance* (London: John Lane/Bodley Head, 1908).
Seymour-Smith, Martin, *Rudyard Kipling* (New York: St Martin's Press, 1989).
Shepard, Leslie A., *Encyclopedia of Occultism and Para-Psychology*, Vol. 1 (2nd edn.) (Detroit: Gale, 1984).
Silver, Brenda R., *Virginia Woolf's Reading Notebooks* (Princeton: Princeton University Press, 1983).
Sinclair, May, *Audrey Craven* (1897) (New York: Henry Holt, 1906).
——— Contributor to "Christmas Symposium on Dreams, Ghosts and Fairies," *The Bookman* (London) (December 1923): 142–49.
——— *The Creators: A Comedy* (New York: Century, 1910).
——— *A Defence of Idealism: Some Questions and Conclusions* (London: Macmillan, 1917).
——— "From a Journal." *English Review* (May–July 1915): 168–83, 303–14, 468–76.
——— *A Journal of Impressions in Belgium* (London: Hutchinson, 1915).
——— Letter, "To the Editor of the *Journal* of the SPR April 26 1917." *Journal of the Society for Psychical Research* Vol. XVIII (May–June 1917): 67–68.
——— Letter to the Editor, *New York Times* (4 November 1912) [On "The Flaw in the Crystal"].
——— *Mary Olivier* (1919) (Toronto: Lester and Orpen Denys, 1982).
Sinclair, May, "The Novels of Dorothy Richardson." *The Little Review* 5(12) (April 1918): 3–11.

―――― *The Romantic* (New York: Macmillan, 1920).
―――― "The Spirits, Some Simpletons, and Dr Charles Mercier." Review of Charles A. Mercier, *Spiritualism and Sir Oliver Lodge*. *Medical Press* (25 July 1917): 60–61.
―――― *The Tree of Heaven* (1917) (New York: Macmillan, 1928).
Smith, Grover (ed.), *Letters of Aldous Huxley* (New York: Harper & Row, 1969).
Sobel, Emilie, "Rhythm, Sound and Imagery in the Poetry of Gerard Manley Hopkins." In Simon A. Grolnick and Leonard Barkin (eds.), *Between Reality and Fantasy: Transitional Objects and Phenomena* (New York: Aronson, 1978), pp. 425–46.
Southam, Brian (ed.), "My Boy Jack." Notes. 6 March 2010. http://www.kipling society.co.uk/rg_jack1.htm (accessed 15 September 2014).
Spargo, Clifton, *The Ethics of Mourning: Grief and Responsibility in Elegiac Literature* (Baltimore: Johns Hopkins University Press, 2004).
Spurgeon, Caroline, *Mysticism in English Literature* (1913) (Cambridge: Cambridge University Press, 1927).
Stableford, Brian, "J. M. Barrie 1860–1937." In E. F. Bleiler (ed.), *Supernatural Fiction Writers: Fantasy and Horror* (Vol. 1) (New York: Charles Scribner's Sons, 1985).
Stashower, Daniel, *Teller of Tales: The Life of Arthur Conan Doyle* (London: Penguin, 2000).
Steell, Willis, "May Sinclair Tells Why She Isn't a Poet." *Literary Digest International Book Review* (June 1924): 513, 559.
Storr, Anthony, *The Dynamics of Creation* (London: Secker & Warburg, 1972).
Strange, Julie-Marie, *Death, Grief and Poverty in Britain, 1870–1914* (Cambridge: Cambridge University Press, 2005).
Straughan, Roger, *A Study in Survival: Conan Doyle Solves the Final Problem* (Winchester: O-Books, 2009).
Surette, Leon, *The Birth of Modernism: Ezra Pound, T. S. Eliot, W. B. Yeats and the Occult* (Montreal: McGill-Queen's University Press, 1993).
Swinnerton, Frank, "The Tree of Heaven." Review of *The Tree of Heaven* by May Sinclair. *The Bookman* (London) (January 1918): 137.
Sword, Helen, *Ghostwriting Modernism* (Ithaca: Cornell University Press, 2002).
Tante, Dilly (ed.), "May Sinclair." *Living Authors: a Book of Biographies* (New York: H. W. Wilson, 1931), pp. 373–74.
Thurschwell, Pamela, *Literature, Technology and Magical Thinking, 1880–1920* (Cambridge: Cambridge University Press, 2001).
Tomka, Bela, *A Social History of Twentieth-Century Europe* (Abingdon: Routledge, 2013).
Turner, Frank Miller, *Between Science and Religion* (New Haven: Yale University Press, 1974).
Underhill, Evelyn, *Mysticism: A Study in the Nature and Development of Man's Spiritual Consciousness* (London: Methuen, 1911).
―――― *Practical Mysticism for Normal People* (London: Dent, 1914).
van Emden, Richard, *The Quick and the Dead* (London: Bloomsbury, 2011).
van Gennep, Arnold, *The Rites of Passage* (1909) (Chicago: University of Chicago Press, 1972).
Wallace, Roy (ed.), "Introduction." In *On the Margins of Science: The Social Construction of Rejected Knowledge*. Monograph 27 (Keele: University of Keele, 1979).

—— "Science and Pseudo-Science." *Social Science Information* 24(3): 585–601.
Warner, Marina, *Phantasmagoria: Spirit Visions, Metaphors, and Media into the Twenty-first Century* (Oxford: Oxford University Press, 2006).
Wilcox, Ella Wheeler, *The Worlds and I* (1918 Reprint) (London: Forgotten Books, 2013).
Wilkinson, Alan, "Changing English Attitudes to Death in the First World War." In Peter C. Jupp and Glennys Howarth (eds.), *The Changing Face of Death: Historical Accounts of Death and Disposal* (Basingstoke: Macmillan, 1997), pp. 149–63.
Wilson, Edmund, Review in *New Yorker*, 2 September 1944, pp. 64–66. In Donald Watt (ed.), *Aldous Huxley: The Critical Heritage* (London: Routledge & Kegan Paul, 1975), pp. 347–50.
Wilson, Leigh, *Modernism and the Unseen: Spiritualism, Mysticism and the Occult* (Edinburgh: Edinburgh University Press, 2010).
Winnicott, D. W., *Playing and Reality* (London: Routledge, 1989).
Winter, J. M., "Spiritualism and the First World War." In R. W. Davis and R. J. Helmstadter (eds.), *Religion and Irreligion in Victorian Society: Essays in Honor of R. K. Webb* (London: Routledge, 2001).
Winter, Jay, *Sites of Memory, Sites of Mourning* (Cambridge: Cambridge University Press, 1995).
Wolfreys, Julian, *Victorian Hauntings* (Basingstoke: Palgrave Macmillan, 2002).
Woodcock, George, *Dawn and the Darkest Hour: A Study of Aldous Huxley* (New York: Viking Press, 1972).
Woolf, Virginia, "Before Midnight." In Andrew McNeillie (ed.), *The Essays of Virginia Woolf* (Vol. 2) (London: Hogarth Press, 1987), pp. 87–8.
—— *Between the Acts* (New York: Harcourt Brace Jovanovich, 1969).
—— *The Complete Shorter Fiction of Virginia Woolf*. Ed. Susan Dick (London: Hogarth Press, 1985).
—— *The Diary of Virginia Woolf*. Vol. 3: *1925–1930*. Ed. Anne Olivier Bell. Assisted by Andrew McNeillie (New York: Harcourt Brace Jovanovich, 1980).
—— *The Essays of Virginia Woolf*. Vols. II and III. Ed. Andrew McNeillie (London: Hogarth Press, 1987, 1988).
—— *Jacob's Room*. Ed. Suzanne Raitt (New York: Norton, 2007).
—— *The Letters of Virginia Woolf*. Vols. I, II, III and V. Ed. Nigel Nicolson (London: Hogarth Press, 1975, 1976, 1977, 1979).
—— *Moments of Being* (New York: Harcourt Brace Jovanovich, 1976).
—— *Moments of Being* (New York: Harcourt Brace Jovanovich, 1985).
—— *Mrs. Dalloway* (1925) (London: Granada, 1983).
—— "Mrs. Dalloway in Bond Street." In Susan Dick (ed.), *The Complete Shorter Fiction of Virginia Woolf* (London: Hogarth Press, 1985), pp. 146–53.
—— *Night and Day* (1919) (London: Granada, 1978).
—— *Orlando* (1928) (Harmondsworth: Penguin, 1993).
—— *To the Lighthouse* (1927) (London: Granada, 1983).
—— *The Voyage Out* (1915) (Harmondsworth: Penguin, 1974).
Yeats, W. B. (ed. and "Introduction"), *The Oxford Book of Modern Verse* (New York: Oxford University Press, 1936).
Zegger, Hrisey Dimitrakis, *May Sinclair* (Boston: Twayne, 1976).

Index

Adult Attachment Interview 13–14
Alexander, F. M. 210, 213
Armistice Day 228
Asquith, Cynthia 4, 129, 132, 134, 141, 231
attachment theory 8–11, 15, 32, 58, 127, 156, 175, 189, 201, 210, 233, 234 n. 3
avoidant-resistant attachment pattern 14–17, 30, 59, 61, 63, 72, 80, 87, 88, 100, 122, 132, 134, 140, 147–48, 152, 156, 160, 165, 185, 199, 201–2, 204, 215, 216, 218, 226, 227, 231
definition 10

Bagnold, Enid 203
Barrett, William 46, 72
Barrie, Sir J. M. 7, 13, 14, 24–25, 27, 124–52, 227, 229, 232–33
attitude towards First World War 133–34
Better Dead 129–30
Dear Brutus 127, 147–48
Greenwood Hat, The 132
Little White Bird, The 143
Margaret Ogilvy 25, 131–32
"New Word, The" 145
Peter Pan 127, 132, 143
"Well-Remembered Voice, A" 124, 127, 148–49, 232
Barrie, Margaret *see* Margaret Ogilvy
Barrie, Mary 132
Bedford, Sybille 209–10
Beer, John 37
Bell, Quentin 165
Benson, A. C. 28, 30, 53, 56, 58
Birkin, Andrew 129, 131–34, 141, 142, 143, 145
Blavatsky, Madame Helena Petrovna 21, 99, 143
Blunden, Edmund 200

Boer War 3, 4, 108, 122, 144–45, 175
Boll, Theophilus E. M. 25, 156–58, 160, 166–67, 169, 183, 229
Bowlby, John 9, 228, 231, 234 n. 3
Brink, Andrew xiii, 8, 10, 11, 17
Brock, Dr Arthur 200, 229
Brock, Sir Thomas x–xii

Caramagno, Thomas C. 160, 174
Cavaliero, Glen 23
creativity and loss 12–13
Crittenden, Patricia 9–11, 14, 90, 122
Cummins, Geraldine 57–58

Derrida, Jacques 17
DeSalvo, Louise 163
Doyle, Sir Arthur Conan xii, 2–3, 7, 13–14, 18, 21–22, 23–27, 86–123, 227, 230, 232–33
"Adventure of the Three Garridebs, The" 120
attitude towards First World War 88, 109–15
Edge of the Unknown, The 115, 120
History of Spiritualism, The 115
"Inner Room, The" 105–6
Land of Mist, The 25, 86, 117–20
Memories and Adventures 25, 88–94, 96–97, 99–105, 108–13, 120, 122
Mystery of Cloomber, The 99
New Revelation, The 113
on telepathy 98
"Parasite, The" 57, 105, 106–7
Pheneas Speaks 114, 116–17
"Poison Belt, The" 109–10
Professor Challenger 93, 102, 117–19
"Scandal in Bohemia, A" 99, 100
Sherlock Holmes 25–26, 87–88, 93, 99, 100–3, 110, 120, 236 nn. 1, 2

"Sign of Four, The" 99, 101
"Study in Scarlet, A" 99, 101–2
Stark Munro Letters, The 94–98, 101, 106, 110
Vital Message, The 115–16
Doyle, Charles 90–91, 94–96, 98, 100–1, 104–5
Doyle, Kingsley 2, 88, 103, 109, 111, 113–14, 116, 122, 226
Doyle, Louisa (Touie) 88, 97–98, 103–4, 107–9, 122
Doyle, Mary (née Foley, Arthur's mother) 90–94, 104
Doyle, Mary (Arthur's sister) 91
Doyle, Mary (Arthur's daughter) 103, 107, 109, 115, 122

ether 47, 50, 52, 63–64, 72–73, 75–76, 83, 109–10

Fairbairn, W. R. D. 8, 177–78
First World War
  burial of soldiers 21
  statistics 4, 15, 228–30
Fleming, Alice *see* Alice Kipling
Freud, Anna 231
Freud, Sigmund 8, 26, 32, 46, 55, 175, 189, 218, 225, 234 n. 5
Fussell, Paul 188

Garrett, Eileen 121
Gauld, Alan 29, 32–33, 53–54, 58, 235 n. 4
grief 12, 18–19
Gunston, Leslie 199
Gurney, Edmund 12, 41, 46–48, 72, 230

Hamilton, Trevor 32–34, 36–41, 44–46, 48, 53–54, 56–58
Hanson, Neil 18, 21, 229
Hazelgrove, Jenny 6, 19–20, 22
Heard, Gerald 212–13
Hibberd, Dominic 187–89, 190–92, 194, 197, 199–200
Hill, J. Arthur 64, 74, 81, 85
Holland, Mrs *see* Alice Kipling
Holmes, Charles M. 209
Houdini, Harry 115, 118

Howe, David 9–11, 13, 15–16
Huxley, Aldous 1, 6–7, 12, 15–16, 19, 21, 24, 26, 31, 57, 81, 117, 120, 135, 201–27, 230, 233
  attitude towards
    First World War 206
  blindness 201, 204
  Brave New World 202, 209
  Crome Yellow 19, 206
  Ends and Means 202, 214–15
  Eyeless in Gaza 1, 81, 202, 209–14, 230
  Heaven and Hell 6, 223
  Island 202
  "Music at Night" 209, 214
  on Myers's *Human Personality* 225
  on telepathy 208, 214
  Perennial Philosophy, The 222
  Time Must Have a Stop 81, 202, 215–22
  World of Light, The 207–8
Huxley, Julia 202–3
Huxley, Julian 203, 205
Huxley, Laura
  This Timeless Moment 223–26
Huxley, Leonard 202–5, 208–9
Huxley, Margaret 206
Huxley, Maria 207, 209, 214
Huxley, Trevenon, suicide of 201, 205–7, 212
Hynes, Samuel 2–3

influenza epidemic (1918) 4

Jalland, Patricia 4, 12, 15, 18, 21–23, 230, 234 n. 3
James, William 4–5, 10, 16–17, 26, 46, 54–55, 74, 225, 235 n. 5
Jolly, W. P. 63–64, 66, 69–71, 73–76, 83–85

Kelly, Edward F. 6, 16, 49, 50–51, 55, 233
Kelly, Emily Williams 6
Kipling, Alice (Rudyard's mother) 134–35, 137–38
Kipling, Alice (Fleming) a.k.a. Mrs Holland 57, 135, 143
Kipling, Lockwood 134, 138

Kipling, Rudyard   xii, 1, 7, 13–14, 19, 21, 23–27, 31, 57, 88, 114, 124–52, 227, 232–33
  "An Only Son"   149–50
  attitude towards
    First World War   142, 145
  "Baa Baa, Black Sheep"   125–26, 137–38
  "Brushwood Boy, The"   142
  "Common Form"   19, 150
  "En-dor"   150
  "Gardener, The"   127, 151
  Letters of Rudyard Kipling   21, 139, 228
  Light That Failed, The   137
  "London Stone"   19
  "Madonna of the Trenches, A"   127, 150–51
  "Mary Postgate"   127, 146–47, 151, 232
  "Sending of Dana Da, The"   144
  "Shock"   124, 150
  "They"   144–45
  "Wireless"   144
Kollar, Rene   22–23

Lawrence, D. H.   57, 207–9, 215, 221
Lee, Hermione   161, 163, 165, 184–86
Leonard, Mrs   79, 84
Levy, Paul   7
Light   56, 98, 112, 236 n. 4
Llewelyn-Davies family   132–33
Lodge, Mary   69, 71
Lodge, Sir Oliver xii, 1–4, 7, 13–14, 18, 21–26, 31, 44, 48, 54, 57–58, 60–85, 88, 98, 105, 108–9, 112, 115, 117, 121, 152, 219, 223, 225, 230, 232–33
  attitude towards
    First World War   75–76
  Christopher   61, 81–8, 235 n. 6
  Conviction of Survival: Two Discourses in Memory of F. W. H. Myers   54, 57–58, 72, 74, 81, 84
  Ether and Reality   83–84, 230
  Ether of Space, The   109
  friendship with Frederic Myers   72–74
  My Philosophy   84
  on telepathy   72, 84
  Past Years: An Autobiography   60–61, 83
  Raymond, or Life and Death   60, 77–81, 152, 219, 230, 232: Doyle on 112, 116, Huxley on 26, 223, 225
  School Teaching and School Reform   67
  Survival of Man, The   75
  War and After, The   75–76
  Why I Believe in Personal Immortality   84
Lodge, Oliver Jr.   78
Lodge, Raymond   1–4, 18, 23–26, 60, 63, 66, 70, 74–81, 83–84, 235 nn. 1–3, 5, 236 n. 6
Longstaff, William   18
loss   10–12
Lutyens, Edwin   18

Marshall, Annie   37–45
mediums
  Cummins, Geraldine   57–58
  Garrett, Eileen   121
  Holland, Mrs a.k.a. Alice Kipling (Fleming)   57, 135, 143
  Palladino, Eusapia   53, 73
  Piper, Mrs   44–45, 48, 53, 73, 77
  Thompson, Mrs   53–54, 57, 74
Mercier, Charles A.   25, 80, 235 n. 5
Meyers, Jeffrey   109
mourning
  wartime   21–22
Myers, Eveleen   40–45, 48, 53, 56–57
Myers, Frederic Sr.   32
Myers, Frederic W. H.   4–7, 12, 14, 16, 21–24, 26–59, 63–64, 72–75, 77, 81–82, 84–85, 88, 98–99, 104, 109, 121, 143, 171, 225, 230–33
  "Fragments of Inner Life"   28, 31–33, 35–39, 43–45, 48
  Human Personality and its Survival of Bodily Death   16, 27, 31, 45, 47–52, 54, 57, 59, 230, 232: Doyle on 99, Huxley on 26, 225, James on   54, Lodge on 54

on telepathy 47–48
"St. Paul" 36
subliminal self 31, 49–50, 52, 55, 225, 234 n. 3
Myers, Leo 26, 41–42, 230, 234 ch.1 n. 1
Myers, Susan 32–34, 36, 38
mysticism 15–17
  definition 4–5
  Huxley on 6, 208–9
  New Mysticism 5, 167–68
  Sinclair on 5–6, 167–68, 179
  Woolf on 168–69, 182

Newcombe, Nora 9, 230
Nordon, Pierre 96, 98–99, 102, 114, 116, 121

object relations 8, 11, 15–16, 233
occultism 6
Ogilvy, Margaret 127–28
Oppenheim, Janet 3
Owen, Harold 199
Owen, Susan 189–92, 196
Owen, Wilfred xi, xii, 19
  "Anthem for Doomed Youth" 4
  attitude towards
    First World War 192, 195–200
  "Has Your Soul Sipped" 197–98
  "Kind Ghosts, The" 195–96
  "On My Songs" 192–93, 196
  pararhyme, definition 189
  "Purgatorial Passions" 194–95
  "Shadwell Stair" 194
  "Strange Meeting" 198–99
  "To Poesy" 193

Palladino, Eusapia 53, 73
Phantasms of the Living 47, 230
Pinney, Thomas 135, 138, 140–42, 144
Piper, Mrs 44–45, 48, 53, 73, 77
post-traumatic stress disorder 3
psychical research, writers' involvement in 21, 56–57
  Doyle on 105
  Huxley on 225
  Kipling on 144
  Myers on 51–53

Sinclair on 169–70
Woolf on 26, 170–71
psychobiography 13, 27
Punch magazine 228

Rae, Patricia 17–18
Raitt, Suzanne 157–60, 169–70, 183–86, 237 n. 4
replacement child, Barrie as 129
Richet, Charles 59, 73–74, 235 n. 5
Ricketts, Harry 25, 127, 139, 145
Russell, Bertrand 12, 17

Sassoon, Siegfried 19, 195
Sheppard, Dick (H. R. L.) 213
Sidgwick, Eleanor 41
Sidgwick, Henry 41, 45–46, 237 n. 5
Sinclair, Amelia 156–58
Sinclair, May xii, 5–7, 12–13, 17, 21, 24–25, 31, 56, 153–86, 229, 233
  and Hector Munro 159
  attitude towards
    First World War 159–60
  Audrey Craven 169
  Creators: A Comedy, The 154, 167
  Defence of Idealism 5–6, 17, 166, 167–68, 170, 175–77
  "From a Journal" 159–60
  Journal of Impressions in Belgium, A 156
  Mary Olivier 25, 156–60, 166–67, 183
  New Idealism, The 166
  "Novels of Dorothy Richardson, The" 25
  on the Society for Psychical Research 169–70
  on telepathy 5, 170, 176–77
  Tree of Heaven, The 156, 167, 174–79, 183
Sinclair, William 156–58
Society for Psychical Research 5, 21, 31, 45–46, 55–57, 75, 85, 105, 142, 169, 234 n. 1, 235 n. 5, 237 n. 7
Spargo, Clifton 17
spiritualism 6, 207, 230
  during wartime 22
  Kipling on 149, 150–51

256 *Index*

Spiritualists' National Union 22, 230
Spurgeon, Caroline 4
Stashower, Daniel 25, 86–88, 91–94, 97–98, 101–2, 105–8, 110–13, 115–18, 120–22, 236 n. 2
Stephen, Julia 162–63
Stephen, Leslie 56, 160, 163–65
Stephen, Thoby 165, 171–73
Strachey, James 170
Strachey, Lytton 57
subliminal 31, 48–50, 52, 55, 225, 234 n. 3
telepathy 234 n. 1
  definition of 47
theosophy 18, 99, 143–44
Thompson, Mrs 53–54, 57, 74
transitional object 8
trauma 3, 7–16, 21, 24, 26–27, 31, 61, 77–78, 81, 83, 87, 92, 106, 110, 116, 126–27, 134, 137, 152, 155–56, 163, 183, 185, 188, 199, 201–2, 205–6, 213, 215–16, 218, 221–22, 226, 229, 231–33

Underhill, Evelyn 5–6, 16, 154, 167, 233

van Emden, Richard 21, 23, 230–31, 235 n. 1
van Gennep, Arnold 9

war memorials xi, 17–19, 27, 228
Warner, Marina 3, 17
Wilson, Edmund 220, 222
Winnicott, D. W. 8, 17, 47, 66, 141, 181
Winter, J. M. 6, 15, 18
Woodcock, George 210, 213
Woolf, Leonard 185–86
Woolf, Virginia 7, 12–14, 18, 24–26, 31, 57, 153–86, 228, 230, 232–33
  attitude towards
    First World War 165
  "Before Midnight" 153
  Jacob's Room 18, 156, 172–74, 184, 230, 232
  "Modern Fiction" 25
  Moments of Being 160–65, 168–69, 171–72, 175, 185
  Mrs. Dalloway 156, 165, 174, 176, 179–83, 184, 237 nn. 6–8
  on telepathy 171
  "Reminiscences" 160–61, 185
  "Sketch of the Past, A" 161, 163, 165, 172, 185
  To The Lighthouse 156, 175, 184–85, 230
  Voyage Out, The 155

Yeats, W. B. 56, 196

Zegger, Hrisey Dimitrakis 25, 171, 175, 237 n. 3

The manufacturer's authorised representative in the EU is Springer Nature Customer Service Centre GmbH, Europaplatz 3, 69115 Heidelberg, Germany. If you have any concerns regarding our products, please contact ProductSafety@springernature.com

Printed and bound by CPI Group (UK) Ltd, Croydon, CR0 4YY

23/03/2026

02076458-0014